Horses

Myth and Fascination

Horses

Myth and Fascination

Susanne Sgrazzutti

Jürgen Schulzki (Photography)

Bath · New York · Singapore · Hong Kong · Cologne · Delhi · Melbourne

This is a Parragon Publishing book

Copyright © Parragon Books Ltd

Queen Street House
4 Queen Street
Bath BA1 1HE, UK

Original edition production: ditter.projektagentur gmbh, Cologne
Picture research: Irina Ditter-Hilkens, Cologne
Concept: Susanne Sgrazutti, Irina Ditter-Hilkens, Jürgen Schulzki
Design: Claudio Martinez, Cologne

English edition produced by: APE Int'l, Richmond, VA
Translation from German: Jennifer Taylor-Gaida and Dr. Lizzie Gilbert
Editing of English edition: Dr. Pippin Michelli for APE Int'l

ISBN: 978-1-4075-0598-5

Printed in China

Contents

Horsepower in All Aspects of Life

Prized Athletes

Growing Up
with Horses 158

Author Susanne Sgrazzutti chatting with Ludger Beerbaum, under the watchful eye of
the young Enorm.

Ludger Beerbaum, born in 1963, is one of the most successful show jumpers in the world. He captured gold for his team at his very first
Olympic Games in 1998 in Seoul, and went on to repeat this success in Atlanta and Sydney. These medals are complemented by two World
Championship and three European Championship team titles, as well as an individual European Championship win and first place in the World
Cup finals (with his best known mare, Ratina Z). Beerbaum continues to rake in awards in major show-jumping contests, including as three-
time winner of the Grand Prize at the CHIO Championship in Aachen, Germany. He is an expert in training horses to become world-class
athletes, and always has an eye open for new talent. Beerbaum is known in the equestrian world as a perfectionist—both in his successful
management of horses and his trusting handling of the animals.

Foreword

Horses are fascinating creatures, not least because they force us to exercise great sensitivity and attention if we wish to communicate with them—all without saying a word. When handling horses, we must be able to read the animals' body language and adjust our own behavior accordingly.

Horses are part of every civilization's cultural heritage. Their existence has often been endangered, but thanks to their adaptability, they have always managed to survive. Many people have a very special relationship with these animals, 60 million of which share our planet.

As an equestrian, I have learned a great deal from horses, which has been particularly helpful in developing my own personality. The time I have spent with Ratina Z. has left an especially deep impression on me. When she came to my stall, I had great expectations for this exceptional mare, who had just won the Silver Medal in the individual classification at the Olympics in Barcelona under the guidance of Piet Raymakers. I, of course, wanted to ride her like all my other horses—with maximum control. But Ratina was at least as stubborn as I am: she didn't like my style one bit and she displayed less and less interest in cooperating. Although I was eager to forge full steam ahead regardless, I had to accept the necessity of changing tactics. I had to learn how to make meaningful compromises, to give Ratina more leeway in everyday riding and on the show-jumping course, and she thanked me for it. After more than a year together, we finally found some common ground and could start to enjoy some successes. To see how relaxed our relationship is today, take a look at the photograph on page 156.

In this book you will embark on an enlightening journey through mythology, history, sports, and culture with Susanne Sgrazzutti as your guide. She has compiled a fabulous compendium of noteworthy facts and entertaining anecdotes, some of which are almost forgotten today. The stories—at times written tongue in cheek—and impressive photographs of these remarkable horses, people, and events are sure to captivate you. Immerse yourself in the fascinating world of horses!

Happy reading!

Sincerely,

Ludger Beerbaum

The Horse in Myth: Truth and Fiction

The Horned Horse

The unicorn embodies invincibility, purity, virginity, and also love. Afraid of people, it can only be caught in the lap of a virgin, so the legend goes.

This fabled creature with its white horse-body and the spiral-twisted horn projecting from its forehead has captured people's imaginations throughout the world. In China, the unicorn is one of four magic animals, along with the dragon, phoenix, and turtle. A legend tells that the unicorn appeared to a young woman in the sixth century CE and without words gave her to understand that she would bear a "king without a throne." This prophecy was later thought to refer to the philosopher Confucius.

From ancient times until well into the nineteenth century, a firm belief in unicorns was passed down in the Christian West as well, spread in part by a book on natural history known as "The Physiologos." This treatise described the properties of flora and fauna, linking them to Christian doctrine. For centuries, all attempts to refute the myth of the unicorn were in vain—even after French paleontologist Georges Baron de Cuvier proved in 1827 that the anatomy of the horse's skull would be absolutely unable to support a horn growing out of the bone of the forehead.

According to legend, the unicorn is a loner and lives in a forest where it is always summer. A lake is an essential feature of its habitat because the vain creature must have adequate opportunities to admire its own reflection.

The Unicorn in the Sky
Not until 1624 was the unicorn inducted into the august company of gods and mythological figures that people envisioned in the starry sky. Mathematician Jakob Bartsch drew the constellation Monoceros, whose five stars are visible in the winter evening sky between Orion and the Great Dog. The Milky Way, the closest galaxy to our planet, passes through the Unicorn, culminating at its center around midnight on January 5 every year.

The singular characteristic of a unicorn is its spiraling horn, with which it fights its enemies, but the unicorn's horn supposedly also has healing properties and can bring the dead back to life.

However, it was precisely this long, pointed, phallic horn with its anti-toxic properties—also frequently described as aphrodisiac—that was so highly coveted. If there was no such thing as a unicorn, what kind of horn was it that was ground into powder and made into amulets, rings, and even drinking cups that were capable of rendering every poison harmless? The answer to that riddle is as bizarre as it is sobering: the horn actually comes not from a horned horse, but from the male narwhal (*Monodon monoceros*), whose left tusk can grow up to 9 feet long. In Europe, these peaceful ocean mammals from Arctic waters were largely unknown, so the rare finding of their extraordinarily long tusks repeatedly fueled the belief in the existence of unicorns. This also explains why the narwhal, of which there are an estimated 20,000 alive today, is also known as the unicorn whale.

The Last Unicorn

The unicorn has also conquered the big screen. The animated film *The Last Unicorn*, based on a book of the same name, was first shown in 1982. It tells the enchanting story of the last unicorn living in the wild searching for others of its own kind. The unicorn learns that the Red Steer is holding his fellow creatures captive at the end of the world and, with three companions, embarks on an adventure-filled quest.

Widespread belief in the healing powers of the unicorn led to its being used as a symbol for apothecaries since the 15th century. In Germany, Unicorn Drugstores are still common today.

However much people may covet the horseshoe as a lucky charm, it is even more important for the horse. It protects the animal's hooves from abrasion, since they wear down more quickly on hard ground.

The Magic Horseshoe

People used to believe that anyone who cast a horseshoe at the feet of the capricious gods would have good luck and be protected from harm. Whence this luck derived, and whether you could enjoy it if you merely tripped over a horseshoe, remains unknown.

It is significant that happenstance plays the lead role, because those who deliberately search for a horseshoe or even purchase one will only end up with a meaningless decoration, without any magical powers. The magic horseshoe itself seeks out the person on whom to bestow its good fortune—luck cannot be taken by force.

The person found worthy of possessing such a lucky horseshoe is then faced with the dilemma of how to hang it. Opinions are divided on this point even today, and applying logic is no help. "Of course, have the opening end upward so that luck can collect in the shoe," say some. Others counter with, "Absolutely not, because luck has to flow from the 'crescent of the half-moon,' deflecting all evil from its prongs." There is an old saying at work here, namely, that everyone forges his own destiny. Those who do not believe in the magic of the

horseshoe will not benefit from it anyway. And there is another thing to remember: supposedly only a rusty horseshoe, ideally with its old nails still intact, can bring true happiness. An ignorant finder might

Horseshoe Nails

It is fortunate that it does not hurt horses to have their "shoes" simply nailed onto their hooves, as it would be difficult to attach them firmly enough by any other means. They are apparently not magical enough to hold on unassisted, so the farrier has no choice but to carefully hammer in nails through the six to ten holes in the U-shaped piece of iron.

Although there may be a few girls who like to wear a horseshoe nail on a leather cord around their neck, there are not many other uses for the 1–1½-inch-long, specially shaped nails—at least, you would think not. But

you would be mistaken! During the Thirty Years War there were reports of a horrible form of torture thought up by foot soldiers—who supposedly hid horseshoe nails in the food of their enemies. These obviously did not go down very well.

Even mythology has laid claim to the horseshoe nail, attributing a peaceful significance to it. It supposedly wards off illness and gives the farrier just the right touch in his work. This is the origin of the old custom of hammering four iron nails into a piece of wood in animal stalls. One was a coffin nail and the other three horseshoe nails.

The wildest legends have been passed down about Dunstan, an archbishop of Canterbury born around 909. When he died in 988, he could look back on a rich and varied life. History records his feats and deeds, both real and imaginary.

Raised by Irish monks, Dunstan learned from them not only how to train his mind and open his soul to the Christian faith, but also all sorts of manual skills, such as working with a hammer and anvil.

And thus began the legendary part of his life: the Devil, usually so clever and canny, unthinkingly put himself in Dunstan's hands. He of all creatures let the most God-fearing smith anywhere in the land nail a new shoe under his hoof. Dunstan recognized what kind of customer he was dealing with and, seeing his chance, hammered violently at the Devil's hoof. Whether he did this out of fear, or to teach a lesson in fear, remains unclear. At any rate, the Devil showed weakness: he meekly asked Dunstan to leave off his hammering. The man of God then seized on this opportunity to make a clever deal with the Devil. He demanded that the Devil spare all those wearing or working with horseshoes. Against his will, the demon agreed to the pact; thus Dunstan successfully helped safeguard the blacksmiths' craft.

In another legend, the Devil came to tempt Dunstan as he worked at his forge by night—only to be taken by the nose with red-hot tongs!

well polish it, thereby buffing away its magical powers for all time. Some people swear by horseshoes from racing horses, since these are allegedly watched over by a particularly lucky star.

Losing a horseshoe is not to be taken lightly. The gods can hardly be expected to regard this as a sacrifice to them. Does this mean that one's luck will evaporate? Well, a certain financial loss is preordained, because everyone knows that quadrupeds cannot walk on three shoes: the farrier will have to make a special visit to fit a single shoe. This is why riders will search even in the swampiest ground to find the lost lucky charm.

Belief in the magical qualities of metal led people in times past to nail a horseshoe over the door to keep demons out. The cult of the horseshoe has survived into the present, although today the luckbringer is more often attached to the grille of a big rig than to house and stable doors.

But why all the fuss about this piece of bent metal, a simple object of daily use? The horseshoe, if one believes the mythology surrounding it, unites three supernatural powers: it is formed in the purifying element of fire from the magical material of iron and is worn by a myth-laden creature, the horse. Roman, Celtic, and Germanic legends all flow together in the symbolism of this one familiar object.

Incidentally, because of its signature shape, the horseshoe has given its name to various flora and fauna, although it has not necessarily conferred its magical powers on them. Horseshoe clover, for example, takes second place to the four-leafed variety when it comes to bringing its finder luck, and the horseshoe bat is quite a commonplace animal.

The Blacksmith's Art

"Man forges his own destiny," said the Roman consul Appius Claudius in 307 BCE, admonishing his fellow Romans to work hard. There were good reasons why he alluded to the legendary craft of the horseshoe and arms smith, who had long since been incorporated into Greek and Roman mythology. The Romans worshipped Vulcan, imagining his divine forge to be located within volcanic Mount Etna in Sicily. They equated him with Hephaestus, the Greek god of fire, the lame smith who was honored by all the other gods due to the magnificent weapons and palaces he forged for them—he even created Zeus' scepter. Only his wife, Aphrodite, the goddess of love, caused Hephaestus concern: while he diligently worked away at his anvil, she sought her pleasure elsewhere. In reaction, the talented smith swiftly forged an indestructible net that he attached to their bed in order to put an end to his wife's extramarital dalliances—and with success.

The handling of fire, water, iron, hammer, and anvil has always been highly fascinating, and not only in Greek and Roman mythology. This also explains why the "smid," as he was known in the early Middle Ages, enjoyed such great respect in society. He was ranked second only to the mayor in the village hierarchy and was authorized to make important decisions in his absence. In emergencies, he even took over the duties of a priest.

Today, the work of the smith is no longer reserved for men. As long as there are horses, equine podiatrists will be in demand—never mind their gender. After all, horses' hooves grow about ⅓ inch every month, and a careful professional pedicure is indispensable to

St. Eligius (588–660 CE)

The cult that arose around the horseshoe and the fabled art of smithery naturally required a fitting patron saint. There are at least ten of these to be found in the Christian faith, differing from region to region.

St. Eligius, who was at first a trained goldsmith and later became the bishop of Noyon, is a prominent example. The chronicles of France make no mention of any outstanding deeds attributed to him, but in Germany, wondrous tales of Eligius were related. He was a farrier and considered himself so gifted that he called himself "Master of the Masters" and even "Master over All."

One day, Eligius hired a journeyman who demonstrated a method to make the hardest physical labor of the smith's job easier: he simply cut off the horse's foot, shoed it directly on the anvil, and then fit it back on the horse again, as if nothing had happened. Since this odd journeyman was not a charlatan, but Christ himself, this frightening method even worked. Of course, Eligius did not know this yet, so he followed his journeyman's lead and cut off, of all things, the foot of a horse that belonged to none other than St. George himself. Once the shoe was on, naturally, he was unable to re-attach the foot to the horse. Thanks be to God, Christ happened by as if by accident and was able to save the day.

From that day forward, Eligius was no longer given to self-aggrandizement, but instead did honest work at his forge and became especially pious. Thanks to his virtuous ways, he even rose to the status of bishop later in his life and was worshipped by many smiths as their patron saint.

In some towns in France and northern Germany, several horseshoes bound together to form a wreath—known as the "bouquet of St. Eligius"—can still be found pointing the way to the local blacksmith's shop.

prevent the hooves from growing longer and longer, and the horse from losing its secure footing. One need only imagine a ballerina whose toenails are too long trying to dance on her points: unthinkable. Horses, who are one-toed animals, can react just as capriciously when their shoes are not properly fit. In addition, the iron horseshoes themselves eventually wear down and must be replaced every six to eight weeks.

In Greek mythology, Hephaestus is the god of fire and the forge—and the only craftsman among the Olympian deities. According to legend, his workshop was located under a volcano.

Every 6–8 weeks, horses need a new set of shoes. First, the smith removes the old shoe with pliers.

Then he uses a hoof knife to remove excess horn before filing the sole flat with a rasp so that the shoe fits.

Making the shoe fit the individual horse's hoof involves heating it and hammering it into shape.

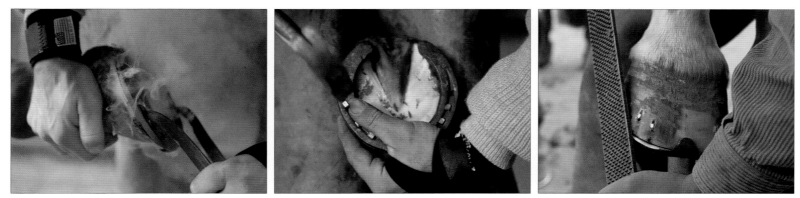

Then it is burned onto the hoof for the closest fit. The farrier must be careful not to burn too deeply.

Now the shoe can be nailed onto the hoof. Outside the white line, the hoof is dead material, so the animal doesn't feel a thing.

The points of the nails are clinched off, bent downwards and filed smooth so that no points protrude that could injure the horse.

The trusted farrier must have a firm grip, because shoeing horses takes quite a bit of physical strength. The shoe must be precisely fitted to each hoof down to the last millimeter. Completed templates are used, from which the farrier has a choice of some hundred different shapes and sizes. The farrier then fits the shoe to the individual horse, drawing on his or her knowledge of horses to correct for any minor motor deficiencies and misalignments. Knowing the needs of every one of their customers intimately is part of the farriers' *modus operandi.*

HOW THE BLACKSMITH HAS SHAPED
OUR LANGUAGE

"Forge plans/links/a treaty/a signature"
"Forge ahead"
"Hammer out a contract or a plan"
"Have several irons in the fire"
"Strike while the iron is hot"
"Iron will/iron constitution/iron discipline/iron hand"
"The blacksmith's horse and the cobbler's wife are
always the last to have shoes."
"The anvil fears no blows."

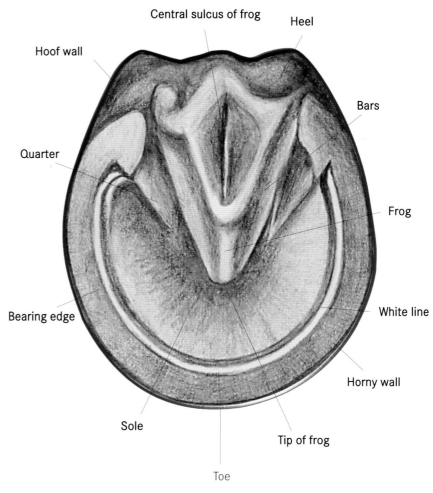

Central sulcus of frog

Heel

Hoof wall

Bars

Quarter

Frog

Bearing edge

White line

Sole

Horny wall

Tip of frog

Toe

Ancient Horse Tales

The horse has played an important role in world history in almost all eras. It made its debut among the Egyptians in 1720 BCE, when their land was literally overrun by the horse-drawn chariots of the Hyksos. It took the Egyptians 100 years to finally cast out the Asian invaders, but they did bring the horse to Egypt, where it was ardently admired and sometimes even honored with mummification.

Hitched in front of a cart or—for much greater mobility—as a trusty mount, the horse first proved its prowess in battle under the guidance of the Assyrians. In 2000 BCE, these aggressive warriors were seen as pioneers of horse breeding and care, and they left behind a record of their knowledge on cuneiform tablets.

Among the Celts, writing was forbidden for cult reasons, which is why we must rely on Roman chroniclers, who considered them very talented horsemen. They also told of the Celts' penchant for cutting off the heads of their enemies and hanging them from their horses' bridles, perhaps as a superstitious way to keep the sky from falling on their heads, an event they lived in fear of. In the powerful waves of the Irish Sea, the Celts saw the horses of Lir and thought they recognized Manannan, the son of the Celtic god Lir, conveying those who had drowned on his fastest horse through the depths of the ocean to the Island of Happiness. Under the spiritual guidance of their fertility goddess, Epona, the Celts rampaged for many years through what is today Europe, fighting and plundering. Epona, who was also goddess of horses, was always shown sitting sidesaddle on a horse and was devoutly worshipped. In Celtic myth, Epona was invincible, and the same mythical figure reappeared as an honored

The Assyrians were probably the first people to use the horse in battle. They left behind records describing horse breeding and care.

patron goddess of the Roman legions, even though the Celts had attacked and plundered Rome.

The Edda, a collection of old Norse myths that dates back to the year 1000, reveals that the Scandinavian gods were also talented riders. The best of all was the chief god, Odin, on the fastest of all horses, the eight-legged Sleipnir. On behalf of the gods, the giantess Nótt and her son, the god Dag, rode around the world in their horse-drawn coaches in order to create night and day. Also steeped in legend is the holy white horse of the Germanic tribes, which supposedly could not even be touched. What has been passed down in factual history is that the Germanic people decided when to launch a

An ancient Celtic coin depicting a horse and rider demonstrates the important role horses played among the Celts.

Caligula and the Equine Consul

Among the most peculiar incidents in history, calling to mind the megalomania to which dictators have always been susceptible, was a special decree issued by Roman emperor Gaius Julius Caesar Germanicus, who is better known as Caligula. Caligula sought not only to be emperor, but also to achieve divine status, and he appointed his magnificent horse Incitatus as his consul.

During his four-year reign from 37–41 CE, Caligula managed to silence all his critics. His addiction to prestige led to a complex network of intrigues that reached as far as Palestine, all in an effort to push the distinctive idea of putting an image of himself in the Temple of Jerusalem.

Caligula ended up falling out with both friend and foe, until one day his own guard murdered him. Incitatus, his consul, survived.

The Legend of St. Martin of Tours

In West Germany, France and the Netherlands, the eve of the day commemorating St. Martin is a special holiday for children. Holding colorful lanterns and lampions, singing and making music, they celebrate the legend of St. Martin, a man on horseback in their midst re-enacting the legend of how the saint rent his cloak in two with a single stroke of his sword in order to give half to a poor man dressed only in rags–a demonstration of selflessness and brotherly love.

Martin was a member of the Roman Legion and the incident in question supposedly took place as he arrived at the gates of Amiens, where Jesus appeared before him in the form of a poor beggar in order to test him. After this experience, the 18-year-old soldier was converted. Martin left the military, had himself baptized in Gaul, and founded the first monastery there, where he lived the modest life of a monk and pursued his vow to help the poor.

Against his will, he was ordained bishop in 371 at the urging of the people. Legend has it that he tried to hide in a stall to avoid taking up this post of honor. The geese in the stall honked wildly, however, betraying his hiding place. Ever since, St. Martin's feast day is celebrated by eating roast goose.

St. Martin attracted great devotion because he Christianized Gaul without resorting to violence and with generous amounts of brotherly love. He lived in extremely humble circumstances until his death on November 11, 397.

He became patron saint of France and his grave in Tours is a national shrine.

---

raid or react against enemy sieges by reading the natural reflexes and behavior of their horses as if the animals were oracles. Even as late as the first half of the thirteenth century, when the first Hanseatic cities on the Baltic Sea were flourishing, the holy white horse was a widely worshipped icon, and there is a museum dedicated to it at a cult site on the island of Rügen.

In their records of their own cultural history, Roman scholars told of triumphant chariot races, not only in the Circus Maximus but also on the Field of Mars after winning a war. The horse on the right in the triumphant team would be sacrificed to Mars, the god of war, as "Equus October"–the October horse. Its head was then hung from the wall of the Regia or suspended from the Mamilian Tower. The blood from the tail of the sacrificed animal was dried and burned as part of a celebration honoring the goddess Pales. People believed that animals and shepherds who leapt through the sacred flames of this fire would be freed of all negative influences.

This Ardre image stone from the island of Gotland, Sweden, shows Odin on his eight-legged horse Sleipnir. Sleipnir means "smooth" or "slippery," a name given to the magical horse because he could glide over land and sea or through the air.

Great Greeks

The Greeks only gradually became aware of the usefulness of the horse in military pursuits. The first chariots, developed around 1500 BCE, made slow progress over the rocky, mountainous terrain and quickly dwindled in significance. Nor did the four-legged creatures attract much interest as mounts for the cavalry. Conflicts were resolved on two legs, and even the news of the Greek triumph over the Persians was conveyed from Marathon to Athens not by a messenger on horseback, but one running on his own steam.

In society, by contrast, the horse played a much more important role. Horse racing in the specially designed Hippodrome was a popular form of entertainment. Winning an Olympic chariot race with a team of two, three or four horses conferred immortality on a driver, and the winning horses even earned themselves a feast sponsored by the state. The 33rd Olympics featured a special attraction: in addition to dressage events, there were some quite free-form races. Naked riders were challenged to ride bareback twelve times around the half-mile Olympic track. Some of the Olympic horses, which had arrived a month before the games to train, were housed by the Greek writer Xenophon (430–355 BCE), who lived on the Skyllos estate near the Olympic stadium. An avid hippologist, he recorded his knowledge in seminal works on horsemanship and hunting that are still of interest today. Although his writings fell into oblivion with the decline of ancient Greece, they were revived during the Renaissance.

The Trojan Horse

One particular horse decoy was to become the embodiment of cunning and trickery: in 1200 BCE the Greeks gained entry to the besieged city of Troy with the help of a wooden structure built to look like a horse. What they had not been able to accomplish in a ten-year siege was suddenly possible because the Trojans failed to see anything suspicious about a horse. They unsuspectingly pulled the vehicle into the city–along with the Greek war- riors hiding inside. The rest is history: Troy was burned to the ground.

The modern version of the Trojan Horse is the computer virus of the same name, which finds its way onto a hard drive unbeknownst to the user. Once there, it can, for example, spy out passwords or control the computer remotely. In order to get rid of this invader, the users sometimes have no choice but to imitate Troy's fate and destroy their hard drives.

Bucephalus, the horse of Alexander the Great, is described in some legends as white, and in others as black. All agree, though, that the stallion dutifully carried the emperor through all his many battles.

It was not until Alexander the Great (356–323 BCE) that the Greeks finally learned the advantages of a cavalry, for this was the only way the great general could unite the eastern and western parts of the known world into one great, powerful world empire. Alexander loved horses, especially Bucephalus, which means "ox head" or "bull-headed." His father had purchased the willful horse, which allowed only Alexander to mount it. This was because Alexander was the only one to notice that the horse bucked so wildly because it was afraid of its own shadow, so he simply turned the horse toward the sun.

Bucephalus may be regarded as the most important horse in history. For eighteen long years, the Macedonian stallion carried Alexander around half the world, from battle to endless battle. Legendary triumphs were followed by equally sensational revelry, in which the king often over-indulged his penchant for alcohol. These unbridled excesses changed Alexander's personality, even causing him in a fit of drunken passion to murder his friend Clitus, who had once saved his life. Bucephalus was spared Alexander's moods, however, and even carried his master all the way to India. Once there, which all citizens would have equal rights. Astride Bucephalus, who is described in this case as a black horse, he fought gloriously and triumphantly until the horse died at the age of thirty in the battle against King Poros at the Hydaspes River. The life and personality of Alexander the Great had already given rise to numerous legends at an early date. On one point, however, all are in agreement: on the spot where Bucephalus died, Alexander founded a city named after the horse in memory of his loyal companion—probably where Lahore is located today.

ARION, PEGASUS, AND THE CENTAURS

Greek mythology is full of horses that served the gods or were themselves apotheosized and ruled over men. Poseidon, god of the sea, sometimes took the form of a horse and with Demeter, goddess of fertility, conceived Arion, the first true horse.

The winged steed Pegasus, another figure in Greek mythology, was born in an instant when Perseus beheaded the Medusa and, so the legend says, the horse sprang with bloodied mane from her trunk. The unbridled Pegasus, who was supposed to bring thunder and lightning to Zeus, the all-powerful father of the gods, was finally tamed by Bellerophon, the Corinthian hero. Emboldened by an excess of pride, the hero rode aloft to Olympus, the seat of the gods. Zeus, dismayed at the arrival of this young upstart, caused a hornet to sting Pegasus, who swiftly conveyed his rider back to earth where he belonged.

Pegasus was the source of future poetic flights of fancy when the beat of his hoofs caused the Hippocrene Fountain to spring forth on Mount Helicon, with water sacred to the muses. Ever since, the legendary creature has inspired poets, thinkers, musicians, and painters. Pablo Picasso painted a modern version of the mythical figure. In Friedrich Schiller's *Pegasus in the Yoke*, the famed steed of the muses ends up at the side of an ox harnessed before a plow, after Schiller's starving poet has sold the animal to a farmer. This famous winged horse is still said to help writers' imaginations take flight.

After catching their first sight of a horse and rider from the neighboring state of Thracia, the Greeks added the figure of the centaur to their mythological stories. With a human upper body and horse's lower body and legs, centaurs were mighty creatures who lived in the forest; loved wine, women, and song; and were wont to tear out trees and cast around boulders as if they were playthings.

Perseus on the legendary winged horse Pegasus shortly after the animal's birth. According to mythology, the horse sprang from Medusa's trunk after Perseus cut off her head.

the poor animal was wounded several times in the battle against the Indian king Poros and finally collapsed under Alexander, dead.

Some histories explain the great general's urge to conquer more and more ground by theorizing that he wished to create an empire in

---

Pegasus and the Centaurs in the Sky

When Pegasus spreads his wings in the night sky, he is a large figure, but quite inconspicuous. The most noticeable point in the constellation is the great Pegasus rectangle, with a smaller equilateral triangle that forms the horse's forelegs but is often mistaken for its head. The Pegasus constellation shares the star in its northeast corner with Andromeda and it reaches its highest point at midnight on September 1.

The centaur figure can be found several times in the sky. The constellation Centaurus with its many bright stars is located south of Hydra and culminates on April 6. In the southern hemisphere, the Southern Cross is readily visible in between the hooves of the centaur.

Sagittarius, the Zodiac sign symbolized by an archer, is based on Chiron, inventor of the bow and arrow and the only wise and peace-loving centaur. Three thousand years ago, people in India thought they could see the shape of a horse in Sagittarius. The eye-catching constellation lies east of Scorpio and south of Aquila at the center of the Milky Way. People in ancient civilizations imagined that after death all souls would reach the Milky Way and pass by Sagittarius, the gatekeeper of the afterlife, on their way.

Powerful Women

OUTRIDERS—THE AMAZONS

No one knows if the Amazons really lived as described by the chroniclers. But whether or not they actually existed, their name lives on—women in the saddle or sulky are still referred to today as "Amazons."

It is a thoughtless epithet considering that, according to Greek legend, the Amazons were a warring tribe of women who cut or burned off their right breast, enabling them to better take aim with a spear or bow, the weapons of choice of the nomadic mounted warriors. The "breast-less ones," which is what the name "A-mazons" is taken to mean, supposedly had contact only with the men of a neighboring tribe, in the spring, dispatching any male children resulting from these liaisons post-haste back to the men's camp and raising only the girls. The Greek historian Herodotus reports that the girls were taught to wield a bow and arrow on horseback for the hunt and, before marrying, had to have slain at least one man in battle. As daughters of Ares, the insatiable, man-killing god of war, the Amazons were honored just like the men for their courage, and mighty Amazon queens such as Antiope, Hippolyta, and Penthesilea appear in many Greek myths. The figure of the Amazon in Greek mythology probably reflects men's fear of women's prowess with horses and weapons—evidently with good reason!

RIDING SIDESADDLE

As a rule, only a few women were found in the saddle until well into the Middle Ages. And even when they were finally permitted to mount a horse, women were not the ones riding the horse, but rather took a seat behind a man. Perched sidesaddle on the horse's croup, they had to struggle to maintain their balance and had only a strap wrapped around the man's hips to hold on to.

When women could no longer be disbarred from riding, genteel society required that both legs be placed on the left side of the horse, with the woman's left foot in the stirrup and her right leg above it resting on a leather support. The entire contortion was prettily concealed by the long skirts women wore at the time. The resulting picture was ever so ladylike, but completely impractical. It was only logical that women then required the assistance of a man in order to mount and dismount. With this posture, there is no leg on the right side of the horse's body to help control the horse, so the ladies had to use a long switch instead. In spite of these restrictions, however, women had at least made it into the saddle, and even took part in the hunt, galloping across the countryside and jumping over small obstacles.

Women had to master the art of sidesaddle until well into the nineteenth century, when they were finally freed to straddle the horse in boyish style and prove that they could match the best of the male riders. They have accomplished this with bravura, as one glance at any list of winners at major riding and jumping tournaments will show.

Penthesilea

According to Greek mythology, Penthesilea, a proud queen of the Amazons, was murdered at an early age in the Trojan War. Achilles is supposedly the one who killed her, and even as she lay dying she was still in possession of her powers as an enchantress: Achilles fell in love with her on the spot and wept over her body in deep grief at his deed.

Romantic playwright Heinrich von Kleist turned this strange legend into a drama that was later even made into an opera. But during his own lifetime (1777–1811), the writer failed to achieve fame with this piece, or any other, for that matter. His tragic depiction of Penthesilea was torn to shreds by prominent poet Johann Wolfgang von Goethe and was rejected by the public. Like the Amazon queen, Heinrich von Kleist found no happiness in his life and died a tragic death—bewildered at his fate, he took his own life at the age of 34.

It took many years for women to gain permission to ride horses. When they did, they were first given a handicap: they were only allowed to ride side-saddle. This was not only uncomfortable, but impractical as well. They could only use one thigh to control the horse, and shifting their weight was also only possible to a limited extent. Nevertheless, women still insisted on joining the hunt and even jumping.

Famous Women in the Saddle

Whether Joan of Arc really won the Battle of Orleans in the saddle, as shown in paintings, is unknown. But we do know that she had the permission of King Charles VII to accompany male troops into battle dressed in men's clothing and armor, and that she paid for her courage later by being burned at the stake. This tragic fate is presumably what brought such widespread fame and ensured her place as France's national heroine.

Empress Elizabeth of Austria, the legendary "Sisi," also met a tragic end: she was stabbed while taking a walk in 1898. Unlike Joan of Arc, we know very well that Sisi was a gifted and daring horsewoman. At the Viennese court she outshone the male competition, often causing her husband, Emperor Franz Joseph, to fear for her life.

Luckier than the Austrian empress were the German Empress Auguste Viktoria and her daughter, Crown Princess Cecilie. They joined parades on horseback and participated in maneuvers.

For decades, the English have enjoyed the sight of Queen Elizabeth in the saddle. She insists on taking part in her own birthday parade on horseback. Her daughter and granddaughter are also successful tournament athletes: Princess Anne took part in the European Championship and the Olympic Games in the three-day event, before becoming president of the International Equestrian Federation for a few years. Her daughter, Zara, is also European Champion in the same event.

Jacqueline Kennedy did not participate in major tournaments, but was nonetheless an enthusiastic horsewoman from an early age and also taught her daughter, Caroline, to ride. She taught her horses, on the other hand, how to smooch with her husband, US President John F. Kennedy, as demonstrated by an old home movie in the National Archives.

For the young heiress of the Onassis fortune, Athina Roussel, participating on the Olympic spring-jumping team is a cherished goal.

Haya, Princess of Jordan, was able to achieve this when she represented her country at the Olympic Games in Sydney in 2000. After marrying the Crown Prince of Dubai at the time, Sheik Mohammed bin Rashid Al Maktoum, she also took up his great passion, endurance riding.

Queen Elizabeth of England riding side-saddle in a parade.

Princess Anne of England competes in the three-day event.

Joan of Arc leading French troops into the Battle of Orleans.

The Unfolding Glory
of the Horse

The Evolution of the Horse

There was a time when horses were only about the size of foxes. Based on fossil evidence found in North America, scientists date this stage of development to 60 million years ago. Back then, the *Hyracotherium*, also dubbed *Eohippus*, a herbivorous ancestor of the horse that measured just 10–16 inches long, made its way through the swampy primeval forest by balancing on four splayed front toes and three back toes. Over millions of years, and as the swamps and deciduous forests receded and the ground became more solid, the toes of the horse's feet were reduced to a single toe—the hoof. The animal's jaw also adapted to tackle the harder foods of the steppe. The back teeth developed into flat-crowned molars. Scientists suspect that the equids grew larger in the course of their evolution because a larger organism requires proportionally less food in relation to its body weight to keep its body temperature constant (for example), and can thus live more economically.

Depending on their habitat and living conditions, a number of various kinds of grass-eating primitive horses evolved. These creatures traveled via land bridges (such as the one formerly existing between Alaska and Russia) from North America to Asia, Europe, and Africa. There they developed independently of each other, while the original horse-like creatures on the American continent died out for reasons unknown some nine thousand years ago. The horse would not return to the continent until Spanish explorers brought horses with them in the sixteenth century.

In zoological terms, the steppe zebra and Grévy's zebra, the African wild donkey and the Asian wild ass, as well as Przewalski's horse, all belong to the genus *Equus*, Latin for horse. Through gradual adaptation to a wide range of living conditions, this line eventually gave rise to the cold-blooded horses in the north and the thoroughbreds in the south, as well as the ponies that spread across Europe and Asia.

Relatives of the Horse: Rhinoceroses and Tapirs

Among the horse's "hunch-backed relatives" are animals such as tapirs and rhinoceroses, which likewise have an odd number of toes and are thus part of the order of odd-toed animals (*Perissodactyla*). Their common ancestor is known as *Condylarthra*, and lived approximately

60 million years ago in the Paleocene period.

Tapirs, which are at home in the South American and Asian swamplands, have hardly changed at all during the last several million years, except in size. Their body structure and particularly their four front and three back toes still strongly recall the forefather of all horses–*Eohippus*.

The *Eohippus* (or "dawn horse") shared its North American stomping grounds with a number of primitive rhinoceros species, which later disappeared from the North American continent, just as *Eohippus* did, for reasons unknown. Until the Ice Age, the rhino-like creatures could still be found in Europe, but today they live only in Africa and Asia, where they are currently endangered.

From the primitive horses, four sub-species developed that are classified as Pony Types 1 through 4. Pony Type 1, a small robust animal sized 47–49 inches tall, lived in northern Europe and parts of eastern Asia. It was protected from the predominantly cold, wet climate by a thick coat, and resembled today's Exmoor Pony. Pony

Mesohippus

- Oligocene: approx. 40–25 million years ago
- Habitat: forests and bush
- Size: approx. 20 inches
- Toes: 3 on all feet, weight mostly on middle toe

Eohippus (Hyracotherium)

- Early Eocene: approx. 60–40 million years ago
- Habitat: forests and bush
- Size: approx. 10–16 inches
- Toes: 4 in front, 3 behind

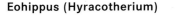

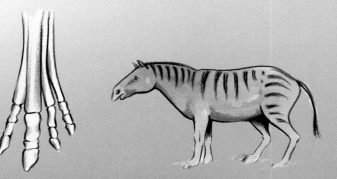

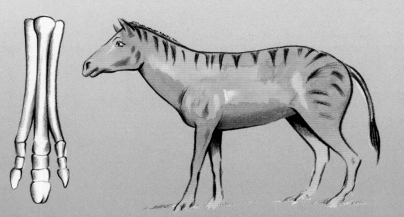

Non-Horses: Seahorses and Hippopotamuses

Any quest for the horse's namesakes might well start with an aquarium or by traveling to the planet's warmer coasts, preferably in tropical waters. This would produce the seahorse, or *Hippocampus*, as it is known scientifically. This egg-laying creature belongs to the genus of the bony fishes and bears absolutely no relation to the horse apart from its similar-looking head.

The hippopotamus has nothing to do with the horse either, apart from its name, which means "river horse." Anatomically speaking, the several-ton hippopotamus and equus have about as much in common as the hippo does with the seahorse–even when the hippo is pulling a sulky, as shown below.

When God Created the Horse

"When God created the horse…" the bedouins of the Middle Eastern and North African deserts and steppes still recount today, "…he said to the South Wind, 'Condense yourself; I want to make a new creature out of you to honor my deities and abase my foes.' The South Wind answered, 'It shall be done, o Lord.' Then God took a handful of the South Wind, breathed life into it, and created the horse."

Type 2 is thought to be the ancestor of today's cold-blooded horses and was at home in the northern reaches of Europe and Asia. It was heavier and stockier than Type 1, reaching a height of 55–56 inches. A modern counterpart of this pony is the Fjord horse. Pony Type 3 inhabited the mountainous steppe landscape of Central Asia, wandering as far as the Iberian Peninsula. It is therefore the ancestor of the Andalusian, Berber, and Sorraia horses. Finally, Pony Type 4 was a steppe horse that lived in the deserts of the Middle East, a predecessor of today's Arabian Thoroughbreds. This fine-boned horse, averaging only 47 inches in height, was capable of great speed and endurance.

On the basis of fossilized remains, paleontologists have been attempting to put together the horse's family tree for over 150 years, and have managed to reconstruct the history of the species almost fully. There are still several open questions, however, since their development did not follow a single, direct line. Rather, it branched off in several directions over millions of years, resulting in a highly complex picture that could fill tomes. The path from *Eohippus* to *Equus caballus*–today's horse–alone encompassed an estimated 15 million generations.

Pliohippus

- Pliocene: approx. 10–3 million years ago
- Habitat: steppes
- Size: approx. 43 inches
- Toes: 1 toe
- Direct ancestor of the horse

Miohippus

- Miocene: approx. 25–10 million years ago
- Habitat: savannah and lowlands
- Size: approx. 35 inches
- Toes: 3 on all feet, only middle toe touches ground
- First grass-eating horse

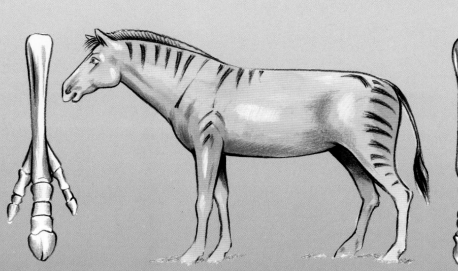

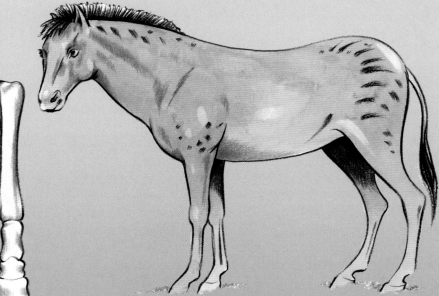

This is the unusually savvy gelding Brutus: as leader of the bachelor contingent in Hortobágy, he caused such an uproar that he had to be put in his own paddock. He now shares his quarters with four mares like a real stallion.

To Civilization and Back

In zoological terms, Przewalski's horse belongs to the horse genus, as did the steppe tarpan and forest tarpan, both of which died out long ago. Przewalski's horse is thus the last living representative of the wild horse species. Typical characteristics are the standing mane and a tail in which the upper third consists only of short hair matching the body color.

The days when the horse with the unpronounceable name existed in the wild were already coming to a close when the Russian general and explorer of Asia, Nikolai Mikhaylovich Przewalski, discovered it in Mongolia in 1879. A skull he brought back and gave to Russian zoologist Polyakov two years later confirmed his suspicion that he had chanced upon a wild horse, which was then named *Equus ferus przewalskii* in his honor. Around the turn of the last century, fifty-five of these horses were caught in the wild, imported into Europe (most of them by Carl Hagenbeck, founder of the modern, natural-habitat zoo), and distributed among various zoos. Almost all Przewalski's horses living in captivity today (and bred to be returned to the wild) can be traced back to twelve horses from this group. The other imported Przewalskis either died young or did not reproduce.

In the year 2005 alone, 17 foals were born. The undisputed star mother in Hungary is the mare Ashnai, who came from the zoo in Cologne, Germany. She has brought seven healthy foals into the world in just seven years.

RETURNING PRZEWALSKI'S HORSES
TO THE WILD

Przewalski's horse, which would have died out long ago if it had not been bred in captivity, is now being returned to the wild, including its original habitat in Mongolia and China.

In 1997, Cologne Zoo helped establish a semi-reservation for the horses in Hungary, at Hortobágy National Park. Today, sixty-seven Przewalski's horses live there in seven harems and one bachelor group; seventeen foals were born in 2005 alone. All the horses are identified and named, and observers keep close watch over them, recording their every move. This data can be evaluated to provide valuable information on the behavior of horses living in the wild.

WILD HORSES

On the plain,
sweet grass grazing
cool streams sipping
horses wild and winsome.
Nuzzling, neck-twining pleasure
clattering, foot-clouting fury
—thus the herd's harmless life.
O unwise man
to bind and burden
with yokes and poles,
with shafts and harness.
Will they not then
burst the traces and
smash the shafts?
Will they not then
tear the tarpaulin and
champ, chew, shred their restraints?
Is it not in this way
that trouble brews?

Chuang Tzu, Chinese Philosopher

Above: The members of a herd keep to themselves most of the time, but they have also learned to tolerate the proximity of other herds.

Below: The stallion Apor among his mares. Apor is the leader of the largest herd in the Hungarian semi-reservation.

Sociable, Undemocratic, and Sensitive

Horses are by no means loners. They seek out the company of others, and have done so from time immemorial. In the wild they live in a herd, a protective community marked by a strict hierarchy headed by the leading stallion. The mares in the herd belong to this highest-ranking stallion. His favorite mare, usually older and more experienced than the others, acts as lead mare, guiding the herd to the grazing areas. When danger threatens, she chooses the direction in which to flee, while the lead stallion takes up the rear, keeping the herd together. Younger stallions that have pretensions to assuming leadership rank and access to the mares have to take on the lead stallion in a head-to-head battle—sometimes to the death. Minor infighting between lower-ranking members of the herd is usually limited to threatening gestures, but must also be resolved at some point. The social fabric of the herd probably seems quite familiar in human terms, at least in its basic workings.

Eyeglasses for Home Alone

In the case of the young Swedish trotter Home Alone, on whom many people had pinned great hopes, an optician turned out to have the answer to a perplexing riddle. After leaving the most elite racehorses in the world in the dust in early races, this stallion suddenly had trouble keeping up and nobody could figure out why. Only after retired optician Kurt Anderson had observed him on the trotting track, diagnosed nearsightedness, and fitted him with a pair of horse eyeglasses with strong corrective lenses, did Home Alone again take the lead.

HIGHLY DEVELOPED SENSES

For the wild horse living on the steppe, speedily perceiving danger (such as the approach of a predator) was a matter of life and death, and they needed highly developed sensory organs. This perceptual sensitivity is still pronounced in today's horses, even though they now live under our protection, grazing in enclosed pastures or housed safely in a stable.

The Sense of Sight

With eyes on the sides of their head, horses obviously have a sense of sight quite different from that of people. Our eyes are close together and thus provide two almost identical images. Horses' eyes, however, see in a monocular manner; in other words, each eye captures a different image, and thus individual points are not perceived completely clearly. This was simply not necessary for survival on the steppe millions of years ago. Instead, the horse had to keep an eye on every angle at once, and for this purpose a sideward view was advantageous. A simple raising or lowering of the head was enough to afford a panoramic view of the surroundings. The human visual field by comparison encompasses only 100°, while that of the horse is three times as broad. The only things horses cannot see are those above their eyes, over their forehead, and directly behind them—and this is precisely what sometimes bothers

Mutual nibbling helps horses care for their coats, and it is a sign of affection and friendship. This kind of physical connection is also part of courtship: a stud nuzzles and nibbles a mare before mating.

A fight between two stallions determines the pecking order in a herd. When the horses are still foals, this kind of jostling is part of play, but later it can take on a more dangerous cast and even lead to serious injuries.

them to no end! It is known that horses can distinguish between colors quite well, especially yellow and green tones. At twilight and during the night they see better than people, even though they adapt only slowly to alternations between light and shadow.

The Sense of Hearing

Horses' ears are several degrees better than human ones, and not only in terms of size and mobility. They are also much more sensitive, and a horse can readily pick out the voice of its rider from a variety of other noises and voices. They prefer quiet, deep, and calm tones to loud, high, and shrill ones.

The Sense of Taste

The taste buds in a horse's mouth are very pronounced and team up with a sensitive nose that once made it possible for the wild horse to tell good from bad instinctively (helping it to avoid eating poisonous plants, for example). Over time, this ability has deteriorated in domesticated horses.

The Sense of Smell

A horse's sense of smell is the most important of all its senses and is much more highly developed than that of humans or even some dogs. Smells reveal everything about other members of the same species, including their readiness to mate, which is signalized in horses by the release of sexual attractants (pheromones). When a horse curls its lip in a reaction known as *flehmen*, it is trying to place a new smell. The odor enters the mouth and is processed by the Jacobson's organ, a small tube on the floor of the nasal cavity.

The Sense of Touch

The sense of touch is also highly attuned in horses. The fact that a horse will try to shake off a fly that alights on it shows how sensitively the surface of the skin reacts to minimal stimuli. The highly responsive sensory hairs around the horse's mouth work like a group of small antennae and should under no circumstances be trimmed. They help the horse examine its feed and sort it if necessary.

The Sixth Sense

Both humans and horses are in possession of depth sensitivity, known as the *muscular sense*. Spindle-shaped receptors in muscles, tendons, and joints convey every change in the musculature to the brain. Without this information on the position of its limbs, it would not be possible for a horse to coordinate its legs, for example, much less to make them obey its will.

Well Built

Horses generally continue to grow until their fourth year. The skeleton of a fully grown horse consists of over 200 individual bones, most of which are connected by flexible joints. Only about 10 percent grow together to form inflexible junctions.

"Don't look a gift horse in the mouth."

Crest with mane · Ear · Poll · Forelock · Eye · Nostril · Withers · Throat latch · Cheek bone · Chin · Lower throat · Mouth · Hip · Flank · Loins · Back · Croup · Shoulder · Dock · Chest · Thigh · Forearm · Tail · Stifle · Barrel · Elbow · Knee · Hock · Castor/Chestnut · Front cannon · Fetlock joint · Fetlock · Coronet · Bulb · Pastern · Hoof

---

"Zeus and the Horse" by G.E. Lessing

One day, the proud and willful horse was no longer satisfied with itself. It trotted up to Zeus' throne and asked the god to make it even more beautiful. Zeus responded by conjuring up a camel and saying: "Look at this: legs that are even longer and thinner, with a long swan-like neck…" He asked the horse, "Would you like to look more like this instead?" The horse said "No thank you," and swiftly sped away, having learned its lesson…

The Exterior

The "housing" of the horse is not its stall but rather its outer appearance, often referred to as its "exterior." When a horse's exterior is judged, those in the know take into consideration a wide range of optical aspects, and what they hope to see depends on the horse's race and gender. Especially important are the shape of the head, the throat, the withers, the chest, the back, the croup, the tail, and the fore and hind legs.

The Horse Dealer

In days past, con artists frequently worked the horse markets, using every trick in the book to sell old, undernourished, unhealthy or otherwise poor quality animals to the unsuspecting public. Most potential customers, however, knew that they had better look a gift horse in the mouth, and look carefully, because the condition of a horse's teeth could tell them everything they needed to know. It is not easy to cheat buyers today: horses usually carry a pedigree with them, along with papers providing information on their provenance, and expert opinions on their physical condition–even the computer helps provide additional fraud-proof data. Nonetheless, horse traders are still seen held a nefarious light. The term is often used in political debates, for example. During an election campaign, Franz Josef Strauss, a fiery speaker, once accused his political opponents of having the manners of horse traders.

Horse Hair

Ropes, belts, harness parts, and bridles were long made of horsehair. The Icelanders perfected the processing of horsehair and regularly cut the manes and tails of their Iceland ponies very short in the spring. Anyone who failed to do so in this land of elves and trolls was considered slovenly. In other countries, horsehair was used to reinforce fabric from which jackets were made, and pillows were often stuffed with a mixture of horsehair and straw, especially in rural areas. These days, people prefer their pillows and fabric a little softer, and down and synthetic materials have replaced the indestructible horsehair, even in mattresses.

In one area, however, horse hair is still in high demand. Stringed instrument players still produce mellow tones with the wiry hair. Used to string a violin bow, horsehair is perfect for music-making.

The White Horse Rider by Theodor Storm
The novella *Der Schimmelreiter* (literally *The White Horse Rider*, published as *The Dykemaster*) is based on an old North Friesian saga. It tells of dyke warden Hauke Haien, patroling night and day astride his white horse. In a tragic accident, he falls, horse and all, into the storm-tossed sea, but finds no peace in death. Whenever danger threatens, Hauke, the White Horse Rider, appears as a shadowy form on his white horse atop the dyke.

and his Andalusian stallion Babieca, Napoleon and his Barb stallion Marengo, General Ulysses S. Grant and his white stallion Methuselah, and the Lone Ranger on Silver, to mention just a few prominent examples.

Those responsible for a horse's body mass and color are its parents, or, expressed more scientifically, their genes. To date, scientists have detected three different genes that carry the white color. The first one causes a foal to enter the world completely white. The second gene causes a horse's coat to become lighter and lighter through the years, and the third is expressed as a white pattern that does not change as the horse grows older. Horses with the last two traits are born with dark skin and have a longer life expectancy than horses that are born white, which have light-colored skin and are very sensitive to sunlight.

Someone who finds the first gray hairs appearing on his colored foal should not jump to conclusions as if the gray hairs had been found on a human head. This is not a sign of premature aging, but simply a natural step in the development of a white horse. The animal will become lighter and lighter over time, with dark and light

White as Snow

A snow-white horse is something special *per se*. If it also happens to be unusually large or graceful and appears in the international sporting arena, it is virtually destined for fame. Calvaro, the high-jumping Holstein gelding belonging to Willi Melliger of Switzerland, was known among his fans as The White Giant. Despite his mighty stature he was an extremely sensitive animal, but Melliger was nevertheless able to reach the World Championship finals in 1998, where Calvaro triumphed. Other dream duos in white have included Joan of Arc riding into Orléans on her donated white warhorse, El Cid

The Vale of the White Horse
And though skies alter and empires melt, This word shall still be true: If we would have the horse of old, Scour ye the horse anew.
G. K. Chesterton's *Ballad of the White Horse* is based on a tradition connecting the massive prehistoric horse cut into the chalk at Uffington, Oxfordshire, with King Alfred's victory against the Danes in 871. In Chesterton's poem, Alfred sees the fading white horse as a moving symbol of his threatened land, of the transience of all things, as an inspiration, and (crucially) as a call to humility. Fortified by this vision, Alfred won the battle and commemorated his victory by decreeing that the chalk horse should be kept clean and white for ever, as indeed it still is.

Most white horses have dark coats at birth. The dappled grey, which is covered in round white spots, is an intermediary stage along the way to a uniform white coat.

A Wedding Coach drawn by White Horses

White horses, white coach, white bridal gown—white is the color of light and innocence. White bridal coaches have long enchanted people in many parts of the world, although for centuries only the high born could afford to ride in a white carriage to the church where the bridegroom patiently waited. Today, this fairytale image has become a rarity.

Lavish weddings like this—with white horses, a coach, and opulently decorated harness—go back to a memorable precedent. First, the prospective groom would appear on foot or horseback in order to announce the upcoming event in the town or countryside. A few days later, the wedding coach and often the horses that would "draw the joyous pair" would be shown around. After the church ceremony, the young groom and bride would then present themselves in the carriage, sometimes accompanied by riders in front and behind the white team. This tradition bred many imitations, but the most elaborately staged wedding parades in the extravagant style of an opera performance have always been reserved for royalty.

mixing in the transitional period, a state that is known as dappled gray. In addition to this, however, nature has invented a whole range of white markings, each of which has a special name: fleabitten gray for small red or black spots all over the body, rose gray for graying horses that have a bay or chestnut base coat. Horses that were once black may end up with a bluish-gray cast that is referred to as steel or iron gray.

If a horse breeder mates a white stallion with a white filly, the result will not necessarily be a white foal, but the probability is 75 percent since the graying gene is dominant. Among the Lippizaners, Andalusians, and Camargue horses, almost all are various shades of white and gray, and Arabian Thoroughbreds often are, too. This coloring is found more rarely in Icelandic horses and trotters. Haflingers and Friesians never give birth to white offspring—and this would be anything but desirable anyway!

Albinos

Light, cream-colored horses are often referred to as Albinos or Pseudo-Albinos. In America, the American Albino Horse Club breeds the American Cream Horse, which is strictly selected for the color of its coat. Foals are born white and can all be traced back to the stallion Old King, who was born in the early twentieth century.

True albino horses, however, which have the red eyes, pink skin, and snow-white hair characteristic of creatures with no pigment at all, are incapable of survival.

This white horse, a fleabitten gray, may never lose the small red flecks on its coat, no matter how much he might like to become a pure-white horse. Although the speckles in the coat are usually red, black is also known.

Black as Night

Back when horses lived in the wild, the colors of their coats and manes served as camouflage. This is probably the explanation for the fact that nature produced primarily brown horses, and other colors such as white, gray, and chestnut only came about through human breeding efforts, along with black horses, which are still something of a rarity.

FAMOUS BLACK HORSES

Black Jack

Amid the muffled roar of bells, drums, and trumpets that processed through the main boulevards of Washington D.C., Black Jack caught the eyes of millions of people lining the streets and sitting before their television sets all over the world as the splendid horse was led behind the gun carriage bearing the coffin of President John F. Kennedy. Hanging from the saddle of the bridled but riderless black horse were a silver sword and two riding boots, reversed in the

A black horse, with or without markings, is always an impressive sight. But not all black horses stay black year round. There are also "summer" or "dull" blacks that get lighter in the summer, when they fade to an earthy or reddish brown color.

The military horse Black Jack—the last horse to serve in the US Army—not only accompanied John F. Kennedy's funeral procession, but also those of other presidents, statesmen, and generals. The two reversed riding boots in the stirrups of the caparisoned (riderless) horse symbolized the fallen hero.

Swiss Rappen

In Switzerland, a centime coin in circulation since the fourteenth century borrows its name from the German term for a black horse, *Rappen*. It was so popular that Rappen fans even founded a Rappen Coin Association, which elevated it to the main coin of the Swiss Federation. This necessitated negotiating a kind of currency treaty with Austria, making the Rappen equivalent to the Austrian Heller. The word gave rise to some local idioms that are still part of today's vernacular, such as *berappen* (to pay something) and *Rappenspalter* (penny-pinchers).

stirrups—a last salute to the assassinated leader of the United States of America. Stamping, and from time to time almost breaking out of the parade, Black Jack kept people guessing if he could be kept in line for the entire length of the six-mile funeral procession. By the time he finally arrived at the president's tomb in Arlington Cemetery, the horse had quieted, and he bowed his proud head along with the surviving Kennedys and the many heads of state attending the funeral. Even when the president's airplane, *Air Force One*, swooped down extremely low over the ceremony, the horse maintained its composure.

Black Beauty

The life of the horse Black Beauty as described in the 1877 novel of the same name by Englishwoman Anna Sewell was marked by suffering and abuse. Sewall based her tale on the reality around her, with her protagonist experiencing the kind of mistreatment at the hands of merciless carters that many transport horses were subject to in the nineteenth century.

Black Beauty enjoyed a far better fate on the big screen in the many film versions of his story. The black stallion with the white sock and white star on his forehead usually winds up in the hands of his owner through a happy series of coincidences, then is lost again through various mishaps, only to find his way back to his true owner after many exciting adventures.

Beloved by young and old, Black Beauty also found his way onto English television screens in a series of the same name that was also shown in Europe in the 1970s.

Fury

Highland Dale was the actual name of the American Saddlebred that stood before the camera in 1946 in the role of Black Beauty and was also booked for several roles alongside Clark Gable, Joan Crawford and Elisabeth Taylor. For his leading role in the feature film *Gypsy Colt*, the famous black horse was even granted the Patsy Award for animal performances in film.

Winning this animal Oscar (which had been swept unchallenged by the collie Lassie for several years in a row) convinced television producers that the time was ripe to create a version of the popular children's series "Lassie" featuring a horse. Thus, on October 15, 1955, Black Beauty, now known as Fury, trotted straight into the viewers' hearts in the first episode of the series, in which the beautiful horse and the orphan Joey Clark became fast friends. When Joey called his best friend, Fury immediately left the paddock and trotted to his side. When the boy suggested they go riding, the horse would kneel down so that he could mount. This touching scene dominated the opening credits of each of the 113 black-and-white episodes in which Fury, Joey, his adoptive father Jim Newton, and his right-hand man Pete experienced all manner of adventures at the Broken Wheel Ranch.

El Morzillo (The Black One)

During his campaign of conquest through Central America, when Spanish conquistador Hernando Cortés had to leave behind his injured stallion, El Morzillo, in an Indian village, he was not sure if he would ever see his trusted companion again. In his diary he noted, "The chief promised to take care of him, but I don't know if he will manage it, or what he will do with him."

His doubts proved to be justified. The Indians, who had never before seen a horse, were fascinated by the huge black animal and tried to do their best by it, but they did not have a clue how to take care of a horse. Treating the animal like a god, they prepared a place in the temple for El Morzillo, showered him with fresh fruit and meat—and were horrified when the horse died despite their best efforts. In their despair, they erected an oversized, sitting El Morzillo statue, which Cortés, if he ever came back, would have been able to see from far away.

The conquistador would never return; instead, some ambitious Franciscan monks arrived in the country 172 years later in order to convert the Indians to the Christian faith. By then, the Indians were worshipping El Morzillo as the god of thunder and lightning, which did not suit the padres at all. They were not prepared to suffer a second god next to theirs and, animated by their strong convictions, tore down the statue. All that remains of El Morzillo, the Black One, is this tale.

The Black Stallion

Beyond the realms of kitsch and whodunits, Walter Farley told the tale of a horse who already won children's hearts with his very first adventure, *The Black Stallion*, published in 1941.

During a voyage from India to New York, the untamed black horse comes to trust a young boy named Alec. When a storm hits, the horse rescues the boy from the sinking ship and they land on an island, where both are finally discovered. The further adventures of the horse and the boy fill a total of fifteen volumes, written by Walter Farley and later by his son Steven. From 1990–1993, the beautiful black horse galloped wild and free across television screens in a series with the same name.

Zorro

His logo was the "Z" that he inscribed with his sword into doors, tree trunks or even bloodily in the skin of his victims after he had completed a heroic deed. His creator, Johnston McCulley, did not have Zorro ride through Spanish-occupied California as an unscrupulous criminal, however, but instead made him into the avenger and rescuer of the oppressed peasant folk. When Zorro, clothed all in black, masked, and mounted on—what else?—a black horse named Tornado, he sowed fear in the hearts of the rich while the ladies swooned with romantic fantasies. This was the stuff of which Hollywood cloak-and-dagger films were made!

The first big-screen heroes under the sign of the Z were Douglas Fairbanks in 1920, who guaranteed the character instant success in the silent film classic *The Mark of Zorro*. In the 1940s, Tyrone Power took up the black cape, and in 1975 Alain Delon donned the mask. In *The Mask of Zorro*, Anthony Hopkins played the aging freedom fighter, who trained Antonio Banderas as his successor. In the sequel, *The Legend of Zorro*, Banderas took his last bow as the hero–supposedly because his back could no longer cope with the many stunts required.

But the legend lives on, still providing plenty of material for the big screen. Bestselling author Isabel Allende of Chile published a Zorro novel in 2005. She too gave the justice-loving hero a black horse, the color of his mount having become an indispensable part of the image.

Herds of horses generally include a range of colors. The horses seem quite content with this—perhaps they feel that variety is the spice of life!

A Horse of a Different Color

Most herds include horses of various colors, and the way the different colorings and markings are described has been standardized for greater ease of identification. A horse's appearance is noted in detail in its pedigree to avoid mistaken identity or even fraud.

Each country originally named the color variants found in horses by making its own associations. For example, red-brown coloring with no black hair is known in most of the English-speaking world as

chestnut. In Germany, it is fox. In fact, the German color system is unusual in that it is entirely attributable to a single man, Eduard Meyer, who certainly showed great creativity in his choices. While English speakers refer to white horses as greys or grays, Meyer connected the color with mold (*Schimmel*) and German grays are therefore, literally, molds.

Meyer was working for the East Prussian Stud Book Society in the 1930s when the imperial minister in Berlin formally commissioned him to find or devise names for all possible color combinations and markings found in horses, in the interest of maximal descriptive uniformity. Although Meyer's line of reasoning is not always obvious today, his descriptions have been mandatory in Germany ever since.

Although the names of the colors and markings are different in every language, they have the same meaning. In English, a horse

Where Did the Tiger Get his Spots?

In German, horses with this spotted pattern are known as *Tigerschecke* (spotted tiger)!

Checked, spotted, painted, flecked, dappled, striped… Retired German State Stud Administrator Eduard Meyer was clearly overtaxed by this case. Perhaps seeing spots before his eyes, he recorded the horse ambiguously as *getigert* (striped or piebald). Thereafter, this catchy but confusing name could not be expunged from either the official document or from memory, and the spotted piebald horse has been known as the tiger ever since. Other languages also referred to various species of big cat for horses with this distinctive look, but arguably chose closer matches, such as *panther* and *leopard*. In England, for example, the leopard is generally known—simply and sensibly—as a *spotted horse*.

with a reddish coat and similar-colored mane without black points is called a chestnut, while one with a reddish or brownish coat and black mane, tail, and legs is called a bay.

Similarly confusing for the nonprofessional is the distinction between duns and buckskins. These two both have a yellow-to-gray coat and dark manes, tails, and points. But the dun always has a dorsal stripe down its back, sometimes along with other darker markings that are not found in buckskins.

Nature's imagination knows no bounds when it comes to spotted and dappled horses. The leopard has any number of irregularly sized spots, while in pintos the variegated patches are much larger. Pintos come in two officially recognized color variants known as *tobiano* and *overo*.

In terms of color, therefore, many things are possible—which also holds true, incidentally, for the whole matter of breeding. Only when a chestnut is mated with a chestnut will a chestnut necessarily be produced as offspring. With all other colors, a differently colored ancestor may pass on its genes, resulting in some surprises. The only thing a breeder faced with this puzzle can do is to concede that beauty is in the eye of the beholder.

Blue, Green, and Red Horses

Franz Marc (1880–1916), cofounder of the artists' movement known as *Der Blaue Reiter* (The Blue Rider), created in the course of his short career a number of unusual animal pictures, many of which express his special fondness for horses. He had his first serious encounter with the equine world during his military service in 1899, when he learned to ride. Just a few years later, in 1905, he executed his first horse sketches, at first consisting mainly of horses' heads.

In his early paintings he was still searching for his own style, but as time went by he became increasingly bold in his use of color, favoring vibrant tones. His horse pictures include *Red Horse in a Landscape* (1910), *The Green Horse* (ca. 1912), and numerous images of blue horses. Marc placed less and less emphasis on a naturalistic depiction of the landscape surrounding his colored horses, painting only large colored surfaces with small gradations between them.

He did not live to see his art defamed as "degenerate" by the Nazis. While serving as a dispatch rider in World War I, Marc lost his life at the Battle of Verdun.

The dorsal stripe, also known as an "eel stripe," is a dark line running from a horse's mane down its back right into the tail. It is found primarily in wild races, but also in Icelandic and Fjord horses and Haflingers.

boots or socks, i.e. with one or more white legs. But this vague description is not nearly good enough—there are precise terms used to refer to almost any kind of marking!

The markings that some horses bear on their heads are also carefully classified and have been given imaginative names such as *blaze*, *star*, and *snip*.

None of these descriptions are mere word games, nor are they superfluous and annoying bureaucracy. They are official terms used just like human traits to unequivocally identify the horse that wears them. The white hairs on head and legs that a horse carries throughout its life are unchangeable identifying characteristics. Interestingly, the skin underneath does not contain pigment. Other markings include cowlicks or whorls, places where hairs growing in different directions meet.

All of these markings can be used to identify a horse and are thus registered in its pedigree documents. Natural variation is so broad that it is highly uncommon for two horses to share identical colors and markings.

Marked for Life

Color is obviously a matter of individual taste: some people have a penchant for a combination of hues while others prefer monotones. A horse lover who sets out looking for a pure, single color, however, will have a hard time finding a horse without more or less conspicuous white markings somewhere on its body. Sometimes nature does a thorough job and sends a horse into the world with

False markings
White hairs that may result from injuries—from the pressure of the saddle on the withers, for example, or from excessively rough use of spurs—are not part of the unchanging markings that are characteristic of an individual horse, and are thus called "false markings."

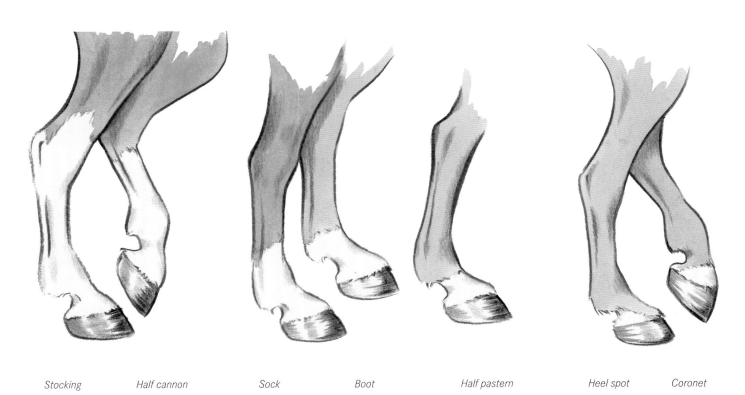

| Stocking | Half cannon | Sock | Boot | Half pastern | Heel spot | Coronet |

Mealy mouth

White mouth

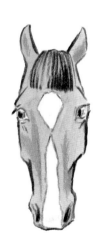

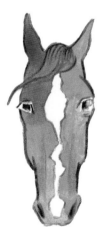

Bald face

Broad stripe

Stripe, race

Blaze

Interrupted blaze

Irregular blaze

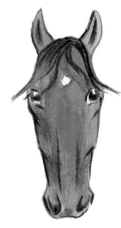

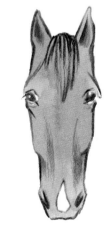

Elongated star

Star

Flame

Flower

Flake

Snip

The state stud farm of Warendorf in North Rhine-Westphalia has been in operation since 1889 and still houses the best sires in the state. Today, the grounds are a protected historical monument.

The National Studs

Many horse owners do not even know they possess one of these animals, let alone have any idea how to breed and maintain them. Because they dutifully pay their taxes, however, they are participants in the national state stud farms. These stud farms, which keep outstanding stallions and make them available for breeding, are in many European countries financed through tax receipts.

These expensive institutions pursue a number of goals: the state tries to maintain some measure of control over horse breeding while working against the spiraling prices that can result from the fact that every private stud farm is able to determine the cover fees for its own studs. This means in practice that the most promising progenitors, whose offspring could very well go on to make a name for themselves, are often unaffordable for the ordinary breeder running a smaller operation. Since these small breeders are vital to the overall success of breeding efforts, however, they must be supplied with equally high quality material. They can rely on the state stud farms to supply a good stud for their mares at a fair price.

Europe has seen several important state stud farms, of which the earliest was perhaps the one at Celle, founded in 1735 by George II,

The semi-state-controlled English stud farm The National Stud is the pride of the English Thoroughbred world. It is located near Newmarket, home to a famous racecourse.

Elector of Hanover and King of England, and developer of the Hanoverian warmblood. At its peak in the 1940s, it boasted 560 state stallions and 35,000 brood mares. It was closed in 1960. The imperial state stud farm established in Mezőhegyes, Hungary, in 1784 barely survived several dramatic vicissitudes. Its 599 founding horses ultimately produced the Nonius, the Mezőhegyes half-bred, the Gidran, and the Mezõhegyes sport horse. State stud books, however, took longer to establish. The Spanish State Stud Book was established in 1847 with the support of Queen Isabella II.

National stud farms are home to whole families of outstanding stallions, mares, and foals, while stud farms run by the individual states limit themselves to housing stallions exhibiting the best traits. Most of these state-owned studs are distributed during mating season to various mating stations. Since breeding is state subsidized, it "only" costs the equivalent of $150–$1,000 to service a mare, plus (if the mating results in offspring) another $75 or so per foal.

When it comes to mating horses, nature is rarely allowed to take its course these days—instead, a veterinarian usually injects the mare in heat with the stallion's semen. Fresh semen can even be delivered by courier if the distance is short enough, and frozen semen ensures that the genetic material of deceased stallions can be passed down to subsequent generations. It is shipped to all corners of the world so that successful lineages can be distributed across the globe. Globalization has thus also left its mark on horse breeding.

The Stud Fee

The amount an owner charges for the stud services of a stallion is known as the stud fee. This amount is freely negotiable among private owners and inevitably increases with the popularity of a particular stud. In the 1930s, for example, the services of the renowned American racehorse Man O'War could be had for $7,000–$8,000, an exorbitant sum at the time. Today's Thoroughbred breeders would find such a pittance laughable, as it now costs hundreds of thousands of dollars to gain access to the top gallopers' gene pool.

The imposing French national stud farm, Haras National du Pin in Normandy, maintains 70 stallions of various races.

Although horse breeding is not state supported in the USA, the country is nonetheless home to countless impressive stud farms, such as Calumet Farm in Kentucky, where gallopers are bred.

An integral component of every stallion parade is the quadrille.

Show Business

Stallion parades are still the most effective way for national and state stud farms to advertise the fine qualities of the horses they have on offer. These were originally designed to give the breeders an opportunity to appraise all the candidates in one afternoon—in the saddle, led by hand or hitched to a coach. Today, these parades have become splashy showcases taking place several times a year to make sure everyone has a chance to evaluate the prime stallions. The stallion parades attract a broad cross-section of the public, luring both casual equestrian fans and experts. Visitors arrive from all over the world to admire the national stallion parade—or simply to have a good time enjoying a program that incorporates elements from all of the equestrian disciplines. By the end of the show, one thing is clear—the organizers know their business, both in terms of breeding and show business.

In addition to jumping and other show elements, the high art of dressage is an important part of the stallion parades. The impressive breeding stallions present their dressage lessons—such as the half-pass in trot shown here—with style and elegance.

Stunts are another highlight of the stallion parade. They demonstrate not only the considerable physical talent of the rider, but also the horse's composure when faced with unusual situations.

Always a sensational sight are the performances of the teams, especially the quadriga. The four stallions lined up before the coach always bring to mind images of Roman chariot races.

When historic coaches such as the brougham are presented, the show takes a more leisurely pace. But the calm interlude is over as soon as the coldbloods appear, coach-and-six, thundering across the arena to the thrill of the audience.

Temperament

The distinction between coldbloods, warmbloods, and Thoroughbreds lies in the horses' temperament, their mental disposition, their drive, and their liveliness. Just like people, they are either high-spirited or they are not; such things cannot be taught or trained. A horse's temperament, character, and willingness to perform reveal something about what is inside, so to speak—the personal qualities of the animal. And these traits vary not only from race to race, but of course from horse to horse, as well.

Coldbloods are robust and not easily excitable. And we should be glad of this, for who could stop these heavy animals if they decided to bolt?

Warmbloods are coveted sport horses. They love to run and are high-spirited, but not overly nervous.

COLDBLOODS

The somewhat infelicitous description "coldblood" has nothing at all to do with the horse's body temperature. The term refers instead to all the heavy draft and workhorses that prefer to walk rather than to gallop. These are by no means icebergs on four legs. Rather, what the name is intended to express is their calm, relaxed temperament.

Coldbloods are hardly what you would call high-spirited—and that's a good thing, because if one of these ponderous animals were a bundle of nerves that bolted in panic every time it heard a paper bag rustle, who could stop it? The breeder, dragged after it like pages ripping from a wall calendar? Since so many horses are easily spooked, it is fortunate that not even such dangerous objects as flowerpots, puddles, and mail trucks can faze these placid four-legged creatures. There are those of us on two legs who would do well to emulate the inner tranquility of the coldbloods.

Bangs and Ponytails

Wigs and hats long spared women the need for a perm—which did not exist until the early twentieth century anyway; and a visit to the hair salon was an exception even then. Women and girls preferred to wear their hair gathered together in a ponytail, sometimes even adorned with a few hairs from a real pony's tail. Bangs (called a *pony* in German) were all the rage even as far back as ancient Egypt. Cleopatra, the last Egyptian queen, set the trend for cutting the hair short at the forehead, like a horse's forelock.

WARMBLOODS

The body temperature of the warmbloods, too, is no higher or lower than that of other horses—ideally between 99.5 °F and 100.4 °F. The term "warmblood" was devised as a blanket term for all horses that like to run, including hacks and cart horses, that are not coldbloods, Thoroughbreds or ponies.

Many countries have their own warmblood lines, including Slovakia, Denmark, and Latvia. The most successful sport horse breeders in the world are the Germans, whose warmbloods enjoy a fine reputation both in Germany and abroad. Thanks to the variety of bloodlines, all the ingredients for a promising show and racehorse have long been readily available. Simply take a little Thoroughbred for speed and spirit, a dose of Hanoverian for show jumping ability, some Holstein for dynamic basic gaits—and the hobby breeder already seems well on the way to fulfilling the dream of creating an Olympic champion. Naturally, everyone would like to breed the ultimate athlete, but not every high-performance cocktail will necessarily become a firecracker. So what happens to all the promising horses that don't make it to the Olympics? They are left with a career as a humble riding horse in amateur and hobby contests—where the hobby rider must be able to handle them. This is why breeders have worked out a common goal known as the German Riding Horse. This horse is envisioned as a warmblood with lively, elastic long strides; it has a noble, generously proportioned figure and correct posture; and, depending on its temperament, character, and willingness to be ridden, it is suitable for anyone. In other words: a beautiful, talented, not too nervous horse for which the chemistry between rider and its partner is simply right.

THOROUGHBREDS

Breeders of Thoroughbreds distinguish between the English Thoroughbred and the Arabian Thoroughbred. Both races have made a name for themselves as the ultimate in speed, endurance, and elegance. They are also popular for interbreeding with warmbloods and coldbloods, exploiting their aptitude for performance and their sensitive temperament.

The cradle of the Thoroughbred horse is the central Arabian highlands, where Bedouins have selectively bred horses with pure Arabian blood for centuries to produce the Arabian Thoroughbred.

Later, in the seventeenth century, the English Thoroughbred was bred purely for racing. It is based on the genetic material of three Arab stallions: Byerly's Turk, Darley's Arabian, and Godolphin Barbe.

The only horses that can be described as Thoroughbred are those whose maternal or paternal ancestors can be traced to these three stallions in *The General Studbook* (kept since 1793). English Thoroughbred and Arabian Thoroughbred crossbreeds are known as Anglo-Arabians.

PONIES

The term *pony* refers to all full-grown horses with a height not exceeding 60 inches. These usually undemanding and hard working small horses with their even temperament are especially suitable for children, and are normally much more robust than large horses.

There are innumerable races of ponies, many of which come from Britain. But demand is also high in other countries, and more and more ponies are being bred these days as the ideal leisure-time companions for smaller children.

All full-grown horses whose height does not exceed 60 inches are called ponies.

Thoroughbreds are tough and tenacious, but sometimes have a more difficult temperament than warmbloods.

Drinkers of the Wind

Race Profile: Arabian

Height: 58¼–61 inches

Colors: all basic colors

Description: elegant, high-endurance racehorse

Origin: Central Asian highlands

Light-footed and graceful movements underscore the beauty of the Arabian Thoroughbred.

We all know there's no accounting for taste, but there is one point on which all horse fans and laypersons agree: an Arabian is a beautiful horse, perhaps even the most beautiful of them all. An ancient Bedouin legend states, "When God created the horse, he said to the splendid creature: '*I have made thee without equal. All the treasures of the earth lie between thine eyes'.*"

The eyes of the Arabian Thoroughbred are stunning. Larger and more fiery than those of any other race, they allow us to glimpse the temperament of this one-of-a-kind horse. An Arabian does not simply

The elegant, well-proportioned head is a characteristic feature of the Arabian horse. The dished profile of the nose, with a marked indentation in the lower part of the nose bone, is typical.

move forward, it "drinks the wind," an appreciative expression referring to the way it gallops with head held high and nostrils flared. Charged with energy through and through, the horse can often seem fidgety or nervous and, despite its gentle and people-loving spirit, it can give the impression of being unapproachable–which is not true.

The Arabians have lovely, delicate heads, with particularly striking eyes and nostrils. The small, sickle-shaped ears are pricked up attentively, giving them an alert facial expression. In profile, one can see the straight or sometimes slightly concave bridge of the nose, the well-known dished profile. This is not a deficiency, but rather a desirable characteristic that is in no way detrimental to the horse's beauty (on the contrary!). The elegance of this horse continues in its slim, elegantly curving neck, the not-too-long but well-muscled back, and level croup. The naturally high carriage of the tail makes its hair flow in the wind like a banner when the horse gallops, further underscoring the dynamic impression of this beauty of a horse.

Mohammed's Mares

An old Bedouin legend tells that the Prophet Mohammed once left a large herd of noble mares in the desert without water. After three days, when Mohammed opened the gates to the watering hole, they stormed in, half-dead with thirst. The prophet, however, simultaneously blew the trumpet summoning them to battle. The horses heard their master's call, but only the mares Abbayan, Habdan, Hamdani, Kuhaylan, and Saqlawi followed him, their sense of duty prevailing over the torment of their thirst. Mohammed judged these five alone fit to establish the breed of Arabian Horses. He blessed them and placed his thumb in their necks to mark them. The small cowlicks that arose where he touched them were passed down to their offspring and are still known as "the Prophet's thumbprint."

Mohammed loved his horses more than anything in the world and therefore called on all the Moslem faithful to take good care of them, *for every barleycorn you give your horse, Allah will forgive you a sin.*

In the holy book of the Moslems, The Koran, the Prophet wrote that the evil spirit would never dare to enter a tent which held a horse of pure blood. Perhaps this explains why Bedouins lived in extreme proximity to their horses and even took them into their tents at night.

Visual considerations are not the only reason breeders like to ennoble warmbloods, ponies, and even coldbloods with Arabian Thoroughbred blood. The Thoroughbred's remarkable endurance and excellent character are also qualities that are worth passing on.

Who knows if the Prophet Mohammed's mares really made this dream horse a reality, or if it was actually the mare Baz, tamed in 3000 BCE by a great-grandson of Noah, who was the original mother of the Arabian race of equines? It doesn't really matter. What is documented is that until his death in 632 CE Mohammed bred especially swift and hardy horses for his followers' use in the holy war. Well-versed in genetics, Mohammed bred his horses in accordance with the severe principle of survival of the fittest. Thus the Arabs came to possess horses that needed little water and food and nonetheless persevered in battle with their riders to the point of utter exhaustion. Purebred Arabians can trace their heritage back to the three main lines of Kuhaylan, Saqlawi, and Muniqi, each of which engendered numerous horse families.

Mohammed's successors, the caliphs, went to war to fight for their beliefs and took with them the verses of the Koran, spreading their creed during the ensuing centuries from North Africa all the way to southwest Europe, along with their horses. This is why Arabian blood flows in many different races of horse.

The purebred desert horse still unites many of the qualities of its predecessors and is held in very high regard. Arabians are only suited to professional sports when they are tailored to their special

Akhal-Tekes

The Akhal-Teke is an ancient breed that has lived on the steppe of southern Russia for eons. It could well be called the "greyhound of horses" because, with a height of 60–62 inches, it has very long legs, and is a swift galloper known for its impressive endurance. Although they are fine jumpers, the Akhal-Teke's somewhat difficult temperament makes it an unsuitable tournament horse. This is why–like the Arabian Thoroughbred–it is ideally employed in long-distance marches.

These horses amply proved their long endurance in a very unusual undertaking representing their own cause. In 1935, to draw people's attention to the gradual dwindling of the race, a delegation of horses and riders conquered the difficult 2,600-mile journey from Ashgabat to Moscow in just forty-three days. Thereupon, the Russian government decided to rescue the noble breed of the Teke people, and extended Akhal-Teke breeding to the dry steppes of Kazakhstan, Turkmenistan, Kyrgyzstan, and Uzbekistan.

capabilities. They are not strong jumpers, so show jumping is not the best arena for them, and their gait is too short for dressage, but in long-distance tournaments Arabian Thoroughbreds are in their element—and difficult to beat.

The Arabian Thoroughbred is known for its great endurance, speed and undemanding character. It is thus tailor-made for use in the desert.

Masters of Spanish Dressage

Race Profile: Andalusian

Height: 61–65 inches

Colors: often gray, but also bay, black and dun

Description: noble racehorse with high knee action and elegant movements

Origin: Spain

THE HISTORY OF THE SPANISH HORSE

A good square deal—that's the Andalusian, the classic Spanish riding horse. Square, because it is about as long as it is tall, a good deal because it is easy to keep and comfortable to ride, with an enormous talent for movement and an even temperament that leaves practically nothing to be desired. From these attributes, it is easy to see why this horse is so popular.

If you have ever ridden an Andalusian, you will immediately understand why it has enjoyed such high prestige among the world's equine races for centuries, and why the most famous monarchs in the saddle chose this proud Spanish horse as their mount: Richard Lionheart and the Prussian king Frederick the Great are just two examples. Everyone who was anyone treated themself to an Andalusian: all agree that bestriding such a fiery horse makes the rider more imposing, too.

As in so many cases, there is little agreement on the historical origins of the Andalusian horse. The most widespread theory is that in the eighth century old Spanish races were crossed with Arabians that had come to the Iberian Peninsula with the Moorish conquerors.

Most likely, however, the Moors were not riding Arabian Thoroughbreds, but rather Barbs, an influence which can no longer be seen in the Andalusian horse. Breeders of the *pura raza Español* (the pure Spanish race) therefore assume that the appearance of the Spanish horses has not changed significantly through the centuries and that all the Iberian horses have their origins within Spain itself. Medieval paintings and equestrian statues demonstrate that Spanish horses ancient and modern correspond in all important attributes: noble head; strong neck; long, sloping shoulders; and muscular haunches. This indicates that there cannot have been much admixing of breeds from outside Spain. Spain has maintained its own studbook since 1912 to ensure the purity of the race. It is entrusted to the Spanish military for safekeeping.

The most important branch in the family tree are the Carthusians. These were bred in three Carthusian monasteries and successfully survived all breeding experiments. On the orders of the king, Friesians and even coldbloods were slated to be used to redesign the race in the seventeenth and eighteenth centuries. But this decree foundered against stiff resistance from the stout walls of the monasteries. Only recently have attempts been made to develop this baroque horse type into a more modern breed—an undertaking that is still highly controversial. The Andalusian itself has passed on its traits to other races with positive results: it was instrumental in the creation of the Lipizzaner, the Frederiksborger, and the Neapolitan.

The most important Andalusian stud farm is located in the city of Jerez de la Frontera, famous for its sherry and the Royal Andalusian Riding School. The horse is every bit as prominent an advertising vehicle for Andalusia as the sherry, and indeed even the flamenco.

THE DOMA VAQUERA

Many cowboys don't realize that their riding style did not originate in America, but in Spain. The *doma vaquera*, the riding method typical of Spanish cattle hands, arrived in America with the conquerors and was picked up by the cowboys, who later modified it slightly. Key elements of the doma vaquera, such as explosive sprints, quick turns, and abrupt stops, had already been mastered by cavalry on the Iberian Peninsula some two thousand years ago. The cattle hands, the *vaqueros*, perfected this art and (along with their horses and steers) became symbols of Spain. Spanish King Philip V

The traditional vaquero horses, the Hispanos, are able to perform all the important tests of classic and Spanish dressage, such as the left half-pass at a trot.

A higher test level for both horse and rider: the right half-pass is performed at a gallop in the illustration below.

(also known as Philippe d'Anjou) limited the deployment of the doma vaquera to the handling of steers in the eighteenth century, banning bullfighting on horseback. So for the next two hundred years the *torero* was forced to stand on his own two feet, with only a red cloth between himself and a raging bull. The doma vaquera continued to be practiced by Spanish riders across all social classes, however, a riding style that has ever since been firmly anchored in Spanish culture. Only Hispanos are ridden for this purpose: Andalusians crossed with English or Arabian Thoroughbreds.

The mounted work of the cattle hands is designed purely for functionality and its highest goal is harmony between horse and rider, which should be achieved with no special effort. The communication between the two appears so effortless that a layperson could easily get the impression that there is a kind of telepathy between horse and rider. But appearances are deceptive here, as training a

vaquero horse takes several years. There is no magic involved, but much hard work based on the principles of classical dressage.

Fortunately, the Spanish saddle is very comfortable, making long full-day rides a pleasure. The vaquero places his feet in wide stirrups that protect him from injury by steer. Of course, he must ride using only one hand, because in the other he holds a 11½-foot pole for driving the cattle (a *garrocha*). Mainly by shifting his weight, he directs his horse through rapid changes of direction, pirouettes, sudden stops, and all the other demands made on it in the course of his dangerous work with the steer. Today, the doma vaquera can be seen in the daily work of cattle hands, at Spanish bullfights, and throughout Europe as a tournament sport.

A vaquero never rides off without his garrocha. He uses this wooden pole to drive cattle or to perform artistic feats.

A vaquero's horse must be nimble in case a bull decides to charge. It can take off in a sprint starting from a stand.

Fearless Bullfighters

Race Profile: Lusitano

Height: 59–65 inches

Colors: all basic colors, often gray, bay or dun

Description: noble riding and carriage horse,
  used in bullfighting

Origin: Portugal

Any normal horse would turn tail and run when charged by a half-ton bull. Horses are by nature flight animals. This instinct is missing, however, in a very special race: the Lusitano, the oldest riding horse in the world.

In the horse's homeland of Portugal, people are justifiably proud of the courageous, agile, extremely strong Lusitanos, which come with a long tradition—complete with the usual legends. Their temperament and power comes (people say) from a drop of bull's blood that runs in their veins. This defies belief, of course, along with the claim that they were already extant before the Ice Age (this is supposedly proven by cave paintings, although scientists reject the theory). What can be confirmed, however, is that this equine race was indeed already extant, and was being ridden, five thousand years ago.

Like many other breeds, Lusitanos originally served their masters in battle until they were no longer needed at the front. Their orientation toward competitive sports was reinforced when horseback bullfighting was banned in the neighboring country of Spain in the early eighteenth century. As a result of this, the Spaniards began to breed lighter saddle horses while bullfighting continued to enjoy great popularity in Portugal.

In the Portuguese bullfighting arena, there is no *torero* facing the bull on foot. Instead, there is a *rejoneador* astride a Lusitano. The object is not to kill the bull, but rather to exhaust it so thoroughly by means of skilled evasive maneuvers that keepers are able to gain control over it. Although the bull initially survives the fight, it ultimately ends up in the slaughterhouse after all, as it cannot be used again. It cannot go on to fight a second battle because it has learned its opponent's strategies and would have no trouble catching the rejoneador on its horns the next time around.

The horse, with its fighter's heart and lightning-fast reactions, is like life insurance for its rider. The pair must also master the most difficult dressage feats in order to fight in the arena, because smooth side steps and agile pirouettes are indispensable.

This is why two famous bloodlines have come about, each of which emphasizes a different appearance and character traits. The Veiga

The imposing Lusitanos are powerfully built, yet at the same time incredibly agile and light-footed. Legend has it that their courage in the bullring comes from a drop of bull's blood coursing through their veins.

In Portuguese bullfighting, the rejoneador *on his Lusitano replaces the* torero *as the bull's opponent.*

line is named after breeder Manuel Veiga, who aims to produce small, compact horses for bullfighting with a maximum measure of 61 inches. Starting at that size, the d'Astrade line ranges up to 65 inches. This line is especially popular for use in *haute école* dressage. The Portuguese love both types of horse and make no attempt to hide their admiration at public events. Only the stallions are allowed to shine, though; the mares must devote their time exclusively to raising their young, which are usually presented to the world as grays. Only the Portuguese Court Riding School keeps rare bay Lusitanos, which are its trademark.

Lusitanos can hold their own in international competition in the disciplines of show jumping, dressage, and carriage driving. The

greatest triumph was earned by the Belgian Felix Brasseur, who became world champion with a four-in-hand team consisting entirely of Lusitanos.

When engaged in a bullfight, a horse's rapid reactions and obedience are effectively life insurance for its rider, the rejoneador. Mastery of the haute école *dressage tests is thus indispensable.*

Alter Réal

The Alter Réal is a close relative of the Lusitano and is similarly a classic baroque horse. If it may be said that the Lusitano has a gift for *haute école* dressage, this applies even more to the Alter Réal, which has an especially pronounced talent in that discipline. Its movements in all gaits are nothing less than extravagant, and make the piaffe, for example–where the horse trots diagonally in place–look particularly spectacular.

The Alter Réal's high sensitivity, which often verges on nervousness, gives it excellent capabilities to learn as a dressage horse but makes it unsuitable for the bullfight.

The line goes back to 1748, when the stud farm Réal de Altér, located in the Portuguese province of Alentejo, founded it with about 300 Andalusian mares from Jerez.

The Alter Réal, with its broad chest and elegant lines, filled the needs of the baroque era and was a much loved riding horse of the Portuguese royal family.

Its qualities were also appreciated by the French conquerors who swept through the country under the command of Napoleon in 1812, snatching up the best horses to take back with them to France. When King Miguel abdicated in 1834, breeding efforts broke down and the royal stalls were closed.

Only a few mares were left, and breeding continued in a haphazard fashion, causing the classic appearance of the Alter Réal to gradually fade. It was not until the end of the nineteenth century that attempts were made to revive the expressiveness of the race by admixing Arabian and English Thoroughbred blood. Hanoverians were also enlisted, but it was only when Andalusians were called into service that the original beauty of the Alter Réal was reborn.

In summer, the Lipizzaners are given a chance to recover from the strains of show business on the fields of the Piber Stud Farm.

The Trained Lipizzaners

Race Profile: Lipizzaner

Height: 61–63 inches

Colors: almost exclusively gray, in rare cases bay or black

Description: baroque-looking horses with impressive movements

Origin: Slovenia (Lipizza) and Austria (Piber/ Steiermark)

Tradition is everything at the Spanish Riding School in Vienna, where the mounted personnel still wear the bicorne hat and have a sugar pocket sewn into the left side of their tailcoat, so that they can reward their obedient Lipizzaners immediately after a performance. The crowning piece of any show is the Grand School Quadrille, which is always led by the single resident bay stallion.

On first entering the riding hall in Vienna, many fall silent at the extraordinary (not to say spellbinding) scene that presents itself.

This is not due solely to the hall's enormous dimensions. The visitor's overwhelming impression is of having unexpectedly walked into a massive, festive ballroom. Measuring 184 feet long by 59 feet wide, with a height of 56 feet, the space is framed by a gallery supported on forty-six columns with an ivory-colored coffered ceiling floating above it all. Below the equestrian portrait of Charles VI (the only color accent in the white hall), is a commemorative marble plaque with a Latin inscription that explains: *This Imperial Riding School was erected for the instruction and exercise of young noblemen, as well as to train the horses in the art of riding and in battle, on the command of Emperor Charles VI ... in the year 1735.*

This alone tells a major part of the story of the Spanish Riding School. But its origins lie in the even more remote past and solve the riddle of why everything in this Viennese institution seems so Spanish. The earliest references to the "Spanish riding stall in the Viennese court" are found in manuscripts dating to 1572. This is exactly when the first Spanish horses came to Austria, and the best

stallions among them went into the Viennese Riding School. Eight years later, Archduke Charles founded the world-famous stud farm in the village of Lipizza, which still exists today in Slovenia. But the proud Spanish horses did not remain isolated for long; they were soon subject to Italian and oriental influences. This stroke of breeding genius created a classic baroque riding horse with its noble body form, graceful movements, and honest character—spirited, good-natured, eager to learn, and with plenty of endurance as well: the Lipizzaner.

Their family tree can be traced back to six stallion lines, the oldest founded by Pluto, a purebred Spanish horse. The next four lines brought in the best traits of the Neapolitans and Kladruby horses through sires Conversano, Neapolitano, Maestoso, and Favory. Finally, Siglavy was an Arabian stallion who refined the appearance of the horse with his small head and slim neck. The beautiful horses that resulted from this breeding strategy became the stars of the riding school and favorites of the aristocracy. Even now, the name of the bloodline is still included in the pedigree of a purebred Lipizzaner immediately before his name: Conversano Banja, for example.

In 1735, Josef Emanuel Fischer von Erlach completed construction of the Winter Riding School, the new centerpiece of the Imperial court, a showplace for ceremonial court balls and rollicking masked celebrations, as well as equestrian games and show riding by the VIPs of the day. Empress Maria Theresia personally led a dressage quadrille that included only noble amazons like herself. In 1814, the Lipizzaners performed artistic feats of *haute école* dressage for statesmen and monarchs attending the Congress of Vienna. The kings later praised this entertainment as the "delight of the Congress." Political figures were not the only guests in the imperial riding arena, however: music also found a fitting context here when Beethoven conducted an impressive concert with an orchestra of 700 players.

The strong arm of history twice threatened to destroy the riding school. After World War I, Lipizza was no longer part of Austria and the Piber Stud Farm in the Steiermark region was forced to take over breeding duties. Then, when Austria was occupied and neutralized following World War II, the riding school was forced into exile in Wales for ten years. It eventually returned to the royal stalls on Michaelerplatz 1 in Vienna, and the charm of this timeless oasis—as it is sometimes called—was revived.

Lipizzaners thrill audiences with their elegance and the precision of their movements, which comes in part from the fact that the stallions are given plenty of time to develop. Their extensive training takes place over six years, but their human partners have to train even

In the quadrille, 8-10 Lipizzaner stallions perform their dressage tests in time to music, either simultaneously or consecutively, with figures choreographed to the last detail. These moves demand the highest level of concentration from horse and rider.

Vienna

"Vienna, Vienna, you alone ..." For centuries, poets, composers, singers and even historians have extolled and glorified the venerable old Imperial city on the blue Danube more than almost any other. Vienna has experienced both halcyon days and less fortunate times, which is why this city has developed an unrivalled brand of melancholy charm. Its residents have always been feared for their acerbic humor—the famous *Wiener Schmäh* (Viennese wit).

Today, Vienna is a vital modern metropolis whose reputation is still strongly predicated on the legends of the past. Prince Metternich once claimed that the Balkans began in Vienna, a notion that can be explained by the lasting influence of the two Turkish occupations in 1529 and 1683. Architecturally, echoes of this era can be found in the minaret columns of the Karlskirche (St Charles' church) and musically, in Beethoven's Turkish March. Beethoven, Mozart and Haydn make up the triumvirate of Viennese classical music, not to mention of course Johann Strauss, whose Viennese waltzes have had the world dancing in three-quarter time since 1867. Tourists still follow the footsteps of the great figures of this era, as well as immersing themselves in Vienna's colorful political past, which still shines in all its splendor at the Belvedere and Schönbrunn palaces.

Downtown, another city landmark awaits: St. Stephen's cathedral; and no visit to Vienna would be complete without a stroll through the Prater park and a glass of wine at a Heuriger tavern, followed by a cozy tour of the city in a horse-drawn hackney carriage.

The haute école "airs above the ground" include the levade (left) and the ballotade (right). In the levade, the horse stays balanced on its hind legs, with the front legs drawn up into the air. The ballotade is a jump with front and hind legs drawn upward.

longer. After five years as an *élève* (or student)—the minimum starting age is 15—candidates can rise to the rank of Student Rider and begin to train their own stallion. Five years later, if the Student Rider has successfully prepared his horse to take part in the performances, he attains the title of Rider. Only a few rise to the post of Chief Rider.

Faced with dwindling public budgets, the state was forced to withdraw from its equestrian hobby in 2001 and privatize the riding school. Since then, the Lipizzaners themselves have ensured the livelihood of their riders and caretakers. Visitors to Vienna will be lucky to catch the Lipizzaners at home—they are usually on tour.

Black Pearls

Race Profile: Friesian

Height: 61–65 inches

Colors: black only

Description: elegant, strong, and expressive

Origin: Holland (West Friesland)

Even as the Friesian has become increasingly refined in appearance over the years thanks to the admixture of Spanish blood, it cannot deny its origin as a coldblood.

Friesian horse breeders are always looking for black, not because they are particularly moody, but for a purely practical reason. A pure black coat allows them to know the instant a foal is born if they have got everything just right, since bays and grays are no longer recognized. The true Friesian horse is as black as the night, and in the sunlight its coat gleams as if lacquered. The long curly mane adds the final touch to give these black beauties their playful air. The Friesian is far from delicately built, but it can nevertheless move gracefully. It is not slim but lithe, and it is clear from the long, silky hair on its fetlocks—the feather—that this noble black horse was originally a coldblood.

Friesian aficianados dismiss any aspersions on the athleticism of this lovely horse. As one of the classic breeds, it goes without saying that the horse is a champion. Friesians number among the baroque horses, along with Andalusians, Lusitanos, and Lipizzaners. In the baroque era (1600–1750), tastes ran to ample and massive forms with plenty of style and verve. Whether in art or in fashion, this ideal of beauty was in demand everywhere, and the Friesians,

Andalusians, Lusitanos, and Lipizzaners embodied it to perfection. Many an aristocrat felt that his or her elevated status could be shown to the greatest advantage when perched on one of these breeds or with one harnessed in front of their coach. Four coal-black Friesians pulling a splendid carriage with their sublime movements were the *non plus ultra*.

The movement of the powerful black Friesians is surprisingly lissome and vivacious.

Despite these advantageous qualities, the Friesian has experienced its share of neglect. Although it represents one of the oldest warmblood races in Europe, it has been threatened with extinction twice in the past. The Friesian horse originated with the Germanic tribe of the same name in the Netherlands and northern Germany, who bred a large-framed horse that went down in history as the warhorse of choice for medieval knights. However, the foundations of today's baroque yet athletic Friesian were only laid in the sixteenth and seventeenth centuries, through combination with the blood of Spanish horses. The multifaceted Friesian has impressed European courts with its classic good looks and elegant gaits ever since—while at the same time being put to work by Friesian farmers. This balancing act turned out to be its salvation, because with the decline of the noble classes, its beauty and grace were no longer in demand, and without its usefulness in the fields, the Friesian horse might not have had a future.

Although the Friesian stud book (*Het Friesch Paarden-Stamboek* in Dutch) finally listed all existing stallions and mares in 1879, the breed continued to decline. By 1913, there were only three stallions left: Prins, Iva, and Friso—living, of course, in their homeland of Friesland. This beautiful and useful breed seemed doomed to die out until its biggest fans and patrons, the Dutch farmers, got together just in time to save the black beauties with renewed breeding efforts. Nowadays, the horses are part of the Dutch cultural heritage and highly prized as leisure and show horses. By order of Queen Juliana, the pedigree now carries the prefix "royal."

With a little patience, Friesians can even be taught some of the *haute école* dressage tests that are generally performed by Lipizzaners at the Viennese Riding School. These are not limited to the "airs on the ground" (pirouettes and piaffes, or trotting in place); Friesians can also learn the "airs above the ground," from the levade (bal-

You might almost think some Friesians are quite aware of their effect on onlookers—even with tousled locks, they have a way of cutting a good figure on the paddock.

Like horse, like rider: performances in historic costume impressively emphasize the baroque splendor of the Friesian.

ancing on the hind legs alone) to that most difficult of all feats, the capriole (in which the horse launches itself upwards as high as possible, kicking out its hind legs, so that it hovers for a moment horizontally in the air). Friesian horses love this kind of performance—or so their owners claim with a proud smile—as they are great show-offs!

The popularity of the Friesian horse is no longer limited to the Netherlands and Europe—today there are Friesians all over the world, from Australia to South Africa.

Tattoos for Friesians

Among the immutable and identifying features of individual horses are the white markings on its head and legs. As a breed, however, this is precisely what Friesians should not have, as they are bred to be completely black.

In order to tell these horses apart, the Dutch Friesian breeders came up with a quite original idea. Every Friesian foal is not only branded on the left side of the neck with its association's insignia, but also with a number tattooed underneath its tongue. This kind of tattoo is unique in the horse world and is otherwise only common among small pets. Cats' and dogs' registration numbers are sometimes tattooed—under full anesthesia—in their ear or on the inside of their thigh. Friesians are tattooed with no anesthesia. The practice is a controversial one in terms of animal rights, and what's more, the tattoo loses legibility over time and can only be read with difficulty after several years.

For these reasons, breeders are increasingly choosing to implant an identification chip under the horses' skin instead. The German Friesian Horse Association, for instance, has been "chipping" its foals since 1991.

Horses of the Camargue often have to find their food under water. They have adapted to the conditions of their habitat and can close their nostrils to shut out water.

Horses of the Sea

Race Profile: Camargue

Height: 53–59 inches

Colors: gray only

Description: strong and robust

Origin: France (Camargue)

One could give Camargue horses many nicknames, the most affectionate perhaps being "divers." Why is that? Because there is only one race of horse in the world that can graze with its head under water. This sounds like a tall story or joke, but it is true. The *Crins Blancs* (White Manes) enjoy far from comfortable living conditions in their homeland, and may truly be called robust. They live semi-wild in herds, sometimes even side by side with black bulls. They never see the inside of a stall in their entire life, and only few are ever trained to accept a saddle and harness. The rest spend their lives grazing on the watery expanses of the Camargue region in France. In this part of the Rhone delta, the horse seldom has solid ground under its feet, much less endless lush meadows; the Camargue is a

swamp. So the clever horse has learned to close its nostrils when pulling out blades of grass under water, so that it can always find something to eat. It follows naturally that the Camargue horse is also a good swimmer.

These horses command respect for their ability to survive in spite of an inhospitable habitat. No other horse in the world could subsist on the extremely salty grass and water that forms their daily fare—let alone in such a harsh climate. Summer temperatures climb to 95 °F without a shade-giving tree in sight, and in the winter, icy winds can drive temperatures down to 15 °F, with the water in the marshlands sometimes freezing over.

The state has not always behaved well in taking care of these unique horses, which undoubtedly trace their roots back to the prehistoric Solutré horse. Under Louis XIV, the army made use of the animals at will and undertook some clumsy attempts at interbreeding with other races. The same thing happened under Napoleon, and the population declined sharply. After the institutional needs of the cavalry declined, at least this source of abuse was no longer a threat. Appreciation for the horses and efforts to preserve their remaining habitat continued to dwindle.

Only the *manadiers* (the Camargue breeders) devoted their attention to fostering the *Crins Blancs*. The cowboys, too (known as *Gardians*), discovered the finer qualities of the small gray horses and made them their partners. But the state stud administration continued to ignore them.

The Camargue

When the cool, dry mistral wind blows over the Camargue, some farmers nail their windows shut, because in winter and spring the cold wind often becomes a storm tearing through the Rhone delta. But neither the wild black bulls nor the robust "white" horses fear this force of nature–unlike the sensitive flamingos that also make their home in the vast marshlands of the region.

Tourists have long been fascinated with this unique area. One of the first visitors, Pope Clement V, chose Avignon as the home base for the exiled Roman Church. As head of the Church, he rode through the sweeping landscape of Provence and the Camargue issuing decrees that have come down to us under his name, as *Clementines*.

The Camargue offers neither inhabitants nor visitors particularly luxurious surroundings, and it certainly cannot be compared with the natural riches of the Cote d'Azur or its cities of Cannes, Nice, and St. Tropez. But the people in the Camargue nonetheless know how to live well–simply but happily.

The best known town is Les-Saintes-Maries-de-la-Mer, the secret capital of the region. The village church with its soaring tower can be seen from as far as 6 miles away, and every year from May 24–26 the town becomes the setting for three consecutive pilgrimages and festivals. On the first day the *Gitans* (gypsies) celebrate the festival of Sarah, their patron saint. Then the two saints Mary of Saintes-Maries are honored, and finally comes the day of remembrance for the Marquis de Baroncelli. He was the founder of the Gardians Association and it was his great dedication that ensured the survival of the cattle herders and their horses.

The Gardians ride their spruced-up mounts in processions on each of these days, but the biggest showpiece of the festival takes place in the arena, where they demonstrate their courage and skill in bullfighting. First, the bulls are brought into town for the *Abrivado*, their keepers flanking them in a V-formation and driving them through the narrow streets of the village, which are lined with onlookers. The spectators make a kind of sport of trying to spook the bulls so they break out of line. They needn't waste their efforts trying to save the bulls' lives, because the animals are not killed during the bullfight. Rather, the goal of the *Course Libre* is for a runner or rider to wrest the cockade from the bull's horns. Ideally, no one gets hurt.

The final act, the *Bandido*, is to drive the bulls over the asphalt at a fast gallop back to the meadows–the idyllic meadows of the Camargue, where some of those bulls live to the ripe old age of twenty years.

The race was only officially recognized with the establishment of a studbook in 1972, and suddenly French politicians began to take an interest in the horses. In 1978, the first offspring of the nineteen selected breeding stallions were born and a decree was issued that recognized the horses' new standing and described the breed exactly. Since then, only horses born "in the cradle of the race"–the Camargue–may be referred to as Camargue horses; horses born elsewhere must at least have a Camargue sire to be registered as Camargue *hors berceau* ("outside the cradle"). Although French pride in this unusual race developed at a late date, it is all the stronger for that.

Camargue horses live semi-wild and are true survival artists. Undemanding and robust, they graze their way through the marshlands in France, standing up to any kind of weather.

The Western Pros

Race Profile: Appaloosa

Height: 57–63 inches

Colors: almost always spotted

Description: strong, sure-footed, and tireless

Origin: USA

Race Profile: Quarter Horse

Height: 59–61 inches

Colors: all basic colors, including dun and palomino

Description: extremely fast over short distances

Origin: USA

Race Profile: Paint Horse

Height: 57–63 inches

Colors: all basic colors, usually spotted

Description: strong and fast

Origin: USA and Canada

APPALOOSA

Horses have relatives all over the world. Depending on who was conquering whom, new horse breeds made their way to different regions and interbred with the native races. When the Spanish tried to conquer the American continent in the sixteenth century, their horses had to weather the long voyage across half the globe. On arrival in America, some of the spotted Spanish stallions evidently interbred with local Mustang mares. Their offspring looked odd to the Spanish, who took no further interest in them. The Nez-Percé Indians of the Palouse Valley were of a different opinion. Well-versed in horse breeding, they took on the speckled race as their own. Through astute selections of studs and mares, they created a horse that perfectly suited their taste and requirements. It was not too big, was sure-footed, and demonstrated extraordinary endurance on long rides—and it was conspicuously spotted. When white settlers arrived in the valley of the Palouse River in Idaho and set eyes on the first examples of this new breed, they reported having seen "a Palouse horse"—giving birth to the name Appaloosa.

This piebald animal with the friendly, gentle character would become one of the most popular races in the USA. True fans cheerfully forgive the fact that even the hooves of some Appaloosas are striped.

QUARTER HORSE

The uncompromising Quarter Horse lover would find the jumbled spots of an Appaloosa dizzying. In the world's biggest equestrian organization, the American Quarter Horse Association, based in Amarillo, Texas, only solid-color horses are recognized. But the oldest race in the USA does share a Spanish ancestry with the Appaloosa; their bloodlines only split later, when the first English settlers came to the USA in the seventeenth century in search of a new homeland. Like the Spanish before them, they brought their horses along onboard their ships. The English horses had similar attributes to Thoroughbreds—which did not yet officially exist. A new race came about in Virginia that offered many advantages to its keepers: easy to handle, eager to learn, and able to thrive under the harsh conditions of pioneer life. What made these horses truly special, however, was their speed and good looks. A Quarter Horse is a real hunk of a horse, with a broad chest, strong back, and highly muscular hindquarters. This impressive rear view is a status symbol for the horses' owners, which is why Quarter Horses are often photographed from behind, to emphasize their best feature.

They have their physical prowess to thank for their name, which was given to them by the English. It was also the English who, at a later date, brought Thoroughbreds to the American continent, along with their passion for horseracing. Meanwhile, since there were no racetracks yet available in America, a quarter mile of the village main street would be blocked off for races. Sprints on this short track could only be won by a horse that could take off at a rapid gallop.

An Appaloosa of the blue roan color, in which white hairs mingle with the black base color of the coat. Blue roans usually get lighter as they age.

Quarter Horses are powerful, fast, and have a gentle temperament. Their character makes them popular leisure-time companions.

Is Little Uncle an Appaloosa? Or perhaps a Dalmatian? In any case, this peculiarly spotted horse belonged to Pippi Longstocking, the strongest girl in the world. Pippi could carry her pet without difficulty from the porch into the garden, which didn't bother Little Uncle much, but drove film critics to distraction. They judged the film's special effect, in which a blue line could be seen all around the horse, as "poorly done," and presumably had their doubts about whether the perfectly round polka dots on the horse's coat were genuine. The filmmakers probably cheated only a little here, because on Sweden's neighboring Danish island of Seeland, large gray horses with many dark spots have been bred since 1812–Knabstruppers, not Appaloosas!

Thus began the Quarter Horse's second career as the cowboys' horse of choice. The "cowpony" made light work for its rider because it demonstrated another important talent: cow-sense. The Quarter Horse is capable of developing a protective guardian instinct toward its charges and can directly adapt its behavior to that of cows and bulls. Whether a cow wanders off and has to be driven back to the herd, or a stubborn steer has to be isolated from the others for branding, the Quarter Horse seems able to anticipate the other animal's every move and react instinctively with sudden stops or turns.

PAINT HORSE

Another member of the family of Western horses is the Paint Horse, which gets its name from the fact that it only comes in the spotted, or "pinto" variety. The different kinds of spot distribution are called Overo (usually dark with white spots, although the back is a single solid color) or Tobiano (white with dark spots that tend to concentrate on the flank). In addition, there are also Paint Horses that are solid color or with only minimal spots; these are known as breeding stock and have their own studbook.

Strictly speaking, Paint Horses do not constitute their own race, but are simply piebald Quarter Horses, but they nevertheless have their own association.

Horses of this new breed were the uncontested champions in these races, leaving all others in the dust by the finish line. As recurring winners of these quarter-mile races, they were dubbed Quarter Horses. Their supremacy, even when later matched against Thoroughbreds, did not last forever, though. With increasing prosperity and progress on the East Coast, the first oval racetracks were built and races could be run over longer tracks on which the little sprinter could no longer keep up.

Paint Horses are robust and obedient. These qualities, along with their interesting coloring, explain why they are favored by many Western riders.

The Big Germans

Bonfire, an Oldenburg (top), and Gigolo, a Hanoverian (above), are two of the most successful dressage horses ever, and were tough competitors across all dressage championships for several years. They took turns sweeping the titles.

Race Profile: Hanoverian

Height: 64–69 inches

Colors: all basic colors, usually bays and chestnuts

Description: riding horse with excellent jumping capabilities
and strong nerves

Origin: Germany

Race Profile: Holsteiner

Height: 63–67 inches

Colors: usually bay or gray, more rarely chestnut
or black

Description: noble sport horse with Thoroughbred traits
and excellent show jumping skills

Origin: Germany

Race Profile: Oldenburg

Height: 66–69 inches

Colors: usually bay or chestnut, more rarely gray
or black

Description: modern sport horse with accurate,
lively movements

Origin: Germany

Race Profile: Westphalian

Height: 65–69 inches

Colors: all basic colors, usually chestnut

Description: sport horse with great show jumping ability

Origin: Germany

The big Germans of equestrian history have names such as Gigolo, Meteor, Bonfire or Rembrandt and represent the races Hanoverian, Holsteiner, Oldenburg (from Lower Saxony), and Westphalian (from the Rhineland). Each associated region produces ever more advertising icons that carry their riders onto the winners' podium at international championships or the Olympic games.

In terms of sheer quantity, German breeders dominate the market for high quality mares and stallions, as testified, for example, by the participants in the 2004 Olympic Games. In those games, a total of 175 horses took part in the disciplines of show jumping, dressage, and the three-day event. Of these, no fewer than seventy-one came from German stables. The second-largest group of breeders, those from the Netherlands, were represented with twenty-six horses in the games.

Of the forty-six jumpers in the individual finals, fourteen were big Germans: nine Holsteiners, two Oldenburgs, one Hanoverian, one Westphalian, and one Bavarian. Perhaps unsurprisingly, the German show jumping team (which won a gold medal in Sydney and a bronze in Athens) rode almost exclusively big German horses. Two Holsteiners were on the team: Otto Becker rode the stallion Cento, while Christian Ahlmann sat the gelding Cöster; Ludger Beerbaum relied on his Hanoverian stallion Goldfever. The fourth member of the team, Marco Kutscher, bestrode the Dutch stallion Motender.

The big Germans are also great dressage artists: 55 percent of all qualifying horses at the 2004 Olympics had big German parentage. Of the fifteen starters in the freestyle event, seven were Hanoverians, one was an Oldenburg, one a Württemberger, and one a Bavarian (ten in all). The winning team shone in the dressage arena with the three Hanoverians Bonaparte (ridden by Heike Kemmer), Weltall (with Martin Schaudt in the saddle), and Wansuela Suerte (carrying Hubertus Schmidt). Only Ulla Salzgeber did not ride a big German. Instead, she rode a Latvian called Rusty. In Athens, Dutch rider Anky van Grunsven repeated her individual Sydney triumph, where she had ridden Bonfire, an Oldenburg. This time around she was mounted on Salinero, a Hanoverian. Finally, a brother of Salinero—Seven up—started for the Korean show jumping team.

HANOVERIAN

In light of the foregoing figures, it is clear that the Hanoverian is the most popular choice for jumping and dressage. Its breeding association boasts a long tradition. Paving the way was King George II of Britain (also the crown prince of Hanover), who founded the state stud farm in Celle in 1735. In his decree, he dedicated the farm *"to the good of our subjects and for the maintenance of a good horse breed in our German lands."* From the thirteen original stallions (some Holsteiner, Neapolitan, and Andalusian blood lines), the breeders set out to create a lighter kind of horse. This may not have suited the farmers quite so well, but it was embraced by the cavalry. After World War II, this kind of service was no longer needed and people began to look for a lightweight sporting horse. The Hanoverian breeders adapted fairly quickly and very successfully to this new set of circumstances.

OLDENBURG

The breeders of the Oldenburg were far less prepared for the changed circumstances after World War II. Their horses were the largest and heaviest of the German warmbloods. Thoroughbred stock was quickly brought in so that the Friesian ancestry of the Oldenburgs (once bred for their sturdiness as carriage horses by the Count of Oldenburg) would become less obvious in these muscular animals. In today's Oldenburgs, Hanoverian and Trakehner blood has also been mixed in to keep the horse well-suited to sporting and leisure pursuits.

HOLSTEINER

The Holsteiners have undergone a similar development. They were always larger than the Hanoverians and made an excellent warhorse in the Middle Ages.

In the course of their transformation to a more modern type, their breeders followed the proven pattern and drew on Thoroughbred traits to stay in business. But the Holsteiners have always been a top export; a studbook has been maintained for them in the USA since 1892. Today, Holsteiners are the top show jumpers.

Otto Becker rode to glory on his gray Holsteiner Cento in show jumping contests all over the world for many years, dashing the hopes of all rivals until his farewell appearance at the 2006 CHIO championship in Aachen.

WESTPHALIAN

In the Rhineland, the Westphalians were long in settling on a consistent identity. Generally, the Westphalian horse world was only interested in farm horses and every breeder worked according to his own plan. The founding of the Warendorf Stud Farm in 1826 was the first step toward bringing order into breeding operations, but experimentation continued, involving Thoroughbreds, Trakehners, Hanoverians, and other races. In 1920, the Westphalian Breeding Association finally decided to set parameters and overhauled their breeding process on the basis of Hanoverian stock. This proved an excellent decision, as Westphalian breeders are now second only to the breeders of Lower Saxony, both at home and abroad—a success that is owed at least in part to astute cooperation with other Rhineland breeders.

Mass Plus Class: The Great Horses

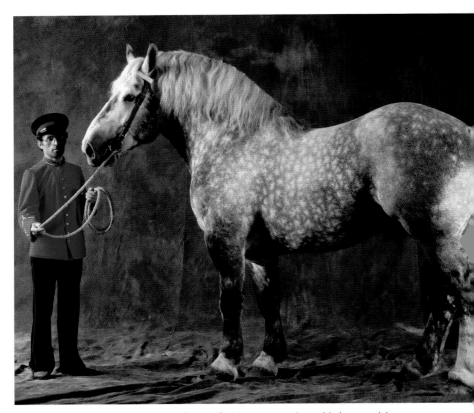

The impressive appearance of the French Percheron, together with its surprising elegance, makes it the most popular coldblood race in the world.

Race Profile: Percheron

Height: 63–67 inches

Colors: gray or black

Description: elegant draft horse

Origin: France

Race Profile: Shire Horse

Height: 69–79 inches

Colors: mostly black, but also gray or bay

Description: powerful draft horse

Origin: England

Race Profile: Noriker

Height: 61–67 inches

Colors: chestnut, bay, black, pinto, gray or blue roan
  with black head

Description: strong work, riding, and carriage horse

Origin: Austria

Race Profile: Brabant

Height: 65–69 inches

Colors: all basic colors

Description: elegant draft horse

Origin: Belgium

PERCHERON

One of the best known and most popular coldblood races in the world is the French Percheron. Despite their mass—they weigh in at over 1300 lb—they have preserved the aristocratic traits of their forefathers. Strangely enough, these included Arabian Thoroughbreds, so the Percheron can move its ponderous body with great elegance, which makes it extremely versatile. Pictures of Percherons pulling the first buses through Paris in 1826 caused a sensation around the world. The horses even became a popular import in countries from North America to Argentina. The French appreciate their large horses—including the gourmets among them.

Shire horses are some of the tallest in the world. Stallions stand up to 6½ feet tall, measured with a yardstick from the ground to the withers.

It is said that slim or thin people tend to be somewhat fidgety and slightly nervous, while heavier ones tend to be more placid and slow-moving, with strong nerves that keep them stolid rather than excitable. The same is true of the larger horses, the coldbloods, which are prized as honest workers with an easygoing temperament to match.

Over the centuries, the coldbloods toiled away in the service of humankind as both farm horses and fighting companions until no one had any further use for them; by the twentieth century, they seemed destined for extinction. Since the early twentieth century, great horses have been in the minority, protected by us in some ways and threatened in others. In the twenty-first century, coldbloods are bred for forestry work and show appearances, while in some countries they are seen as abundant meat producers, because despite their massive bodies, with proper care and sufficient exercise they are very lean.

SHIRE HORSE

Shire horses are among the tallest horses in the world—stallions can attain a height of up to 6½ feet at the withers, which can make mounting them something of a challenge. These well-proportioned horses have a fine gait, which they owe to the enormous strength that allows them to carry their ton-plus bodies with ease. That strength also makes them very fine draft horses. There are reports of draft horse competitions in which Shire horses driven tandem pull 18.5-ton carts over wet cobblestones. More impressive still, in the curve, the rear horse takes the entire load unaided!

The Shire horse had its heyday in the Middle Ages, effortlessly carrying knights with their heavy armor into battle and, thanks to its strong nerves, letting nothing faze it. In the ensuing centuries, however, there was ever less need for the huge animals and the breed was able to survive only in small numbers, in the service of agriculture. It was not until their rediscovery as show horses for tournaments, processions, and country fairs that the gentle giants came back into fashion among the coldblood breeders in their English homeland. Interest in the world's biggest horse has now spread as far afield as America and Australia.

NORIKER

The Noriker is another member of the long-established coldblood aristocracy. Thousands of years ago, in the Roman province of Noricum (what is today the Austrian state of Carinthia), a large and sturdy horse was bred. Its somewhat unprepossessing appearance mattered little to the vigorous knights of the late Middle Ages, since the ungainly head was not visible underneath their protective armor anyway. And these warhorses were certainly not lacking in power and tenacity.

In the eighteenth century, farmers continued breeding Norikers to help them work in their fields in the challenging mountainous terrain of Austria, giving them even greater strength and endurance in the process. A finer and more elegant line was developed some four centuries ago under the thoughtful guidance of the Salzburg archbishops, who procured Neapolitan and Spanish studs for this

The Rhineland horse is very similar to the Brabant in character and appearance.

purpose and, while they were at it, bred selectively for the speckled coat that is typical of Norikers.

Its physical capacity has helped ensure the continuation of the Noriker race, although other qualities are also admired in it today. In Austria and Bavaria, where it was traditionally used to haul logs in the Alps, its quality as a racehorse and as a carriage horse have now been rediscovered.

BRABANT

At just over a ton, the Brabant is almost the equal of the Shire horse in weight, but has an entirely different body type and is sometimes characterized as rather tubby.

In terms of dimensions, the Belgian coldblood is not one of the biggest horses. It averages 67 inches in height, has a small head and short neck, and a trunk that bears an unfortunate resemblance to a barrel. But when eight Brabants draw a wagon full of beer barrels, one can only congratulate the brewery on its choice of mascots. The slim and the lithe are not, after all, the only good advertising icons!

In its homeland, the Brabant is popular for precisely that stoutness. In the USA, it is bred as the "American Belgian," and it has also had a strong impact on the Rhineland coldblood, which owes its current popularity to Brabant stock.

When the heavy-set Norikers—here blue roans with black heads—gallop across the fields, the ground shudders beneath them.

The American Cream

The only great horse originating in America and now endangered (approximately 300 are known), the American Cream draft horse goes back to a single mare, Old Granny, foaled sometime before 1905. Mixing Old Granny's unknown stock with Belgian and Percheron established the breed, which reaches a height of over 65 inches and weighs in at just under a ton. Its most distinctive feature is its pale cream color, "champagne," teamed with white mane, tail, limbs, and face, and unusual amber eyes—a sure crowd pleaser!

Haflingers are extremely robust, sure-footed horses. Their strong nerves make them perfect for leisure riding.

Blonde Beauties

Race Profile: Haflinger

Height: 53–57 inches

Colors: chestnut with blonde mane and tail

Description: robust work and riding horse

Origin: Italy

These chestnut horses with blonde manes and tails are named after their birthplace in the southern Tyrol region of Italy. Their small size classifies them among the pony or small horse races. Characteristic traits include strong legs and hard hooves that are essential on the steep, rocky paths of the Alps. Their ancestors include mountain ponies the Eastern Goths left behind around 555 BCE. After some interbreeding with Oriental stallions, these formed the basis of today's athletic Haflinger horse. Despite this refining touch, they are fairly calm animals and also extremely sure-footed, which makes them perfect for use in difficult terrain.

It would be a mistake to think there is no more to the Haflinger than this: it is far better suited to sporting pursuits than one might think. The "Hafis" may not rise to the highest level of dressage, but they often make it effortlessly to the M class, thus showing up some of their larger cousins and their riders. At Western tournaments, too, it is not uncommon to meet compact Haflingers who score points with their nimbleness, especially in the trail and cutting disciplines. Thus it is only partly in jest when they are sometimes affectionately dubbed "Alpine Quarter Horses." But where the blond beauties really shine is in the equestrian sport of driving. There are several Haflinger teams among the top ranks of international competition.

Mare's Milk

The ancient Greeks and Romans told of legendary equestrian peoples who milked their mares in order to benefit from the special properties of the milk or products made from it. They believed, it was said, that mare's milk would give them greater strength, endurance, and health.

While tall tales may have had more currency back then, there is a kernel of truth in the fabled properties of mare's milk. Today it is even a recognized natural remedy, although there are only a few stud farms that specialize in producing it. Mare's milk has a composition very similar to that of human breast milk. It is nutritious and fortifying, and at the same time has the property of stimulating the circulation.

People who have suffered lengthly illnesses or are exhausted are especially likely to gain renewed strength from mare's milk. It is available unpasteurized (in which case it must be consumed within two days) or pasteurized for longer shelf life. A popular product made from fermented mare's milk is *kumiss*, a slightly alcoholic and wonderfully refreshing beverage.

These blonde Haflingers are one of the breeds especially well suited for milking since they are quite patient and have a long lactation period.

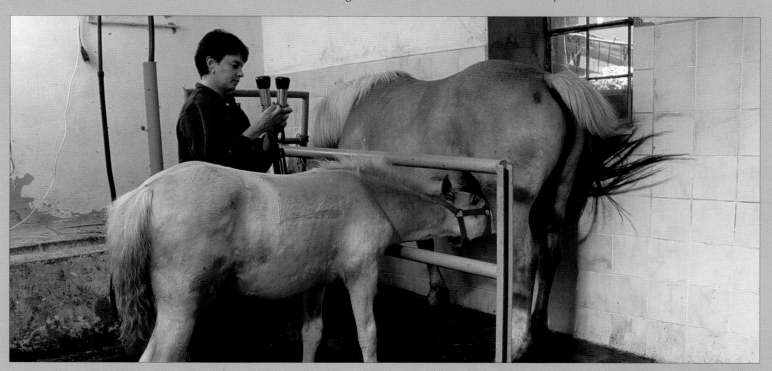

Unlike cows, mares only produce milk while the foal suckles, which is why the foal must be close by when the mare is at the milking stand.

The milk is pumped by a machine specifically designed for the position of the horse's udder. The process takes considerable skill and sensitivity, but goes smoothly when done right.

In the milk chamber, the fresh mare's milk is first poured unfiltered into a measuring cup and then into special bags. If not pasteurized, it must be consumed immediately.

Taking It Up a Notch

Race Profile: Icelandic

Height: 49–57 inches

Colors: all basic colors, including pinto

Description: robust, eager, and high-endurance horse
    with a good-natured, charming character; in addition
    to the usual gaits it can also do pace and tölt

Origin: Iceland

When the Vikings anchored their dragon boats off the island of fire and ice in the late ninth century, they had only their most valuable animals aboard with them. These included Germanic horses from their Norwegian homeland and a few Celtic ponies that they had taken on board during a stopover in northern Scotland. Irish immigrants had also brought their horses with them, and the medley of these disparate races resulted in the Icelandic horse. The conquerors of Iceland were so pleased with this robust and good-natured horse

The tölt is similar to the walk but much faster and has no moment of suspension. This means it is almost completely smooth and very comfortable for a rider to sit.

Putting a Horse Through its Paces

In addition to the walk, trot, canter and gallop, some gaited horses have a couple extras in their repertoire: the liquid tölt and rapid pace. There are about forty horse races around the world that do the tölt, including Paso Fino, Mangalarga Marchadores, Tennessee Walking Horse, Aegidienberger, and Töltiberer. The best known remains the Icelandic pony (called a "natural tölter" because it breaks into this gait unprompted at times). This should please its rider, as it is the most comfortable way to move quickly, ensuring a non-jolting ride. The tölt is similar to a walk, but faster and perfectly smooth. Horses that have mastered tölt and pace make great riding horses and are thus highly coveted and very expensive, even in Iceland.

Pacers fascinate riders, who can feel their lightning-quick movements while sitting calm and collected in the saddle. Flying pace races, in which horses practically fly along the 800-ft track, can result in record speeds: in September 2000, the Icelandic gelding Gamur fra Kritholi reached the finish line in just 21.73 seconds.

that by 930, they resolved not to allow any other horses onto the island. The import ban was regarded as unwritten law until finally set down officially in 1939—by which time the Icelanders could already look back on a thousand-year breeding tradition.

Just how close Icelanders have always been to their horses becomes clear with a glance at the island's terrain: the glaciers, geysers, boulders, deserts, and lava fields could hardly have been navigated without the help of the sure-footed Icelandic ponies. Midwives, doctors, and priests could only reach the far-flung home-

Above: The Icelandic pony is the pride and joy of the North Atlantic island. It has become one of the most popular races of pony anywhere in the world and is now bred around the globe.

Below: Icelandic horses are classic, robust horses, exceptionally easy-to-please, tough and undemanding. They are often kept in semi-wild conditions in their homeland because they are not bothered by inclement weather.

steads on horseback. All supplies, up to and including coffins, were transported with the help of the robust little horses. Not infrequently, a horse even accompanied its rider in death. According to a Celto-Germanic belief, a man needed his horse—harnessed and saddled—on his last ride into the underworld. Horses were the "gift of the gods," beloved of all who spent time with them—and the descendants of the Vikings still live according to this creed. On the outskirts of the capital Reykjavik, the people of Iceland have erected an enormous horse village for several thousand horses with stalls, bridle trails, and meadows.

Word of the special qualities of the Icelandic horse long ago made its way abroad. In the early 1970s, the Icelandic horse became a popular German import, in part because of a popular TV series in which the girls had so much fun with their "Isi's." Owners and riders praise the horses' eagerness to please and their amenability to life in the open stall or herd; they have also discovered the horses' potential for equestrian sport.

World championships for Icelandic horses are conducted every two years to determine the best of the best in the pace and tölt gaits. Strangely enough, this event can never take place in Iceland itself, as the old embargo on importing horses still applies—even if they are only brought in for the games.

Management Training with Icelandic Horses

"May I introduce you to your new co-workers!"

This is how a group of managers are introduced to a herd of Icelandic ponies—their new charges—at the beginning of a training seminar. But who is actually in charge and who the subordinate is not really clear until horse and manager look each other in the eye in the *picadero* (an enclosed arena). There are a few small tasks to be done here, ones that should be no challenge for a top manager: the business leaders must learn to make the horse walk over to them, follow them or keep a certain distance—without using a rope or any other aids. In short, They have to prove their managerial qualities.

This is easier said than done, because the animals only do what is asked of them if they receive unambiguous signals. They are highly sensitive to whether the body language and expression of their trainer are believable, picking up on any uncertainty and giving a prompt and unmistakable behavioral response. The horse becomes an unerring mirror of its master's powers of persuasion and leadership abilities.

Icelandic horses make good training partners because they live independently of people, who have been unable to change them much in over a thousand years of breeding. They grow up like wild ponies in a herd, which is very similar to a human community in its social fabric. Even as young foals, they learn natural social behavior and get a feeling for hierarchy. This closeness to their fellow horses means they do not rely on feedback from humans.

Before the management team is let loose on their two-legged co-workers again after their three days of horse training, every participant has the opportunity to appraise his or her own leadership capabilities by means of video analysis. Some decision-makers are truly amazed at what a horse can teach them about themselves and others.

The smallest and most popular of all pony races is the Shetland Pony. It makes an ideal companion for young children since its typical pony stubbornness is accompanied by an amiable and dependable character with a high level of endurance.

Little Treasures

Ponies come in all colors, shapes and sizes—as long as they are no larger than 58 inches tall. The word "pony" does not signify a particular race, but rather a way of distinguishing them from the larger horses, and is a special trademark as well.

Children love ponies since they don't seem as threatening as an adult warmblood. This makes the pony an ideal companion for the under-10 sector, and a good way for youngsters to learn how to handle a horse and to ride. Some ponies hardly differ at all in traits and demands from a large horse, except that ponies are usually more robust. Of course, there are also small, pot-bellied lawn mowers, hardly any larger than a German shepherd. But the catalog of races includes many other varieties, too, ranging from A for Acchetta to Z for Zemaituka.

The Acchettas are at home on the island of Sardinia, where they have probably lived for 2,000 years. They measure 47–51 inches tall; they are easy to keep and are usefully versatile. They have never really made a name for themselves beyond the their island home.

The Aegidienbergers are even fun for adults to ride. These ponies are a unique creation—their breeder, Walter Feldmann, left nothing to chance. Dreaming of a new race of gaited horse that would be larger and more elegant than the Icelandic pony, he mixed Icelandics with

Paso Peruanos and actually achieved the results he desired. Standing 55–59 inches tall at the withers, these are spirited and expressive natural tölters that are fast and sure-footed to boot. He named the new breed after his Aegidienberger Stud Farm in the German state of North Rhine-Westphalia.

The British Highland Pony is growing in popularity. It is robust, strong, and (with an average height of about 57 inches) relatively big. The long shaggy mane is typical of this breed.

Record-breaking Strength

Astonishingly, the strongest pony in the world is the tiny Shetland. Relative to its size, this smallest of the small can pull much more than its own weight. The Shetland Islanders prized their diminutive horses as pack and draft horses, using them to transport peat from the moors and seaweed from the coast. Unfortunately, their size and strength also made them ideal for use in the coalmines of Great Britain—a dark chapter in their history.

The Fell pony, which looks like a miniature version of the Friesian horse, is named after its homeland on the fells (or hills) of northwest England, near the Scottish border. These compact, muscular animals have enormous strength, and in the nineteenth century they were put to work drawing baskets of lead or slate weighing up to 450 lb from the mountains to harbors on the Irish Sea. Today they lead a much less strenuous life as family horses, and are especially popular in England.

Other interesting races can be found on the British Isles as well, such as the Exmoor pony, the Dartmoor pony, the Scottish Highland pony, and the Welsh pony. One race enjoying increasing popularity as a riding horse for youngsters is the Hackney pony, which arose from the love affair between an excellent English carriage horse, a Hackney stallion, and an unknown pony mare, whose offspring turned out to be only 51 inches tall.

But the most popular of all for children is the island Shetland pony (the American Shetland is a more elegant variant cross-bred with Hackney ponies), whose ancestor is presumably the Tundra horse. Known affectionately as Shetties, and only 34–42 inches high, they are perfect riding companions for smaller children. For the smallest riders of all, there is even a Dwarf Shetland pony, which must be even shorter than 34 inches. Shetland ponies are robust and have great endurance. They are among the strongest of all horses relative to their body size, which is why they have often been used as pack animals in the past, especially in mining.

The only pony breed from Ireland comes from County Connaught. This is the Connemara pony, a descendant of the Ice Age and Celtic ponies that for a long time lived semi-wild on the inhospitable moors and were used for riding and as pack animals. The quality of the

The Lewitzer Pony is one result of the ambition to breed a "German Riding Pony." This is a relatively new race that was bred on the Lewitz Stud Farm (owned today by international sporting horseman Paul Schockemöhle) in the former East Germany in the 1970s. One race characteristic is the coloring: these ponies are always pinto.

ponies, which are 55–59 inches tall, was improved considerably by mixing in Andalusian blood in the sixteenth century. Later addition of Thoroughbred blood made the Connemaras gifted sporting mounts, especially skilled in show jumping.

The German Riding pony is modeled on the English Riding pony, and was developed to meet the increasing demand for high caliber sport horses for children. In 1965 a working group of pony breeder associations was established to develop this pony. Welsh ponies were imported and crossbred with Arabians, Anglo-Arabians, and Thoroughbreds. Through this parentage, the pony character was preserved—small head and ears—but was muted somewhat by crosses with warmbloods such as Trakehners and Hanoverians. The resultant ponies are as skilled as their bigger cousins in the disciplines of show jumping, dressage, and the three-day event, and can be found every weekend presenting their talents at tournaments.

Ponies, the ideal leisure riding horse for children and smaller adults, can be found all over the world. In addition to the breeds described above, there are also the Australian pony, the Bali pony, and the Chinese Guoxia, the Galiceno from Mexico, the Norwegian Fjord horse, and in Greece the Skyros. All of which goes to show that bigger is not always better!

Exmoor Ponies come from southwest England, where they have been living in the wild for thousands of years. They are relatively small, measuring only 43–47 inches, but all the more adaptable for that.

Colts that were born the year they were rounded up remain a further year in freedom with their mothers. A few renegades must nonetheless be driven back to the herd.

For the yearlings, there is no escaping their fate. They don't make it easy for their pursuers, though, fighting for their freedom as long as they can.

The Wild Horses of Dulmen — An Annual Event

To separate the yearlings from the rest of the herd, all the horses must first be rounded up into the arena.

Race Profile: Dulmen Pony

Height: 49–53 inches

Colors: duns in all variations, without markings

Description: versatile riding and carriage pony

Origin: Germany

Once each year, on the last Saturday in May, the wild horses of Dulmen in Germany's Münsterland region are rounded up. Following a tradition that dates back to 1907, the horses living freely in the Merfelder Bruch nature reserve are driven into an arena, and then the colts are separated from the rest of the herd. Controlling the numbers of colts is essential. Because the horses' habitat is quite limited, too great a number of pubescent stallions would get into bitter fights, often ending in death.

Once the young horses have been gathered together, the rest of the herd is let loose again, while the colts are immediately branded.

It usually takes several men to wrestle the unwilling youngsters away from the herd and steer them where they are supposed to go.

The Dulmen wild horses have lived in the Merfelder Bruch reserve for centuries. They were first documented in 1316.

A few of the most promising colts are reserved for the Duke of Croy (who owns the Merfelder Bruch reserve) for breeding purposes. But most of the young horses are auctioned off, and in some cases raffled off, the same day. Although the stallions lose their freedom, they can look forward to a much more comfortable life being pampered by human companions—even though they presumably don't realize at first how lucky they are.

Before the colts are put up for auction, they are branded on their left hindquarters with their race insignia.

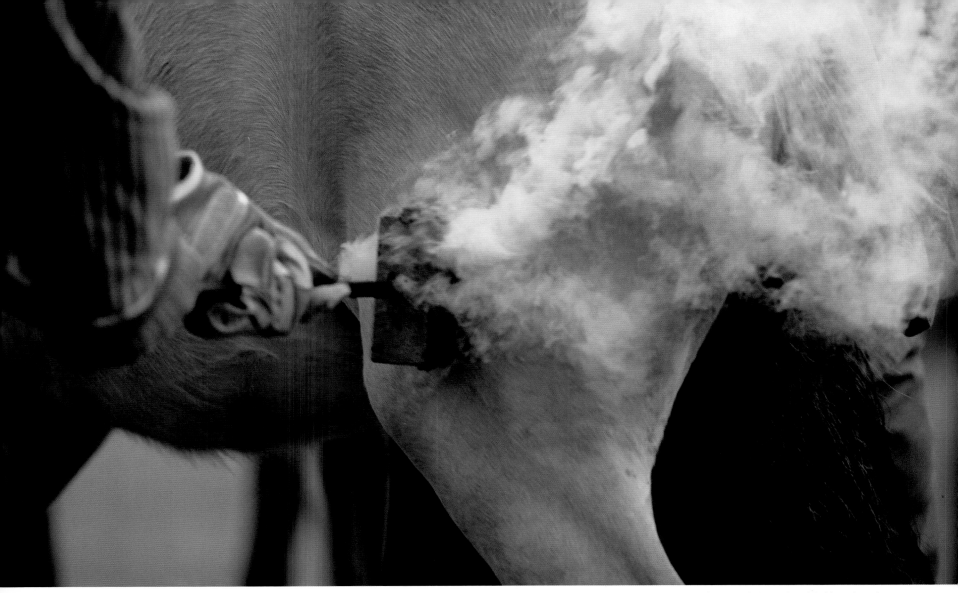

In hot branding, the branding iron, a kind of stamp, is heated and held against the horse's hide for several seconds—usually on the left hindquarters. The resulting scar remains visible for the animal's entire life.

Various Identifying Marks

The Egyptians were not merely playing with fire when they burned lasting marks into the hides of their livestock as early as 3000 BCE. It was in people's own best interest to label their property in order to be able to prove their ownership.

There is evidence that branding for horses was introduced in England and Germany as early as the eighth century, obviously hundreds of years before the branding iron was first used on a large scale in the American Wild West—where horse and cattle thieves were still feared well into the nineteenth century. In extreme cases, US ranchers even gave their animals four brands, showing the breeder, year of birth, father, and mother.

Branding has always been a painful procedure—and no wonder, since the red-hot iron stamp is pressed into the animal's hide for a few seconds, injuring hair and hide to the extent that the scar remains visible for a lifetime. Branding produces third-degree burns, because only then is the brand legible.

In the seventeenth century, brands that turned out too faint were made more distinct using "etching water" that alchemists mixed up from verdigris, pulverized mercury, and yellow mouse poison and applied to the shorn hide of the horse three times daily. This

Gentler Alternatives to Burning

There are several reliable ways to identify horses without hurting them. Markings, or patches of white, as well as cowlicks provide 99.8% accuracy as identifying features, and thus form a viable alternative to branding, whether hot or cold. The entire Thoroughbred breeding community uses this method and as a rule does not brand its horses.

Hair analysis is the second method used to identify horses, and requires only a single hair. Large-scale use of this method is impractical, however, since, as with DNA analysis, the laboratory costs are prohibitive.

Looking to the future, identification by means of iridology (mapping the iris of the horse's eye) would seem to present a plausible alternative.

procedure is similar to today's cold branding, which uses acid instead of heat to burn the mark into the hide.

The third method is freeze branding, practiced since the 1970s. Here, the branding iron is dipped into dry ice, alcohol cooled down to -94 °C or liquid nitrogen cooled to -320 °F, and applied to the hide for 15–90 seconds. The longer application time is especially necessary for gray (i.e. white) horses, since the brand only remains legible if all hair roots in the area are destroyed. If the branding time is too short, the roots remain intact and the hair will grow back—but only in white. This makes the brand visible against a dark coat but not, of course, on a white one.

Before the branding iron can be effectively used, it must be heated in an open fire until it is red-hot.

Comparative studies of the stress caused by branding in foals have shown that freeze branding evidently causes less pain than hot branding, although the resulting wound takes longer to heal and the healing process itself is far from painless. The higher costs and time needed are other factors that have prevented freeze branding from gaining much popularity, so that hot branding is still the method of choice when several animals are involved. In Germany, some 50,000 foals ranging in age between 3 and 6 weeks are hot-branded annually, along with around 20,000 older horses that are branded for tournaments.

For some owners, the brand is more than just a visible proof of their ownership, because the renown of some breeding areas has made the corresponding brand into a true trademark. The brand itself has, in some cases, become a status symbol in its own right.

ID Chips

Once limited to microwaves, cameras, and television sets, microchips are now found in horses and cattle as well. The miniature data chips (about ½ x ⅟₁₆ inch) disappear without a trace into the layer of fat under a horse's mane, and their unique fifteen-digit code can be read at any time with a special scanning device. After America's initial experiments in 1985, the Italian racehorse association began marking its foals electronically just two years later to prevent Mafia interference on Italian racetracks. After the implementation of ID chips, fraudulent betting (in which horses are switched at the last minute before a race) was uncovered time after time.

Nowadays, the racing scene in every country around the world uses these chips, and some racehorse breeding federations also register the horse's gender, color, markings, and even a blood sample.

To date, Spain has chipped the most riding horses, and the Dutch Friesian breeders have also begun using the chips alongside the traditional tongue tattoo. This gives them double assurance, since the tattoos tend to fade over time.

Introducing a needle containing the bioglass-encased chip under the skin is an uncomplicated medical procedure performed under local anesthesia and is relatively painless. A worldwide system is planned in which all domestic animals will be registered using chips.

Every race of horse has its own brand mark. This is the brand for wild Dulmen ponies.

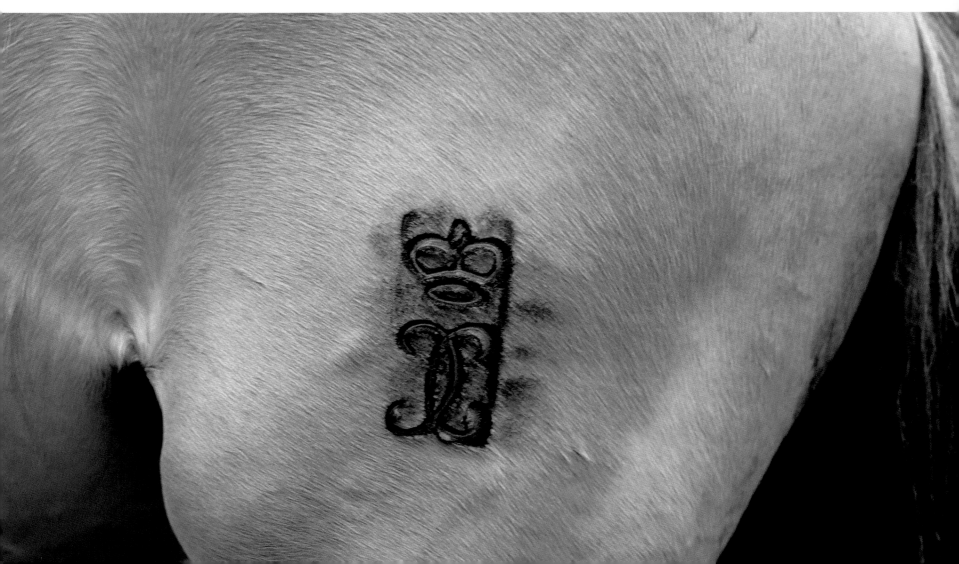

Horsepower in All Aspects of Life

This is one of the Stone Age horse paintings in the caves of Lascaux. Although the paintings cannot be dated precisely, experts estimate that the image above was executed between 20,000 BCE and 15,000 BCE.

People and Horses: Friend or Food?

The first encounter between horses and humans was less than congenial, especially for the horse, who ended up in the cooking pot. The people, on the other hand, were happy to feed themselves such high quality meat. In terms of cultural history, therefore, we are less interested to know whether the horse was first harnessed to a wagon or ridden—we are far more interested to discover when people stopped seeing horses merely as a source of nourishment.

Paintings of horses on cave walls in Altamira, in northern Spain, or Lascaux in southern France, are the earliest testaments to the growing veneration humans evidently felt for the horse. They are perhaps the earliest evidence of religion anywhere. The Lascaux cave paintings were executed between 20,000 BCE and 15,000 BCE and are unanimously classed among the greatest legacies of our Stone Age ancestors.

Marcellino de Sautuola was the first to discover the colorful Ice Age images in the Altamira caves, in 1879. Although their prehistoric origins were not recognized for quite some time, they did provide cave explorers and historians alike with an important motivation to delve further. In the course of the ensuing years, excavations in Europe have brought to light more than four thousand such works of art.

"There is something about the outside of a horse
that is good for the inside of a man."

Winston Churchill

The Acceptance of Horsemeat

In many European countries, it was once commonplace for every town to have its own horse butchers, as well as restaurants that served horsemeat. Further back in history, the equestrian peoples of Asia even rode the meat under their saddles tender before consuming it.

But all that has receded into the rather distant past, and horsemeat is far from everyday fare today, having been rejected for a variety of reasons. Horses are an integral part of our culture; people feel particularly close to these creatures and regard them as leisure companions and sports partners rather than a source of food.

In our own time, the consumption of horsemeat is fraught with emotional issues. Children raised on stories such as those of Black Beauty and Fury could never separate their love for these glorious adventurers from the food on their plates. Many dream of spending summer vacations on pony farms (as their parents did before them). It would be unthinkable to try and eat such creatures. Tears and tantrums would be the inevitable result—you might as well suggest char grilling Lassie!

Despite these reservations, however, horse butchers have not completely disappeared and may be even be making a slight comeback. Their sales are of course modest; many are open only three or four a week or sell their wares from mobile stands, traveling from market to market.

This marginal existence could be coming to an end, though. In these days of BSE, hoof and mouth disease, avian flu, and scandals involving spoiled or contaminated meat, horse butchers are regaining some of their former respect. They confidently sing the praises of their product, explaining to interested consumers that horsemeat offers high-quality nutrition with an average of only 2.7 % fat. Lean beef, in comparison, has 7.2 % fat, while its normal fat content can be as high as 22.1 %. The protein content of horsemeat is likewise on a par with other meats. In terms of taste, the dark red meat is somewhere between beef and game. It is used mainly for making sausages, but is also available in the form of steaks or roasts.

Horsemeat is eaten in parts of Europe (France, Germany, Italy, Switzerland), Japan, Canada, and Argentina. Until it is slaughtered, the horse has a more pleasant life than a cow, pig or chicken, because it is normally kept in ideal conditions, with plenty of room to move, normal nutrition and human affection. The best horsemeat is said to come from America and Argentina, precisely because the horses roam free.

Stone Age paintings of horses are also found in the prehistoric cave of Tito Bustillo in Spain. They probably date from around 15,000 BCE.

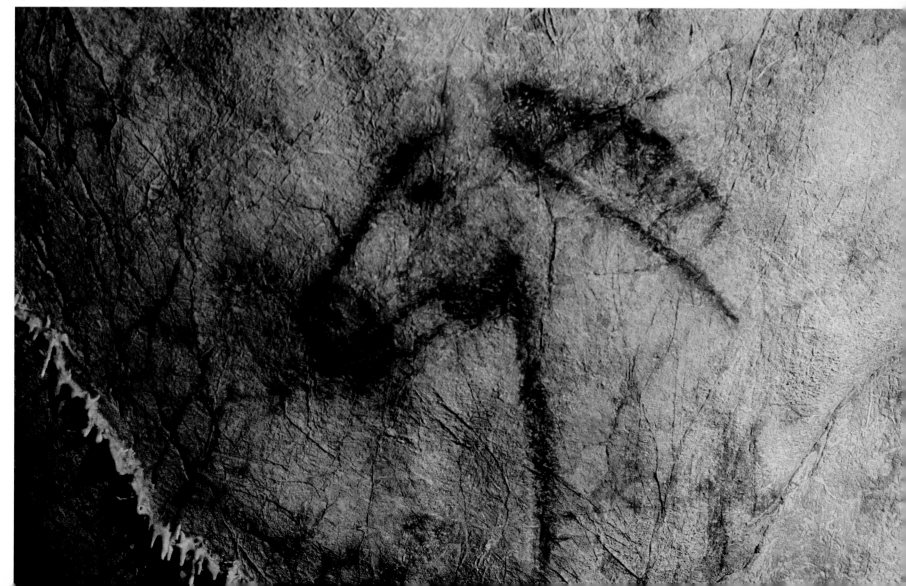

The Development of Mutual Trust

The horse's transformation from hunted prey to domestic animal was not stimulated by humane scruples so much as plain convenience. The herds on the steppes were dwindling rapidly and the supply of fresh free-range meat threatened to become scarce. The hunters, who had had ample opportunity to study the flight and herd behavior of the horses, had gained enough experience to be able to catch them alive, and the process of domestication began.

The first horses must have been difficult to tame. But as they became accustomed to living close to people, they would have developed more trust as they began to see their keepers as more than hunters. Nevertheless, the step from the first friendly encounters to genuine domestication must have taken several generations; taming happens one individual at a time, and is not automatically transmitted to an entire species. Depending on their origin, horses would

> "A horse is a creature that sacrifices his own being
> to exist through the will of another.
> He is the noblest conquest of Man."
>
> Count de Buffon, French naturalist

have been accustomed to living alongside other animals, such as zebras, antelopes or ostriches. Instinctively, they would hardly have approached humans.

Most horse historians believe that the first attempts at domestication were made around 6,000 BCE in the Ukraine. By choosing only tamed stallions and mares for breeding, early breeders could initiate—and gradually solidify—the genetic change to domestic animal. This also ensured the further existence of horses.

People did themselves a great service by ceasing to regard the horse as nothing but a food source. The living, domesticated horse offered them a whole range of new opportunities in life, and without horses many things would have unfolded differently in world history.

Horsemen of the Apocalypse
Swift horses with unearthly riders, the Horsemen of the Apocalypse are seen as a symbol of plague, war, starvation, and death; and they embody an old nightmare that seemed to come true in the fifteenth century. People were suffering from epidemics across wide swaths of Europe and a doomsday mood spread, predicting the end of the world would come in 1500. Albrecht Dürer, artist and engraver, created his well-known woodcut of the Horsemen of the Apocalypse in 1498 in Nuremberg, where the plague was rampant.

People rode horses for hunting, for example, which put them at an advantage over much of their prey. Traveling long distances in a short time to deliver important messages, or even completely relocating to settle in a new place, presented far fewer problems on horseback. When people needed to transport heavy loads, horses made themselves useful. The new servant also proved indispensable for farming, pulling the plow and harrow. People steadily discovered uses for their equine charges, without regard for the consequences. Thus, inevitably, horses ultimately found themselves going to war with their keepers. Having repressed the horse's natural aggression, people acted out their own ever more freely from its back.

Native Americans demonstrated horses' usefulness in hunting for prey particularly impressively. Hunting buffalo would have been impossible without their help.

One of the most famous knights of all time was the legendary King Arthur with his Knights of the Round Table. His story is the subject of countless books and films.

The medieval knight's charger had to carry not only its rider and his armor, but also had to bear up under the weight of its own elaborate protective plating.

THE VALIANT STEEDS OF THE MEDIEVAL KNIGHTS

Being a knight's charger meant withstanding enormous challenges, starting with simply bearing up under the weight of the noble warrior in his heavy armor. In battle, horses were exposed to the risk of serious injury, often losing their lives on the battlefield. Knights in individual combat were forbidden to thrust a sword at the opponent's horse. But the infantry were involved during war, and they were able to put even an armored horse out of action with their weapons. The horse's unprotected legs were defenseless against the fearsome billhooks: sharp, sickle-shaped blades attached to long poles with which the horse's sinews could be severed.

"A horse! A horse! My kingdom for a horse!"

Riders love to quote this line from Shakespeare!

But the words written by the great dramatist and poet stick in the throat when read in the context of the tragedy of *Richard III*, for Shakespeare's fictional portrait of the English king was not only of a rider and a knight, but also a murderer. Shakespeare created a bloody historical saga to tell the cautionary tale of the rise and fall of a king who was not prepared to sacrifice the empire he had gained through extortion for anything–least of all for a horse! He slaughtered friends and relatives left and right until

he himself was conquered and killed in the Battle of Bosworth in 1452.

The film version of Shakespeare's *Richard III* became an avant-garde big-screen hit and brought world fame to its director, Sir Laurence Olivier, who also played the leading role.

Bayard the Magical Horse

Many a horse has saved its master's life in battle. According to one French legend, a stallion named Bayard performed this miracle not just once, but four times over–all at the same time! The Duke of Aymond had four sons, all of whom were knighted by Charlemagne. The emperor gave the oldest, Renaud, the stallion Bayard as a gift. When, in the aftermath of a fight, Renaud killed the emperor's nephew in battle, he and his brothers had no alternative but to flee, fearing the ruler's revenge. When the horses ridden by Renaud's brothers collapsed of exhaustion, Bayard remained strong enough to carry all four of the men to safety.

Peaceful interludes harbored fewer dangers, although they were no less strenuous: knight's tournaments were quite fashionable for a time. These were designed to keep horse and rider fit for battle, but without hostile intentions. At the great European courts, rulers and their elite coteries entertained themselves by admiring the bravery of the knights who were willing to risk their lives for the honor of their beloved lady. If the knight could later accept the winner's prize from her hand, the risk had been worth it.

To minimize losses of horses and men in these tournaments, both wore full armor. The horse's armor included pieces called the *chanfron* and *crinet* that covered the head and neck; the *petral* over breast and shoulders; *flanchards* protected the ribs and abdomen below the saddle; and the *krupper* protected the rump, thighs, and hindquarters. With all this heavy metal, little could be seen of the elaborately embroidered blanket the horse wore underneath. Even the reins were covered with metal plates to foil attempts to sever them. Thus outfitted, the rider had little influence over his mount, preoccupied as it was in simply carrying the incredible weight. The knight's armored legs could only reach the horse's belly to give it a signal through spurs with extra-long shanks; however, these were reserved for true knights. Only when officially knighted had a man "earned his spurs."

Jousting, one-to-one combat using lances in which each knight tries to unseat his opponent, remains one of today's most popular tournament competitions.

Modern Knights and their Tournaments

Occupation: stunt horse. This would be an apt description for the horses that take part in contemporary knights' tournaments. Both the four-legged and two-legged contenders give it all they've got, putting their full strength into the shows and a big dose of ambition, too. The insufficiently prepared will end up risking more than is good for them. In medieval tournaments, the knights were willing to risk their lives for the favor of their one chosen love. To that end, they gave no thought to their own well-being or that of their horse. Today's performances look no less spectacular, but are at least less dangerous.

Behind the scenes, the actors prepare the illusions carefully, setting up a breaking point for each lance. In fact, the wood does not break from the force of the collision, but because it has been sawn through in advance. Everything is designed to look as real as possible, but the spectacle is never carried to the point where blood flows.

Modern destriers and their knights do not enter the tournament without first donning plenty of padding, but they do go without the full medieval armor (in which the rider was as about as agile in the

What is Chivalry?

The great class of knights in medieval Europe came from various noble orders. Mounted on horseback and wearing heavy armor, they took up their swords and rode off to war. The doctrine of knightly, or chivalric, virtue combined ancient Greek and Roman ethics with Christian morality. To live up to this creed, a knight was required to remain true to his ideals, to fight for them courageously and to defend justice. He was also directed to grant mercy at the right moment, which in concrete terms meant renouncing vengefulness.

In Rome, knights were given preference for official judiciary and administrative positions, a status that was legally enshrined. Imperial knights had territorial lordship, meaning that subjects living on the knights' estates were their vassals. This situation remained so until Heinrich Friedrich Karl, Baron vom und zum Stein (prime minister of Prussia), put an end to it. The title "knight" could still be inherited in Austria and Germany until 1945.

Modern knights embody the ideals of modesty, courtesy, and respect, especially toward women and weaker members of society.

St. George

There are numerous legends surrounding St. George, patron saint of horses and their riders, who supposedly lived around 300 CE.

The most famous story is that of his fight with a dragon. The monster lived in a lake and terrorized the city of Silena with its bad breath. And the odor must have been really foul, because the inhabitants sacri-ficed lambs to the dragon every day. In the end, even the king's daughter was called upon to serve as a sacrifice to appease the beast. Fortunately, on that very day, St. George showed up on his trusty steed and heroically slew the beast.

Thanks to this and a number of other legends dating from the twelfth century, St. George became the personification of chivalry, especially in England. As personal patron saint of Richard the Lion-heart and ultimately of the United Kingdom as a whole, St. George was celebrated on April 23 every year with folk customs including processions and horse blessings. In agriculture, too, St. George's Day had great significance: on this day, servants could switch masters, and interest fell due.

saddle as a sausage in a can). Helmet and breast plate are still mandatory, but the remaining clothing can be lighter and more comfortable, as long as it looks sufficiently authentic. The horse is still pretty well hidden as in the days of yore, with race and color kept under wraps. It disappears completely under an embroidered blanket and is also padded in sensitive areas such as breast and flanks. Thus the horse, too, stays much more nimble than its jousting forefathers.

The modern warhorse thinks for itself; when surrounded by enemies, it is not afraid to jump through fire, and it even remains calm when its rider falls off yet again. The dramatization only works, of course, when the audience is completely immersed in the medieval atmosphere. That is why the lord and lady of the castle and their retinue can be found sitting in the loggia, while merchants loudly hawk their goods all around the tournament grounds. The tournament becomes an all-encompassing experience for visitors.

Modern knights with their horses put on a good show for enthralled audiences. Always impressive are stunts with fire that demonstrate the fearlessness of the horses and their trust in their riders. Hunting games are also very popular. The tournament champions are celebrated just like the knights of old.

One of the key show events at every tournament is ring jousting, in which the knight galloping by on his horse, without slowing down, tries to hook a small ring hanging from a pole with his lance.

Willing Servants

"This is not a race horse and it is not a walking horse—in short, it is a farm horse." The question is, does that constitute a compliment or an insult? It certainly seems less than complimentary at first. The farm horse is no icon of beauty, and despite its well-packed muscles, it is no Schwarzenegger either. Often slightly bulky, ponderous and inflexible, these horses definitely have some finer traits as well, and we are not only talking about inner qualities. But this is where we will begin: the farm horse is singularly undemanding and does not take long to get down to work. With great determination, it plows its tracks through the fields, not stopping until the job is done. Farmers

> "Only a man harrowing clods
> In a slow, silent walk
> With an old horse that stumbles and nods
> Half asleep as they stalk."
>
> Thomas Hardy, English writer

used to harness a horse in front of a team of oxen to set the pace. Direct comparisons have shown that horses accomplish 50 percent more than oxen, even voluntarily pulling overtime. When the oxen are already lounging around back at the stall, exhausted, the horse is still out in the fields for an hour or two longer. This is probably the origin of the expression "to work like a horse."

But do horses have to be compared with oxen to be accepted as farm workers? Of course not! A glance through history shows that humans have benefited from horses in many ways, but especially in

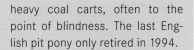

Mining Ponies

The exploitation of children in English mines is one of the darkest chapters of the industrial revolution. Child labor was not outlawed until 1847. Taking their place in the mines, increasingly, were Shetland Ponies.

When we think of workhorses, these enchanting little ponies are probably not the first animals that come to mind. But they were the ones working in the coalmines and pits of England, pulling heavy coal carts, often to the point of blindness. The last English pit pony only retired in 1994.

agriculture. Once people realized that it was a pity to waste a horse's talents by seeing it as a mere source of sustenance, they began to explore a wide range of potential equine services.

From the sixth to the eleventh centuries especially, farmers needed all the help they could get. As the first towns arose, more and more food had to be produced to supply the growing numbers of citizenry that were no longer self-sufficient. The horse was indispensable for this. No longer harnessed before the plow or harrow with mere ropes, but with the modern horse collar, it could perform even better than before. Farm equipment became ever larger and heavier, and the horses did, too. Around 1890, a combine harvester used in the USA was ca. 40 ft wide and weighed 15 tons. No fewer than forty-two horses were needed to move it. These were the same horses that also carried the farmer safely and comfortably to town or market.

In the days before machines, horses were invaluable partners for farmers. The muscular, hard-working animals made the work far easier.

Race Profile: Black Forest Chestnut

Height: 57–60 inches

Colors: dark chestnut with blonde mane

Description: spirited and robust, with great stamina

Origin: Germany

Black Forest Chestnuts are ideally suited for forest work under difficult conditions and are still employed in Germany's Black Forest. They are also increasingly popular as leisure horses for riding.

As time went by, the classic draft horse breeds—such as the Brabant, Black Forest Chestnut or Shire horse—were replaced by the tractor. But they proved to be very flexible and have secured their continued existence in Europe by helping to transport wood or by

Many breweries continue to keep a team of coldbloods, and groom and dress them elaborately to pull beer wagons in processions where they can really prove their worth as draft horses.

putting in extremely impressive appearances as part of a large team pulling brewery wagons in parades. In developing countries, the reputation of the industrious farm horse lives on not merely through stories of days gone by, but in actual daily work in the fields. This is also true in Amish parts of Pennsylvania, where horses seemingly frozen in time continue to pull the plow.

Horses in Forestry

Where it walks, no grass grows! One could be forgiven for thinking so when faced with a massive coldblood pulling 1,000-lb tree trunks from the undergrowth. Far from destroying the forest, these gigantic helpers are real nature conservationists, because their measured footsteps replace the tractor that would otherwise flatten the forest floor. Using horses thus preserves an important habitat for microorganisms—and the grass can keep growing.

Still, by the early twentieth century cost considerations had brought an end to the thousand-year teamwork between man and horse. Since tractors and machines called forwarders were more effective, the up to 1-ton coldbloods with their muscular build and enormous willingness to work were suddenly no longer in demand.

It has only been recently, as people become more aware of the need for ecological forestry, that horses have returned to the woods. With their load attached to a hook, they carefully walk over obstacles on the forest floor, even skillfully dodging young saplings. For ecologically-minded forest owners, the horse remains indispensable for harvesting wood and preparing the ground for new planting.

and bandits taking advantage of the defenseless new arrivals in the West. Attacks on stagecoaches and even trains were rampant.

When the settlers finally arrived and set up home, they had to deal with the Native Americans whom they were gradually displacing. The newcomers were amazed by their non-violent handling of horses and their light, easy riding style. They knew nothing of heavy saddles and sharp bits; they usually rode bareback, placing a simple rope around the animal's neck. Unfortunately, relations between the two peoples never remained friendly for long, as the cavalry was making its way westward at the same time and driving the Native Americans before it. Although their resistance was

The greatest of the cowboy cartoon figures is Lucky Luke, who is a quicker draw than even his own shadow and whose main pastime is chasing the Dalton brothers. At the end of all of his adventures, Lucky Luke rides off singing into the sunset on his faithful horse, Jolly Jumper.

At the Battle of Little Bighorn on June 25, 1876, General Custer's American cavalry regiment was routed by an association of Indian tribes under the leadership of Chiefs Sitting Bull and Crazy Horse. Their bloody triumph made history.

The Wild West

The conquest of the Wild West has long provided plenty of fodder for films, novels, legends, and stories, both true and invented, telling of white settlers and persecuted Indians, of battles, vigilantes, the Gold Rush, sheriffs, and bandits. After America won its independence in 1783, the new country began to expand westward bit by bit. Single men and whole families gathered all their belongings in covered wagons and made the long and arduous journey through uncharted territory. Horses and mules pulled the heavy wagons, flanked for protection by armed riders. Owning one or two good horses was like having start-up capital, which is why horse thieves lurked everywhere. If there was money to be made this way, there was also tremendous risk from the vengeful rage of their victims: getting caught could well mean lynching. There were also plenty of other crooks

ultimately in vain, they did win some spectacular battles in the meantime. The American Army experienced its worst defeat in June 1876 at the hands of the biggest association of tribes ever. Under the leadership of Sioux chief Tatanka Yotanka—Sitting Bull—the Hunkpapa and Teton Sioux joined forces, along with the Arapaho and the Cheyenne, to resist being forced off their land and onto reservations. Sitting Bull worked with another chief, Tashunka Witko—Crazy Horse—a tactic that paid off. In the famous bloody battle at the Little Bighorn River in Montana, the Native Americans succeeded in surrounding confident, unsuspecting General George Armstrong Custer and the 7th Cavalry Regiment. Popular tradition (which is almost true) has it that all 225 US soldiers and their horses met their deaths—with one exception. The only survivor on the American side was a horse named Comanche, who was still standing by his rider's side, bleeding, two days after the battle. Soldiers who arrived after the battle were able to save Comanche and proclaimed the horse a hero. The animal was released from military service and proudly shown off in parades. He spent his last years at Fort Riley, Kansas, allowed to roam free (see box, p. 157).

WESTERN HEROES AROUND THE WORLD

Author Karl May brought the legends of the Indians and settlers to Germany in a series of popular novels. His immortal characters Winnetou and Old Shatterhand, a proud Apache and a German surveyor, are enemies when they first meet but over time become blood brothers. On their black steeds, Iltschi (Wind) and Hatatitla (Lightning), they ride across the country battling against injustice.

Few cowboys have ridden off into as many sunsets as the enduringly popular Franco-Belgian comic book hero Lucky Luke, a best seller all over continental Europe. His horse, Jolly Jumper, was a very clever animal that helped its rider solve many a predicament. Lucky Luke could shoot faster than his own shadow, but that alone couldn't save his life every time, and without Jolly Jumper he would certainly not have lived to a ripe old age. The white horse with a crooked spine never let anyone make a fool of him, neither the nasty Dalton brothers and their nagging mother nor the high-strung women in frilly dresses Lucky Luke liked to court. At the end of each adventure, the pair rode happily into the sunset, Lucky Luke singing at the top of his lungs: "I'm a poor, lonesome cowboy, far away from home."

What Lucky Luke did for comics abroad, John Wayne accomplished on the big screen at home. He had already been in the movie business for ten years when he was discovered as the ideal Western star. No one in Hollywood could walk bow-legged better than he, or sit a horse with the same casual nonchalance. He had his own special brand of roughneck charm, whether sitting in a saloon knocking back whiskey to wash the dust from his throat or talking to his horse (who understood him better than any lady).

Sitting Bull was chief and medicine man of a Sioux tribe and played a decisive role in winning the Battle of Little Big Horn against the US cavalry. Shortly thereafter, he and his people were forced to flee from the US Army to Canada, where he lived for a few years in exile before finally returning to a reservation in America. He later performed in Buffalo Bill's Wild West Show.

The Marlboro Man

What ever happened to that ultimate denizen of the Wild West, the Marlboro Man? For years it was his mission to convince the world that smoking was the secret to his suave assurance, promising consumers the tantalizing taste of freedom and adventure.

But cigarette advertising has now been banned from television in many countries and relegated to short stints on the big screen, at most. In the United States the Marlboro Man met with the worst fate of all: the oversized, 80-ft tall billboard figure that once reigned over Sunset Boulevard in Los Angeles eventually became the target of those suffering the after-effects of smoking. People who had contracted lung cancer sued the tobacco industry for millions, even billions of dollars. The Marlboro Man was forced to beat a swift retreat and make way for anti-smoking campaigns.

This fall from cult figure to pariah was hard on him. Legend has it that, somewhere in the hills outside Hollywood, a lonesome cowboy sits sadly before his campfire, a nicotine patch behind his ear…

A sign in Sacramento, California, the starting point of the very first Pony Express courier, who rode on April 4, 1860, commemorates the messengers on horseback and their achievements.

The Pony Express

Before the telegraph was invented in 1837, the fastest way to send a message was by horse and rider. The most elaborate postal service ever was the Pony Express. Its founder, William H. Russell, dis-

patched the first relay team from Sacramento, California, on the 2,000-mile-long journey to St. Joseph, Missouri, on April 4, 1860. He hired only young men under 18, who weighed no more than 130 lb and were willing to ride 300 miles before passing the mail to the next rider. The hard-running ponies carrying 22-lb mailbags were exchanged every 15 miles at a total of 165 stations. The riders had

The Midnight Ride of Paul Revere

"Listen, my children, and you shall hear / Of the midnight ride of Paul Revere, / On the eighteenth of April, in Seventy-Five; / Hardly a man is now alive / Who remembers that famous day and year."

H. W. Longfellow

Paul Revere did make the midnight ride immortalized in Longfellow's poem, though he didn't shout *The British are coming!* as tradition claims. By his own account he borrowed "a very good horse" that he could not return. Some say it's name was Sheherazade. Revere said nothing, but its owner called it Brown Beauty.

A commemorative coin was minted in homage to the Pony Express, showing a pony and rider in rapid gallop.

The Late Harvest Messenger

In the eighteenth century, vintners in the German Rheingau region were forbidden to harvest the ripe grapes in the fall without written permission from the Prince-Bishop of Fulda. Only when he gave his blessing could the wine harvest begin. Every year, a messenger on horseback was sent from Johannisberg Castle to Fulda to fetch the official consent. In 1775, the messenger's return was delayed for two weeks. The vintners waited impatiently for the courier, as the overripe grapes were already falling prey to a fungus known as "noble rot." When the rider finally arrived, there was widespread doubt about how this wine would turn out. Against all expectations, however, the late harvest produced an especially delicious wine that has become a signature of the German winemakers' repertoire: Spätlese (late harvest)!

only two and a half minutes to switch horses, because the whole route had to be covered in nine to ten days.

A superhuman accomplishment was credited to the 15-year-old William Cody, later known as Buffalo Bill, who was forced to ride 322 miles of the route on his own when two relay riders failed to take over at their assigned posts. He covered the stretch in 24 hours and 40 minutes—corresponding to an average speed of over 13 miles per hour.

The 400 Express ponies soon knew the way and what was expected of them. In those rough days, the riders often fell victim to a gunshot or stray arrow, but their mounts would gallop on undaunted until they reached their goal. In the entire eighteen months of operations, only a single letter went missing. Nonetheless, the Pony Express ultimately had to be shut down because the new trains and stagecoaches were faster and less expensive, and could also take on paying guests.

England was far ahead of the developments on the new continent. John Palmer had already founded the Royal Mail in 1784, almost eighty years before the Pony Express made its first deliveries. But the usually badly-mounted couriers quickly disappeared and were replaced by postillions.

In France, the mounted coachmen wore the proverbial seven league boots, which did not make them especially fast, but derive their name from the fact that the coachmen only dismounted from their horses and touched the ground at the postal stations—every seven leagues.

Buffalo Bill

What did the legendary Buffalo Bill actually look like? In the imaginations of countless children playing cowboys and Indians, he looks like genuine trapper, dressed from head to toe in leather with scuffed boots, his hat pulled down low over his eyes. He is a desperado without a home, he is no friend to the Indians, and he is good for nothing but sharp shooting and promoting himself as Buffalo Bill.

Much of this picture is accurate. Buffalo Bill, a cult figure of the Wild West, was a real person, born on February 26, 1846, in Scott County, Iowa, as William Frederick Cody. His family moved on to Kansas when he was still a young boy, and he grew up on the prairie. He worked for the Pony Express while a teenager and then became a cavalry officer at 22, fighting the Indians for many years. Later he was swept up in the pioneer spirit and became a famous scout for the American Army, working that dangerous job for five years.

As the Transcontinental Railroad was being built in 1867-1868, he took a position as a supplier. The laborers had him to thank for nutritious, if somewhat one-sided fare: buffalo meat, buffalo meat, and more buffalo meat! William Cody could supply as much of this as the men could eat—he claimed to have killed 4,280 head of buffalo in just eighteen months, which is how he got his nickname, Buffalo Bill.

A photo taken around the turn of the century shows not a weathered adventurer, however, but a well-groomed gentleman in shirt, tie, and frock coat with a carefully twirled mustache.

By this time Buffalo Bill was married and, as the father of four children, was making his living less dangerously by marketing himself as a living legend. He toured with his Wild West Show through America and Europe, thrilling audiences everywhere with his own sharp shooting and performances by other famous figures, such as Chief Sitting Bull. When, after thirty years, public interest began to flag, the big show was over at last. Buffalo Bill Cody died a poor man in Denver, Colorado, in 1917.

Horses Everywhere

"I believe in the horse. The automobile is only a passing fad!"

Emperor Wilhelm II

The coachman knows the way!
Many passengers must have comforted themselves with this thought on the arduous several-week journey across America. Traveling on the postal carriages, known as stagecoaches, was anything but comfortable, because the suspension system made for quite a rocky ride. On September 17, 1858, the first stagecoach (run by the Butterfield Overland Mail Service) made its way over the dusty road from Tipton, Missouri, to San Francisco. When the coach reached its destination after twenty-four days of travel, it had covered 2,800 miles. It made 165 stops along the way for changes of horses and coachmen. Only the passengers remained the same, who were likely thoroughly shaken and exhausted by the end of their journey.

It would be hard to imagine a big-city street in the nineteenth century without horse-drawn wagons and carriages. Transport of passengers and goods alike depended on what was at the time the least expensive method of travel, the horse. It pulled the milk wagon, the fire engine, the taxi, the hearse, and—as it still does today—the brewery wagon. Trams and buses were also horse-drawn until the invention of the automotive engine.

Horses and Canals
Long before the invention of the motorboat and steamship, workhorses were used to tow barges upstream. Egyptian wall paintings show how boats were towed from the shore with the aid of long ropes, and the Romans also used draft horses to transport goods and stone upriver for use in building streets. Modern canals were a by-product of the early industrial revolution with its demand for reliable and cheap freight transport, which the horse could still fulfill—although it ultimately lost out to the railways.

Towing ships was hard labor: a 10-ton load could be hauled by up to ten men or one horse, but some jobs required twelve horses making their way along the towpaths on either bank of the river. Not infrequently, the trip had to be continued in shallow water when the poor condition of the towpaths prevented the horses from making headway. Horses are still used for towing today, but the boats are usually full of tourists, not freight.

This seemingly idyllic scene with horses everywhere is deceptive, however. Many draft horses pulling buses and streetcars did not survive the arduous work longer than four years.

Major cities like New York and London, in which more than 200,000 horses lived in 1885, also had major problems disposing of the huge quantities of horse manure that accumulated—up to 1,630 tons a day. It was particularly unpleasant on hot and humid summer days when the city was blanketed in a thick layer of horse dung and dust. After a heavy rainfall, the unpaved streets became muddy cesspits full of horse droppings and urine. Despite these drawbacks, however, it was not until the major wave of motorization that horses were replaced in their duties.

Before the invention of motorized vehicles, horses were indispensable for public transport. They pulled anything and everything on wheels, from fire engines to streetcars.

In post-war Berlin, an ill-fated switch from horse to motorcycle prompted an unexpected tragedy. Based on his valuable service, Soviet Colonel General Nikolai Bersarin was named town major of Berlin. His trusty steed had accompanied him all the way across Russia, Poland, and East Germany to take up his post. On June 16, 1945, Bersarin, who had been officially promoted to the status of a "hero of the Soviet Union," climbed onto a German motorcycle that was part of the spoils of the war. He got ready to take his first motorcycle ride and proceeded to drive at full speed right into a truck. He was killed instantly. Stalin greeted the news of his demise with more indignation than horror and grief, as a staff officer remarked, "Stalin thinks anyone who rides a motorcycle is a rowdy." In the Generalissimo's opinion, "A commander on a motorcycle violates the disciplinary code; horses have better judgment." Stalin even begrudged the

Before the advent of the railroads, stagecoaches not only transported the mail, but also passengers.

"Soviet hero" an honorable funeral, but the political administration managed to see to it that Bersarin was transported to Moscow and given a state burial in the most prestigious cemetery.

> The saying "He's gone to the dogs" originally referred to someone who was so poor that he had switched from draft horses to mules, and then on downward to dogs.

The Fiaker

The horse taxi has been part of the Viennese cityscape since 1693, but actually took up its first passengers thirty years earlier in Paris (where carriages were available for hire at the Place de St. Fiacre). St. Fiacre was an early Irish monk who by the seventh century was venerated as the patron saint of horses, and later the horse taxi by association. The fact that the French original went on to become a Viennese archetype is attributable on one hand to the two horses pulling the elegant coach, and on the other to the fiaker, or coachman. Fiakers have long ceased to be mere drivers and horse caretakers; they also serve as tourist guides. In the fiakers'

heyday, from 1860 to 1908, they were even known as accomplished singers and whistlers. At that time, around a thousand fiakers plied the streets of Vienna. They are commemorated in the Fiaker Song and immortalized in the character of Fiakermilli, the singing coachwoman in Richard Strauss's opera *Arabella*.

Today, fiakers have to do more than bridle up a pair of *Würschtel* (sausages), as they affectionately refer to their horses. Since 1998, they have been required to pass a test proving their knowledge of local streets, their ability to drive and maintain the horses, their skills as tourist guides, and their grasp of traffic regulations. Between fares, incidentally, fiakers may take a

break and enjoy another kind of fiaker, pure black coffee in a water glass. The alcoholic version

with rum is reserved for after hours, once the horses are safely in their stall.

The reigning Queen of England in her opulent carriage, drawn by the Windsor Horses.

Great Carriages

BEN HUR

Ben Hur was a fictional figure, a daring charioteer who lived at the time of Jesus. He was made famous first by a popular novel of his life, and then by a classic Hollywood blockbuster film. The novel's author, former Union General Lewis Wallace of Indiana, told how Ben Hur survived a series of adventures at sea, in the desert and between Rome and Jerusalem.

In the film, the high point is the chariot race. The chariots are drawn by teams of four, Ben Hur's team is white, Messala's is black. Ben Hur wanted revenge on his betrayer Messala, but there was also a great deal of money at stake in the packed arena. The crowds got their money's worth in drama and excitement when Ben Hur caused Messala to fall from his seat and the other chariots ran over him, trampling him to death.

For the audience, Ben Hur was not the only hero of the film. The 24 horses of the chariot teams put up a magnificent performance with their panicked reactions, providing great entertainment and suspense.

DRACULA'S COACH

Count Dracula and his cohorts of sun-shy vampires prefer to ride in a black coach drawn by black horses. And when the bloodsucking count invites "guests" to visit him at his castle, he also dispatches his black team, which finds its way without a coachman. The horses are devoted to their master, taking him all over Transylvania wherever the best supply of fresh blood can be found, and always standing at the ready to whisk him off to the safety of darkness before the first rays of sunlight creep over the horizon.

THE QUEEN MOTHER AND QUEEN ELIZABETH

It's true that the Queen Mother once flew in a Concorde (her dearest birthday wish some years ago) but this vigorous monarch's favorite means of transport when in London was a horse and carriage. In 1940 she refused to abandon the city despite the constant bombing

One of the most famous coaches ever was Ben Hur's quadriga, a chariot pulled by a team of four, in the monumental film that bears his name. The movie received a special Golden Globe in 1960 for the spectacular staging of the chariot race.

The Queen Mother was an enthusiastic carriage rider all her life and took regular tours through England's capital, cheered on all sides.

and stayed in residence against the will of the Churchill government and her husband, King George VI. The Londoners never forgot her valor: right until her death in 2002, they broke into cheers every time their "Queen Mum" rode by in her coach on her daughter's birthday. Naturally, Queen Elizabeth II also has her own carriage, drawn by the Windsor Horses—a privilege reserved for the reigning monarch.

THE QUADRIGA

In 1794, King Friedrich Wilhelm II of Prussia (Frederick the Great) commissioned Gottfried Schadow to create a statue of the goddess of peace pulled by a quadriga and set it on Berlin's Brandenburg Gate. But in 1807, Napoleon, who was in the process of sweeping through Europe and scoring triumph after triumph until half the continent was under his dominion, had the quadriga pulled down from the Brandenburg Gate after his march into Berlin and took it back home with him to Paris as a trophy. Prussia did not recover from this affront until 1814, when Napoleon was defeated at last and the quadriga could be returned to its rightful home.

Then, the Prussians renamed the goddess Victoria—after the Roman goddess of victory. And her original classical laurel wreath was replaced by one of oak leaves with an iron cross and the Prussian eagle. When it was remounted on the gate, the quadriga was set in the opposite direction, away from the west where the triumphant

> "My sister, and my sister's child,
> Myself, and children three,
> Will fill the chaise; so you must ride
> On horseback after we."
>
> William Cowper, English lawyer and poet

French emperor had ridden. Instead, it now faces east, which makes more sense as it thus commands the full length of the grand boulevard Unter den Linden, which runs between it and the statue of Frederick the Great.

The monument was heavily damaged in the final days of the Second World War. It was later restored, but sustained damage once again in the commotion of the fall of the Berlin wall in 1989. The quadriga had to be removed, refurbished and replaced on top of the gate—where it can again be admired from all sides.

The quadriga on Berlin's Brandenburg Gate was first placed there in 1794. Since then, it has seen good times and bad, including several episodes of damage and restoration.

Pacifists at War

The idea that wars would have been more humane without the use of horses in the battlefields is ludicrous. After all, the idea to go to war stems from men, not horses (despite popular advice to leave the thinking to horses because their heads are bigger).

In the twelfth century, the Mongols were the masters of the surprise attack. They would overwhelm their enemy and vanish before the victims even got around to realizing what had happened.

300 years later, the Hussars, a Hungarian elite troupe of horsemen, were equally agile. The name, "húsz", means twenty and refers to the fact that every twentieth inhabitant of a village was forcibly recruited to the ranks of the Hussars. Because horses far outnumbered horsemen in Hungary, a Hussar could was often to be seen standing astride a pair of horses while driving a third horse before him. Variations on this daring feat can be seen today in horse shows and is known as the Hungarian Post.

In the sixteenth century, horses were used as heavy artillery wheelers: when Frederic II of Prussia first employed artillery in battle, six horses were needed to draw each gun wagon. The cavalry was also indispensable for sending scouts ahead to view the situation for the troops.

THE BATTLE OF WATERLOO

Napoleon Bonaparte had slept well and enjoyed a good breakfast when he mounted his horse on June 18, 1815, in anticipation of sure victory. He had chosen his gray mare Desirée for the ride up the low

Today the Hungarian Post is a feat of equestrian display, but it was once part of real life: the Hussars, elite Hungarian horsemen, would frequently not sit on horseback but instead ride astride two horses!

hills near the Belgian village of Waterloo; his gray stallion Marengo was reserved for later in the day. He was juggling figures in his head, estimating his chances. He had 72,000 men and 246 guns at his disposal, whereas his enemy, the English Duke of Wellington, had only 68,000 soldiers and 156 guns to set against him. Luckily for Napoleon, Wellington's Prussian allies were nowhere to be seen: he

The Battle of Waterloo in Belgium, 1815, was the last major cavalry battle in history–and Napoleon Bonaparte's last battle, too. After this devastating defeat, he finally had to abdicate and went into exile.

had just defeated them at Ligny. The English Duke, Arthur Wellington, had mounted his best horse, a stallion called Copenhagen. He was desperately in need of help. Legend has it that he moaned, "Night or Blücher! Night or Blücher!" Blücher was the Prussian general—night or Blücher would put an end to the desperate battle.

The first minor attack charged by the French was only meant as a diversionary maneuver, but it quickly transformed into such a severe battle that Napoleon soon gave orders for the main attack. The troops of the French marshal, Michel Ney, were well-positioned: 2,000 riflemen on horseback made up the front, followed by 100 red lance-bearing cavalrymen and 40 squadrons of cuirassiers. They engaged in a frontal attack; 9,000 horses were included in the confusion. Ney had four horses shot dead under him and was beginning to have doubts about the successful outcome of the battle when all of a sudden the Prussians appeared, led on by their "Marshal Forward!," as Gebhard Leberecht von Blücher was nicknamed.

The last major cavalry battle in history culminated as a tremendous disaster for Napoleon, with terrible losses on both sides. Napoleon

At the National Tin Figure Museum in Omme, the Netherlands, the Battle of Waterloo is reenacted with colorful tin figures. One can even identify the various generals, such as Napoleon, above.

had sacrificed 25,000 men, Wellington 15,000, and Blücher 7,000. It is estimated today that 20,000 horses were killed in that battle.

Copenhagen, Duke Wellington's horse—who carried his master faithfully for more than 18 hours—survived. As a reward for his loyalty, Wellington discharged the horse from cavalry service and sent him to his estate in Hampshire, where he lived ten more years. True to form, the Thoroughbred would still kick out at any who tried to get near him. Copenhagen didn't even show much respect for Wellington when he came to see his horse. However, many Englishmen would gather to see the horse, collecting a hair from his coat as a souvenir. When Copenhagen died aged 28, Wellington had an inscription made for his tomb that reads: "There may have been many faster horses, no doubt many handsomer, but for bottom and endurance I never saw his fellow."

Napoleon's Horses

Napoleon did keep more than 130 horses in his stables, but this hardly proves that he was a genuine lover of horses. He is said to have gone through at least 19 gray stallions in 60 major battles. Only once, in 1800, when the impetuous Frenchman defeated the Austrians in the decisive battle at Marengo in Italy, did he thank God and his horse—which thenceforward took on the name of Marengo and became his favorite horse next to the roan Vizir. When mounted on a good horse, there was no stopping Napoleon. He was Europe's foremost adventurer at the time, rampaging everywhere from Austerlitz, where he beat both Austrian Emperor Franz and Russian Czar Alexander I, to Moscow and back. He was utterly unmoved by the loss of men or horses. He once wrote, "At night, 10,000 horses died. Our Norman horses are not as robust as the Russian ones, nor are the soldiers." En route (doomed by the Russian frost) 48,000 horses lost their lives, but Marengo, a horse with an exceptional constitution, stayed at Napoleon's side. At Waterloo, where Napoleon lost his last battle, the little gray Arab stallion served his master one last time, but when Napoleon had to flee he left his exhausted horse behind. Marengo was the prize of the English who took him to the stud farm of New Barnes, in Ely, where he produced a great many descendants before dying at the impressive age of 38. His skeleton is still kept at the Military Museum in Sandhurst, proof of England's great satisfaction at the legendary victory over Napoleon. Napoleon himself spent the rest of his life in exile on the island of St. Helena, where he died in 1851 (aged 52) as a result of a stomach ulcer. Shortly before his death, he is reported to have said, "I feel so good, I could ride 15 miles cross country!"

Cannon Fodder: Horses in the World Wars

Up, up, my brave comrades! to horse! to horse! Let us haste to the field and to freedom! To the field, for 'tis there that is proved our hearts' force... Friedrich Schiller's *Recruit's Song* was very popular among German cavalrymen. Many members of the cavalry would sing fervent hymns before going to war, a good way to avoid contemplating the horrors awaiting them at the front line.

Ever since the Prussian king Frederick the Great had introduced a well-trained cavalry, the Ulanen (lance-bearing horsemen) were feared on every battlefield. They even went to war in World War I, although the enemy infantrymen with their rifles could kill them easily. The German dragoons (mounted infantry on light horses) entered the battlefields with twenty-eight regiments and, as usual, charged with naked saber at the ready. But they, too, saw their end

rolling toward them when the French used tanks and armored cars for the first time.

But the German army could not make do without horses. In total, 1.4 million war mounts were put into action. Some of these had to draw the heavy artillery: six horses were harnessed to the light guns, and eight to twelve were needed to wheel some of the heavier guns. Gray horses were dyed without compunction to make them look like bays and prevent their light coats from betraying them to distant field glasses.

In times of war, the English had special equine hospitals where up to 2.5 million animals were treated. A good three-quarters of these were, in fact, saved. Yet, the English lost 265,000 horses, most of which froze or died of famine.

However, the cavalry helped the British to a decisive victory in the campaign in Palestine, 1917–1918. The British Chief Inspector of the cavalry, Sir Edmund Allenby, assumed command in the campaign to expel the Turks. He put together a mounted desert corps consisting of soldiers from Australia, New Zealand, India, and Britain and marched against the Turks, supported by troops with machine guns and the Royal Horse Artillery. In October 1918, he took Aleppo

On June 14, 1940, the German troops entered Paris. The cavalrymen rode triumphantly along the Champs-Elysées, without a clue about what World War II would bring them within the next few years.

and thus conquered Palestine. The British Prime Minister praised the horses, calling them as invincible as their horsemen, but the Britons were in fact not very grateful to their loyal comrades-in-arms and instead sold 20,000 cavalry horses to the Egyptians.

Although horses did not stand a chance against modern war machinery, more horses were used in World War II than ever before. The Russians sent 3.5 million into battle, some of them accompanying tank missions. The German armed forces, too, were far from being "entirely motorized," as Hitler's propaganda had it. There were 2.75 million horses at the front lines, and they died in large numbers—52,000 horses and their riders fell at the Battle of Stalingrad alone. Between 1939 and 1945, an average of 865 animals died each day. Utterly hopeless acts of desperation were a daily occurrence. When at the outset of the war the Germans rolled into Poland with their tanks, a whole brigade of Polish mounted horses stormed toward them and was destroyed entirely. 1941 saw a similar catastrophe in Russia, when a division of the Mongolian cavalry stormed the German infantry. It was easy for the soldiers inside tanks to defend themselves: they simply opened fire. Within minutes, 2,000 horsemen and mounts were killed or wounded. Though the Germans suffered no losses during that attack, they did face their final defeat later in Russia. The German forces staved off their downfall for over a year, but in 1944 they had to retreat from the Crimean peninsula. The soldiers were given brutal orders to leave no live animals behind—which meant that thousands of horses were slaughtered.

The armies of every country that participated in World War I employed horses for transporting the heavy guns.

An odd situation arose during the war in Southern Russia. German General Field Marshal Erich von Manstein had his headquarters guarded by an unusual troupe of horsemen. It consisted entirely of Cossacks—who took not the slightest interest in world politics—and their legendary horses.

In World War I, not only soldiers were supplied with gas masks to protect them from poison gas, but horses, too.

Kurt Waldheim's Horse

For years, Austrian president Kurt Waldheim tried to shrug off accusations of having been a supporter of the Nazis. An international committee finally concluded that the statesman had, in fact, been part of the mounted corps of the SA (storm troopers) but had not been involved in any war crimes. The Viennese responded with typical black humor that clearly it had not been Waldheim who had been a member of the SA, but his horse.

In Exile

Race Profile: Trakehner

Stick Measure: 63–66 inches

Colors: all basic colors

Description: elegant, athletic riding horse

Origin: Eastern Prussia (former German Empire)

Fleeing Eastern Prussia

In the winter of 1945, tens of thousands of refugees leaving eastern Germany witnessed the astonishing endurance of this horse as they fled the Red Army, which was charging toward Berlin and Frankfurt. Among the refugees was Marion Gräfin Dönhoff, who had grown up on the Gut Friedrichstein estate in eastern Prussia. Her book, *Weit ist der Weg nach Osten* (Long is the Road to the East), includes graphic descriptions of her experience as a refugee and the horrors of this particular trek, which took place in the cruelest frost and left many people injured or even dead.

The late countess, a well-known author, journalist, and editor of German weekly paper *Die ZEIT,* never forgot that "in those days, a horse was worth a kingdom!"

"His Majesty orders all commanders of the cuirassier regiments to concentrate all their work, education, and training on turning a common man into a good and talented horseman."

Shortly after taking up the regency in 1740, the Prussian king, Frederick the Great, realized why his regiments were defeated by the Austrians. The problem was not the horses, but the riders and their poor training. To remedy this, he had the daredevil Friedrich Wilhelm von Seydlitz released from prison in Austria and promoted to the post of cavalry captain. Von Seydlitz made the Prussian cavalry the most famous and feared cavalry of its time: when the Hussars rode to attack, their enemies wished they had never been born.

It was thanks to the father of Frederick the Great, Frederick William I, that these courageous horsemen had the right horses to match their spirits. To ensure provision of specially trained horses for the military campaigns—horses that were exceedingly courageous and had an exceptional stamina—Frederick William had almost 15,000 acres of marshland near Königsberg drained. There he founded the royal stud of Trakehnen, with 1,100 horses of various

During World War II, both the inhabitants and the horses living in eastern Prussia were driven from their home. On this trek through snow and ice, countless people and horses lost their lives, although the horses gave an extreme show of their immeasurable toughness and stamina.

bloodlines. In its heyday, the stud was referred to as *Königreich der Pferde* (Horse Kingdom). The complex even had its own school, post office, hospital, and the Hotel Elch (elk). Because this was the only part of the entire kingdom where elks lived, elk antlers were chosen for the brand, which is now world famous.

The Trakehner horse developed into an elegant bloodline with a muscular croup and ground-covering action. Outside blood is no longer permitted in the studbook, although Trakehnen horses are very popular today for revitalizing other breeds. In January 1945, the Trakehnen horses gave a dramatic performance of their courage, stamina, and robustness when they were forced to leave their home in eastern Prussia, fleeing the oncoming Russian army tanks. The trek of refugees was many miles long and rolled on day and night. Coupled mares pulled covered wagons weighing over two tons each over the frozen ground, in temperatures well below zero. There was hardly any food or water at hand. Only 800 mares and forty stallions survived with their owners and made it to western Germany.

Right: The studbook of the elegant Trakehner breed is closed, but these horses are frequently employed to upgrade other breeds.

Below: The magnificent stud master's house with a statue of the Trakehner Tempelhüter in his prime. It dates from the heyday of the stud farm. Today, the whole estate has fallen into disrepair. The original bronze sculpture now stands in the Equestrian Museum, Moscow.

Below: The Trakehnen horse brand shows an elk's antlers. The breed is therefore sometimes known as the Pferde mit der Elchschaufel *(elk-antler horse).*

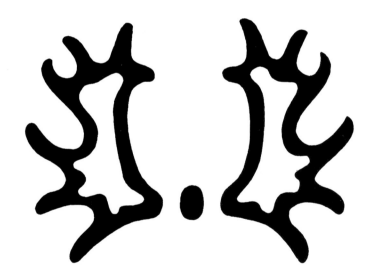

Tempelhüter

Tempelhüter's sire was Perfektionist–at least that was his popular name, and it was fitting, as he produced some excellent offspring. This impetuous English Thoroughbred came to the state stud of Trakehnen in 1904, but after an accident in his stall only three years later he had to be euthanized. In the few years of his active life at the stud, he sired 131 foals, of which thirty-two stallions and thirty-seven mares were used for the breeding program.

The mare Teichrose was a perfect match for Perfektionist. One of their progeny was the stallion Tempelhüter (Temple Guard)–worthy both of his name and his progenitors–whose stellar career as state stud began in Braunsberg. His renown was so great that in 1916 he was ordered back from the main stud and brought to Trakehnen, where by 1933 he had fathered an amazing number of exceptional horses. Among these were fifty-four stud stallions, sixty brood mares, and a hundred horses for riding and eventing.

The breeders especially prized his trunk length–65 inches. With a height of 62½ inches that can certainly be considered long! These measurements fit exactly with people's visions of the ideal Trakehner at the time. And because Tempelhüter was also beautiful in every other way, the main stud farm dedicated an equestrian statue to him. It was confiscated by the Russians following World War II, however, and since then can be admired in front of the Moscow Horse Museum. With much diplomatic skill and targeted donations, the German Horse Museum in Verden at least managed to obtain a copy of the sculpture so that Tempelhüter could live on in the memories of others besides his offspring.

In places such as Barcelona, Spain, mounted police are used to control the traffic. Above, an imperturbable Andalusian at work.

Horses and Crowds

Recently, the situation around European football stadiums has grown steadily worse. Fans of rival teams come together, often leading to fights and disputes. In these situations, a police riding team can work wonders. When riot police arrive on horseback, hooligans quickly take flight. Many a hooligan seems to fear the four-legged civil servant more than a biped armed with a baton.

The same is true of demonstrations. Neither anti-riot water cannons nor several hundred police with shields can disperse a rioting mob as effectively as a riding team, and this usually happens without any use of violence. Most urbanites instinctively back away from horses because they know that horses shy easily and that their reaction is unpredictable. This is why large-framed, imposing warmblood horses are chosen as police mounts: their appearance increases the psychological effect. The truth is, though, that these big horses are usually calmer and more stress-proof than other breeds. They may not have been that way as fillies and colts, but on entering police service they go through extensive training, after which they stick by their riders through thick and thin. Police mounts have absorbed a solid training in jumping and dressage and are as good as unflappable. They do not panic when shots are fired, and don't even twitch when objects are thrown at them or when they have to face a howling mob waving flags and banners. Coping with situations like these is all part of their training.

The use of mounted police is not limited to these special assignments, however. Everyday life on patrol is much more relaxed and friendly. Every chief of police knows perfectly well that horses draw a lot of sympathy, which means that mounted policemen have a great advantage compared to their colleagues patrolling on foot. From their viewpoint in the saddle, 8 feet above the ground, they also have a panoramic view of pedestrian areas, and when there are crowds on special occasions, such as Christmas markets or fairgrounds, they are much quicker at catching pickpockets than their

This Israeli policewoman and her horse are well-equipped. Both wear protective shields to reduce the danger of injury in case they are attacked.

From Police Mount to Olympic Champion

No pair has been juried as often as German Chief Inspector Klaus Balkenhol and his police mount Goldstern. The two were team champions of the Olympic dres-

sage competitions in Barcelona and Atlanta, and took bronze in individual competition.

Klaus Balkenhol himself discovered the big-framed sorrel gelding, and bought and trained him as a grand prix horse fit for the Olympic Games. Stationed with the mounted police of Düsseldorf, Germany, he was given full freedom to focus on sporting events (so Goldstern was not employed for patrolling the streets).

Goldstern, who was officially property of the state, and his comrade Balkenhol were both in active service until 1999. The team then retired from state service and enjoyed life together in the countryside, near Münster. Goldstern died in 2003.

Most people instinctively treat mounted police with respect, which means that their mere presence often suffices to ensure order.

pedestrian colleagues. Indeed, the potential of the mounted police is so wide-ranging that their relative scarcity is quite astonishing.

A riding team is both ecologically sound and in touch with the people. Depending on the season, they can serve taxpayers in many ways, thus securing their safety. Combing parks and recreational areas in summer disperses potential muggers and trouble-makers of

various kinds, while in town burglaries can be prevented by patrols of mounted police in neighborhoods.

Whether in London, Tokyo, Barcelona, Jamaica or the Fiji Islands, mounted police are employed all over the world. Without question, the most photogenic of these must be the Redcoats of the Royal Canadian Mounted Police, whose tradition goes back to 1873. The Mounties, as they are affectionately known in Canada, are both popular individual figures and a national symbol.

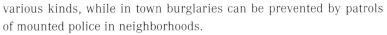

The Royal Canadian Mounted Police are Canada's mounted federal police. The Mounties are famous for their red and black parade uniform.

A Horse on the Crest

FORD MUSTANG

Extraordinary scenes unfolded in the car showrooms when the first Ford Mustang was presented to the public on April 17, 1964. In San Francisco, one truck driver was so fascinated that he couldn't tear his eyes from the advertising poster and promptly crashed into the showroom. In Texas, fifteen customers almost came to blows because each of them had their heart set on the floor model. One gentleman from Dallas bid highest and locked himself inside the car to wait until the following morning when the salesman could establish the validity of his check. A vendor in Chicago had to lock the Mustangs on display because the eager customers simply would not accept that eight people could not check out the inside of a car built for four, all at the same time.

The auto manufacturers in Dearborn, Michigan were more than satisfied: the Mustang became the best-selling hit in the history of the enterprise. Numerous extra features, a profoundly solid construction, and the exceedingly tame price tag are some of the factors that led to the Mustang's being nicknamed Pony-Car. The interior design included one optional extra feature: a band of Mustang horses embossed on the backrests. Naturally, this instantly transformed the Mustang Pony-Car into a luxury model.

The first Ford Mustang was launched in 1964. Over the years, it has drawn such a huge community of fans that it is still produced, although there have been some fundamental changes in the design since then.

PEGASO

The Spanish car manufacturer Pegaso did not add wings to its Z-102 racing model but did make sure it had plenty of hp. Launched in the 1950s, it was designed as part racing car and part chic, Italian-style design object. Although its top speed of 160 mph impressed many of its competitors, very few clients actually bought the car—only 100 models were produced altogether.

FERRARI

Wickedly expensive and only truly acceptable in bright red: the cars manufactured by Scuderia Ferrari are among the world's top luxury goods—and they are only authentic with their crest, a black stallion from the Italian town of Ravenna on a yellow background. Legend

Standard Oil Company of New York, or SOCONY, traces its origins back to the 19th century, when it used a white Pegasus for its logo. The name was changed to Mobil in 1920 and the red Pegasus debuted in 1939. It was used until the new (reversed) version was introduced in 1965. Vintage signs survive throughout the world.

Although Enzo Ferrari was given the right to use the prancing horse as an emblem for his manufacture as early as 1923, it was only used for the first time nine years later.

has it that the company founder, race driver Enzo Ferrari (1898–1988), had been given the crest as a lucky charm when he won the match race in Ravenna in 1923. Prior to that, the *cavallino rampante*, as the little rearing horse is called in Italian, had been featured on the coat of arms of the Piedmont cavalry regiment.

PORSCHE

Sporting luxury cars are carefully designed in the minutest detail and they can be confusingly similar. So Porsche makes its logo distinctive with a horse, a symbol of dynamism and speed. It is taken from the coat of arms of the German city of Stuttgart, where the Porsche manufacture is based. The black horse has been gracing the hood of these Swabian automobiles since 1948.

MUSTANG JEANS

To the war-weary Germans, the blue jeans that first came to Europe after World War II were the epitome of freedom. However, American originals were rare and were sold at horrendous prices on the black market. For the majority of people, they remained a coveted ideal beyond their reach. This changed in 1949 when the first German-made jeans were sold. Frankfurt-based pioneer Albert Sefranek had simply swapped six bottles of liquor for six pairs of jeans, copied the

cut, and then started producing his own American-style jeans. Initially, however, he had to make do without the denim that distinguishes true jeans. When the original US denim was finally imported in the late 1950s, Sefranek struck a major international career with his Mustang Jeans. They are now sold all over the world.

MOBILGAS

Pegasus, the winged horse and symbol of poetic inspiration, was used as the trademark for Socony Mobil Oil, the first oil company in Australia and a highly successful brand in the United States, especially in the 1940s and 1950s. It became an extremely well-known corporate logo and even today tin signs, posters, and prints featuring the red winged horse are in high demand. Even Edward Hopper included such a sign with the red horse in one of his famous lonely street scenes, *Gas, 1940*, showing an attendant at a Mobil gas station.

Porsche's prancing black horse logo is similar to the Ferrari crest. This prestigious brand was designed by Ferry Porsche, son of the company's founder.

Prized Athletes

The Sport of Kings

Royalty and members of high society have always had a penchant for noble horses, and racing has long been seen as the sport of kings. Indeed, even the handsomest and fastest steeds were hardly good enough for them.

The fast gallop is an inborn trait in horses. When they lived in open pastureland and on the steppes, it was essential to be able to flee enemies at a flat-out gallop. Domestication has protected horses from many dangers, but their instinct for flight survived. Even today, a horse's first choice is to flee, not to fight, and for good reason: on further investigation, the apparent cowards turn out to be extraordinary sprinters with great staying power.

It comes as no surprise that it quickly occurred to people to turn this trait into a form of entertainment. In antiquity, only chariot races were part of the Olympic Games. The first races under saddle were held in 720 BCE. The Romans were responsible for the development of horse racing and the breeding of suitable horses, but the true cradle of horse racing lies in England. In 208 CE, Roman emperor Lucius Septimus Severus decided to settle in the British Isles after his military campaign against the Britons. A great horse race enthusiast, he had horses brought over from the Middle East because there were only sturdy native ponies on the island. This is where the story of the English Thoroughbred begins.

The key initiators of today's flat-race sport were members of the English royalty in the seventeenth and eighteenth centuries. During the times of Charles I, Newmarket developed as an important center for horse racing and the breeding of racehorses, and this is where the first auction house for Thoroughbred horses was founded. After the crown was abolished and Charles was executed, the puritan Lord Protector Oliver Cromwell put an end to public horse racing in 1654. Six years later, however, the monarchy was restored under Charles II and the racecourses were opened once more. The breeding of Thoroughbreds expanded to such an extent that a central organization was required. The result was the English Jockey Club, founded in 1752, which continues in full force today. From Newmarket, the Jockey Club took on the organization of horseracing and control of Thoroughbred breeding. Many a member of the nobility held race meetings as part of their entertainment program for countryside parties, and this is how the classic race meetings came about. One of these is the Oak Stakes (Epsom Downs), named after a hunting chalet—the first race to admit three-year-old mares only.

The *General Stud Book*, the British studbook in which the pedigree of every English Thoroughbred is registered, was established by the renowned James Weatherby and first published in 1791. The standard volume is updated and published regularly by Weatherbys and is indispensable for horse breeders: without it, tracing the pedigrees of these noble horses would be impossible.

From the British Isles, the fascination for horse racing slowly spread throughout the world. The first organized flat racing began in Long Island, NY, in 1665. Thoroughbreds were only imported in the eighteenth and nineteenth centuries, however, and the first

When entering the home stretch, it is vital to have a good position. The riders on the inside lanes depend on a gap to open up in front of them. One can also overtake from the outside, but this costs much more energy.

Thoroughbred racecourse of in the United States was the Union Course, built on Long Island in 1821. After the Civil War, horse racing advanced to become a major sport in the USA. The Kentucky Derby was inaugurated in 1875.

When the going is soft and a large field of racehorses thunders along the racetrack, little is left of the green grass afterward.

The King of the Sport

Though he is world famous for his unique "flying dismount" performed after each victory, it is not this artistic jump that has made Lanfranco (Frankie) Dettori king of the flat-race course. He has won more than 100 Group 1 races, as the top-class meetings are called, and is without question the most successful Thoroughbred racing jockey in the world. Be it Ascot, Paris, Hong Kong, Dubai, Tokyo or New York, there is virtually no major race on this planet that Frankie Dettori has not won.

And because this jockey never rests long on his laurels, we can expect to enjoy his gleeful flying dismounts on more major race-courses in the future. On September 28, 1996, he achieved the unprecedented feat of winning every one of the seven Ascot races held that day. But one man's meat is another man's poison: Dettori's dedicated fans bankrupted many bookmakers because they had foreseen this coup and had bet sums that amounted to a profit of billions.

The sunny boy himself with his idiosyncratic flying dismount has no financial worries. He wears the royal blue colors of the Godolphin racing stables owned by the sheik family Al Maktoum from Dubai. They have given Frankie an exclusive retainer as their jockey in appreciation of his unquenchable will to win, his elegant riding style, and his exceptional talent for inciting the highly responsive Thoroughbred racehorses to record performance. Dettori is adamant that a race is 80 percent decided by the horse.

The famous jockey, who is 5 ft 4 inches tall, inherited his talent from his father, Gianfranco, also a very successful jockey–a thirteen-time Italian champion who won around 4,000 races. When Dettori senior gave his son a Palomino pony for his eighth birthday, the boy set his heart on his future career: to become a jockey, too. He rode his first race at the age of 9. At 15, he moved to Britain to learn the tricks of the turf in Newmarket. England has become his second home; in fact he received an honorary MBE (Member of the British Empire) from the Queen as a token of appreciation of his feats.

This exceptional jockey credits his guardian angel with preventing his career from taking a sudden and tragic end. In June 2000, he sur-vived the crash of a small private aircraft relatively unharmed, with only a fractured leg. After a mere two months this father of five was back to his old form. He now says that when his time comes, he hopes to die on horseback during a flat-race meeting.

During the season, Thoroughbred racehorses merely have to be kept in condition. The morning after a difficult race, a light warm-up training is enough exercise.

Featherweights in the Saddle

Small, wiry, and as light as possible—that describes the jockeys, not the horses! A jockey has to be a true fighter, not only on the racecourse, but in private life, too, always ensuring that his or her body weight never surpasses 110 lb.

Being a professional jockey is a demanding job that few people choose as a career. Since it includes traveling the world and meeting interesting people, however, a successful jockey's career can also be very fulfilling. If they can make it to the top, the pay is also far above the norm, but it takes time to get this far. Training courses are offered by various international racing schools and associations such as the British Horseracing Board. It is not necessary to be able to ride beforehand, but experience with horses is useful.

A professional jockey is a freelancer who signs a contract with the owners of a racing stable. Including purse money (prize money), a top American jockey can earn $90,000–$100,000, although most will see $35,000–$40,000 in addition to about half of the negligible mount fee (riding fee). Still, money cannot buy the feeling of winning—outdoing all others, standing in the stirrups, fully balanced, cushioning the jolts of every galloping stride for that perfectly-timed final sprint. It's not about being carried by a horse, but flying across the finish line as one, hearing the crowd cheer and the exultant yells of those who placed a bet on you—whether a dollar or a small fortune—this is what motivates a jockey to face the tedious everyday chores. Incidentally, the oldest contemporary jockey is Hungarian Pal Kallai who is still active as a flat-race jockey at the age of 73.

The profession of jockey is dominated by men but there are a growing number of female jockeys. Many of these, however, switch over after a while and become racehorse trainers. In fact, behind the scenes, most grooms and trainers are women.

Fair Balance: The Handicap

The handicap was introduced to equalize the chances in horse races and give slower contestants an opportunity to win against accredited champions. This is a lead weight that must be carried by all horses deemed to exceed the average.

The amount of weight each horse has to carry is settled before the race, based on its previous performances and the specific race distance. For a sprint race (less than ¾ mile) a ratio of 3 lb per furlong would apply, for a medium distance (up to 1.4 miles) a ratio of 2 lb per furlong, and for longer races the ratio is 1 lb per furlong. The exact weights are assigned by the racing secretary, and a general rating of each horse is issued at the end of the season.

In theory, every race should end in a dead heat, with all contestants crossing the finish line at the same time. Ultimately, though, it is a horse's form on the day of the race that counts.

Racing saddles can weigh anywhere from a mere 250 g (= ½ lb), which is called a featherweight, to 2 lb.

1.Lot		2.Lot		3.Lot	
Sherekan	J.Quinn	Macara	F.Minarik	Simoun	J.Quinn
Laudrops	K.Bonhoff	Shalako	J.Quinn	Carrera	F.Minarik
Sumaco	F.Minarik	Marcelino	J.Sobotka	Advocatus	K.Bonhoff
Basento	J.Rogowski	Terek	A.Richter	Liberty Set	M.Rigo
Williamstown	A.Marciniak				
Sumitas	S.Wirths	Indian Ruby	J.Helmeczi	Mr.Bombastic	Z.Rab
Hurricane Thong	K.Erven	Eisprinzess	B.Fueleki	Llanadas	J.Saradin
Borsato	J.Sobotka	Boreal	S.Eder	Sosela	V.Cernohorska
Ofarim	S.Perov	Borabay	K.Bonhoff	Idjen	M.Sadowski
Wellington Hall	J.Saradin	Kasus	J.Rogowski	Fragonard	S.Perov
Catella	Z.Machu	Indian Star	K.Erven	Mendosino	J.Sobotka
Masai	R.Heiders	Zöllner	J.Kluczynski	Ammonias	S.Sluka
Lamani	L.Jurackowa	Iberus	Z.Machu	Irulan	J.Rogowski
Tareno	S.Sluka	Doraline	J.Saradin	Flamingo Sea	B.Fueleki
Laplace	M.Rigo	Balrog	S.Perov	Batang	J.Helmeczi
Bernardon	J.Helmeczi	Macanillo	R.Heiders	Last Rebell	Z.Machu

The jockeys ride with much longer stirrups when training than they do during an actual race. With no rivalry, they gallop comfortably next to each other.

Without a strict itinerary, chaos would rule. This sign board shows each professional horseman when to ride which horse during the warm-up periods.

It is always busy in the jockey's quarters on race day. While dressing and preparing themselves, they watch the current race on the monitor.

Without the help of ground staff, jockeys would be unable to get their horses inside the starting box. Horses that refuse outright must wear a hood over their eyes.

During the final spurt, the jockeys demand the utmost of their horses. The whip is usually shown rather than used, because excessive whipping is penalized.

Dick Francis

Winston Churchill, who was a proud horseman before he became Lord Admiral and later British Prime Minister, once made the audience laugh at a racecourse when he stated that not every visitor to a race meeting was a criminal, but every criminal would surely be met on a racecourse.

Audacious flat and hurdle race jockey Dick Francis took this comment to heart and, following an accident, quit his career. He became a racing correspondent and spent time investigating bookmakers' offices and racing stables. Finding indications of many illegal activities that he could not prove, he decided to pour his knowledge into novels instead, and has been writing thrillers set against the background of the horse racing world ever since.

Francis has received the Mystery Writers of America's Edgar Award for Best Novel three times, as well as the Grand Master Award, the highest honor bestowed by the MWA. He received an OBE (Officer of the Order of the British Empire) in 1984.

A Microcosm: The Racecourse

The racecourse is a lively, colorful, self-contained world that attracts all kinds of people from all social classes. They come together because they share a passion that is unmatched in the sporting world, making the racecourse a veritable microcosm of society.

The ABCs of the Racecourse

When two runners cross the finish line nearly simultaneously, a photograph is indispensable. Both steward and bettors accept this as proof of victory or defeat.

Bismarck: A horse that is a favorite with bettors but which the bookmakers do not expect to win.

Blinkers: Nervous racehorses wear blinkers attached to a hood to prevent them from seeing sideways or backward during a race, or from shying when the jockey swings the whip.

Canter: The canter is a smooth gallop that brings the horses to the starting boxes. It serves as a warm-up to loosen the horse's muscles.

Dead Heat: When two or more horses cross the finish line at the exact same time. In such a case, the prize money and money won through wagers is divided between the winners. A dead heat with three horses has occurred just once in the history of horse racing.

Draw: The day before a race meeting, the starting position from numbered stalls or starting boxes are drawn. A horse starting on the inside barrier has less distance to make up.

Favorite: Term for the anticipated winners of races or the best horse of a racing stable.

Going: The going refers to the surface of the racetrack. The surface is usually grass in Europe, and called turf, while in North America races are also held on a dirt track consisting of sand and clay. The condition of the surface, the going, is extremely important and can have an direct impact on the outcome of a race. Before each race meeting, the going is measured and assessed by an official. There are seven surface grades for turf and five for artificial surfaces. Some horses prefer firm ground, while others run better when the going is soft—known as heavy-goers and soft-goers, respectively.

Handicapper: An official member of the race meeting organizers who determines the specific weight each horse has to carry.

Morning Glory: A term used for horses that have impressive form on the home gallops but fail to perform accordingly on the racetrack.

Pacemaker: A horse that sets the pace by running in front, often for a stable mate, to help it keep up a quick pace.

Photo Finish: The moment the runners cross the finish line is documented by a camera. In case of doubt, the photo finish will help the steward decide on the actual winner. The photo is then enlarged and displayed for the spectators.

Purse: The first four horses across the finish line are awarded a purse (race prize), 60 percent of which goes to the owners.

Racing Colors: Every racehorse owner has an officially registered, unique set of colors. During a race, the jockey wears these colors on his silks (blouse and helmet).

Racing Results: The steward decides the official racing results, assessing whether a runner has won easily and by how many lengths.

Rails: These are light boards used to cordon off the racetrack.

Show Ring: One of the most important locations on the racecourse,

On a sunny day, a race meeting such as this on the flat-race course in Cologne, Germany, attracts thousands of spectators enjoying the atmosphere and excitement.

At the show ring, bettors can take a good look at the horses. An experienced bettor might make a final decision here, having assessed the runners' form.

Few people have to step on the scales as often as a jockey.

this is where the horses are presented to the public before each race. This allows even an amateur spectator to get an impression of a horse's condition on the day of the race. Both the owner and the trainer are present when the horse is saddled. The jockey is then given last-minute tactical advice before mounting and riding from the ring to the racetrack.

Stayer: A horse that performs best over long distances.

Steeplechase: A cross-country race that includes fences and other obstacles.

Steward: Usually, a horse race meeting is organized by an association that employs three official stewards or organizers to ensure a correct and fair race. The outcome of a race may be decided with the help of a photo. Stewards can enforce rules and issue a penalty for horse or jockey if, for example, the jockey has interfered with other runners or is a non-trier (which means that the horse has not run on its merits).

Weigh-in: Before each race, the jockeys are weighed in their complete gear, including the saddle. Jockeys whose overall weight is less than what had previously been assessed by the official handicapper must carry extra weight to compensate. To double-check, the jockey is weighed once more after the race.

Glamorous Society

There is always a good reason to spend a day at the races. Some go to win money by betting or to catch a glimpse of the celebrities who are always present at a race meeting. Aristocrats and rich entrepreneurs make a hobby of keeping expensive racehorses. In the best case, they will stand beside their winning horse during the ceremony, the women resplendent in haute couture and a ravishing hat, and then stroll over to the grandstand for a glass of champagne to celebrate with the trainer.

Owning a racehorse is incredibly expensive. Many owners of flat racers only manage for a year or two, and there are very few families that have owned a racing stable through generations. One such clan is the Rothschilds, who own banks in France and Switzerland in addition to an important stud in Normandy.

Aga Khan IV, the spiritual and worldly leader of the Ismaili Muslims, is also a constant visitor to the turf. The title is hereditary, and the current Aga Khan, Prince Karim al-Hussaini, was appointed by his grandfather. He has been the Aga Khan in the fourth generation since 1957. The Ismaili are a Muslim sect with about 20 million members, each of whom pays 10 per cent of their income to their leader. The Aga Khan is by faith obliged to use this money to help the poor, and is thus founder and chair of the world's largest private development organization. Recently, for example, he invested $80 million to help rebuild Afghanistan, where many Ismaili Muslims live.

The Aga Khan is also a very successful and extremely rich private businessman. Apart from the Imamate, he also inherited his grandfather's love for horse races and the family's breeding empire in France and the UK. With approximately 500 horses, worth an estimated $250 million, he also runs one of the world's largest racing stables.

According to the Ismaili faith, the Aga Khan is infallible in all his actions. So his followers were probably not overly surprised when his stallion Sinndar performed a miraculous feat: within one season, this exceptional runner won both the English and the Irish Derby as well as the French Prix de l'Arc de Triomphe. The Aga Khan could afford to retire his stallion to stud at the age of three.

Sheikhs from the oil-producing countries are also frequently seen on the world's major racecourses. General Sheikh Mohammed bin Rashid Al Maktoum, crown prince of Dubai, strove to play a major role in the racing world of the twenty-first century. With his brothers, he founded the racing yard Godolphin in 1992. Its headquarters is the stable Al Quoz, based in Dubai, where the Thoroughbreds spend the winter recovering from the strenuous racing season and preparing for upcoming events. When the climate gets too hot toward summer, the horses are sent back to their second home, Newmarket in England.

There was hardly anything the sheikh loved more than his Thoroughbreds. When the world-famous stallion Dubai Millennium broke a leg

in August 2000 during a training in Newmarket, he had a specialist flown in from Dubai and attended the five-hour operation himself. The wonder horse was soon back on his legs, but died six months later due to the mysterious grass sickness. The sum paid by the insurance company, some $60 million, was cold comfort to the man who loved his horses so well. "I do not think my love for horses is exceptional. It is part of my blood, my soul, and my history. This love stems from my country."

Like today's Aga Khan, his grandfather Aga Khan III was also a great lover of horse racing.

The hats devised for Royal Ascot's Ladies Day defy the imagination. The Royal Meeting is known throughout the world, and the royal family evidently enjoys the event greatly. Above, Queen Elizabeth and the late Queen Mother.

Great Races

ROYAL ASCOT

There is still a whiff of the old glory days of the British Empire about the racecourse of Ascot when England's Queen Elizabeth turns onto the racetrack in an open state carriage drawn by four or six horses as the national anthem is played. As Her Royal Highness reaches the grandstands, the royal standard is hoisted and the crowd, consisting of passionate bettors and partiers, chimes in soulfully with the lyrics. The ceremony concludes with overwhelming applause while Her Majesty greets family members and the royal entourage. On this day the gentlemen dress in morning suit, gray tailcoats and top hat,

while the ladies indulge in grand and expensive designer hats. Ladies' Day, Thursday, is the fashionable peak of Royal Ascot week.

This has been a tradition since 1951, when King George VI was introduced at Ascot with his wife, who would be known and loved as the "Queen Mum" after her daughter ascended the throne. Ascot (a thriving town in southeast England), owes its fame entirely to this traditional Royal Ascot Week held every year in June on the Ascot moors. The 2-mile track was inaugurated by Queen Anne in 1711, and the first race (Her Majesty's Plate) was held in August. The royal family has made a point of attending Royal Ascot week ever since.

The highlight of the Royal Meeting is the Ascot Gold Cup, held on Ladies' Day and first run in 1807. In 1875, the crowd witnessed a truly exciting win by 17-year-old jockey Fred Archer. Archer continued on as King of the Derby until, weakened by continual dieting and the death of his wife, he committed suicide at the age of just 30.

The Grand National—the Most Arduous Steeplechase of All

It is the biggest betting race in the UK, notorious among jockeys, is protested annually by animal rights activists. The Grand National Steeplechase is the most demanding in the world, and has an ambivalent reputation indeed. Nowhere in the world do outsiders have a better chance of winning than on this racetrack at Aintree near Liverpool. Dismounts by the dozen are normal, with abandoned horses ca-

reening along the track and bringing the running field into confusion shortly before the finish. At times a horse crosses the finish line *sans* jockey (which does not count as a win, of course). The winner must arrive with their jockey—though some insist that anyone (or any horse) that makes it that far should be called a winner.

The most notorious fence, where many are dismounted, is Becher's Brook. A certain Captain Becher won the first Aintree Meeting in

1836, after negotiating forty-two obstacles. But Becher is famous for his mishaps, rather than this victory. In 1839, he fell from his mount in the first circuit, managed to remount, but fell off again in the second circuit, at the same fence. This time, he took shelter in the small brook, waiting for the remainder of the field to thunder over him. Ever since this curious incident, the fence has been named after him.

The grounds of the Grand National have been sold several times

and have frequently come close to being shut down, but the risky meeting remains one of the top racing events today.

England's golden boy and everyone's favorite on the turf, however, was an 18-year-old jockey who appeared out of nowhere in 1954 and immediately trounced all his competitors—Lester Piggott.

The yearly pilgrimage of a dazzling crowd of celebrities make Ascot the most famous racecourse in England. The duty to see and be seen is never so assiduously performed as during Royal Ascot week, with its aristocratic tradition and glorious race horses. International high society here displays its art of easy living: 120,000 bottles of champagne, 75,000 bottles of wine, over 2 tons of beef and 5 tons of salmon, 6,000 lobsters, and 4½ tons of strawberries are consumed by the upper crust during the Royal Meeting—let's not begrudge them the pleasure. Ascot will always draw crowds of spectators, and it is not only high society that gathers here. Ordinary people and visitors from all over the world arrive to witness one of the main social and sporting events of the year. Their most important accessory: a hat.

THE TRIPLE CROWN

The Triple Crown originated in England in 1853, and is now established in the USA, Ireland, Canada, Japan, and Hong Kong. It developed around the Derby (a race for three-year-olds) in tandem with two Stakes races. Inaugurated in 1780, the Derby was named after an English aristocrat. The choice between Lord Derby and Sir Charles Bunbury, the first president of the British Jockey Club, was decided on the toss of a coin.

THE AMERICAN TRIPLE CROWN

In 1919, Johnny Loftus rode Sir Barton to victory in three successive races, thus giving rise to the American Triple Crown. The races are held in three states over five weeks. The youngest, founded in 1875 with an original track length of 1¼ miles, is the Kentucky Derby at Churchill Downs, KY. Conceived as the equivalent of England's Epsom Derby, it has long been attended with all the accoutrements of that great race—hats, champagne (or, rather, mint juleps), ceremony, and traditional song. In Pimlico, MD, the Preakness (named after a great race horse) has been raced over various lengths since 1873 (it is currently 1³⁄₁₆ miles, or 9.5 furlongs). Finally, the third jewel in the crown is the Belmont Stakes, founded in 1867 and named after the first president of the American Jockey Club, is run at Belmont Park, NY, on a track that is 1½ miles, or 12 furlongs, long—a severe test of endurance for horses that have already raced the two shorter courses in recent weeks. Over the years there have been only eleven Triple Crown Winners, the most recent being Steve Cauthen on Affirmed in 1978.

THE BREEDERS' CUP

The highlight of American flat-race meetings is the Breeders' Cup, where there is less focus on tradition than the incredibly high sums of prize money. The Breeders' Cup is held at a different venue every year and is America's most important event in flat racing.

LONGCHAMP

The racecourse at Paris is fabulously situated on the banks of the Seine in the Bois de Boulogne park. With a distance of 1¾ miles and a track that includes a hill in the home stretch, Longchamp is among the longest and most demanding racecourses in the world.

Nearly all classic race meetings take place at Longchamp, including the most important Group 1 race, the Prix de l'Arc de Triomphe. The winner of this race is voted best racehorse of the year and unofficially recognized as the European champion Thoroughbred.

The most modern Thoroughbred racecourse in the world is in the United Arab Emirates. Of all the races in the world, the Dubai World Cup has the highest sum in prize money.

The Prix de l'Arc de Triomphe in Paris-Longchamp is one of the most important and arduous races in Europe. Participating horses need to have exceptional stamina.

The Breeders' Cup is the highlight of the American racing season. The venue varies— there are tracks in Kentucky and in New York, for example.

THE MELBOURNE CUP

In addition to hosting the Australian tennis cup and the first Formula 1 race of the season, Melbourne also hosts Australia's most important flat-race meeting. The Melbourne Cup holds the entire country in its thrall. It takes place on the first Tuesday in November, which is a national holiday; thus everyone is off work and eager to place a bet. It is the bookmakers' busiest day of the year, with over two million Australian dollars in circulation. As for the fashion scene on Flemington Race Course, the ladies prefer to appear Ascot-style— which means that, more than anything else, what you see is hats.

THE DUBAI WORLD CUP

Once a year, the best Thoroughbred racehorses in the world are sent into the desert. Thanks to Sheikh Mohammed al Maktoum's generous financial support, the Dubai World Cup is a high-class race with the world's biggest prizes, amounting to $6 million.

Legends of the Turf

In the world of horse racing, many a story is told about famous horses. Some are touching, some tragic, and every now and then there is a funny anecdote to tell. Just as ordinary people make up the minority among the spectators of a horse race, Thoroughbred racers with an everyday personality are also hard to find. Generally, it is the headstrong mounts that grow to become famous and, by word of mouth, their stories turn into legends.

It was a complete sensation for the 40,000 spectators when Seabiscuit effortlessly galloped ahead of War Admiral in Maryland, defeating the official favorite by four lengths.

Man O'War (1917–1947)

No racehorse has ever achieved so much in so short a time as Man O'War. When he was born in Kentucky in 1917, his breeder, who was serving in the war at the time, was told that the young colt seemed to consist of nothing but legs, long and beautiful legs.

These legs went on to become the fastest of their time. In his very first race, Man O'War beat the second horse by six lengths. During his first season, he won nine out of ten races and even as a 3-year-old his competitors didn't stand a chance. There was no important race that he didn't win. In fact, there was hardly anyone who dared let his mount compete against him. He was an undisputed star, leaving the field behind at every race and rushing toward the next victory, with perhaps one or two horses in his wake.

Man O'War finished the season without once having been defeated and was retired from active racing after a career lasting only 16 months. He became a greatly coveted sire because of his prepotency merits, actually succeeding in passing on his amazing talent. His many fans from the racecourse, who could not forget him even many years later, often visited him in the stable.

When this most exceptional horse of the twentieth century died in 1947, a ceremonial burial took place and a life-sized statue of him was erected as a memorial. Over 2,000 people came to pay their last respects and the ceremony was broadcast live on the radio.

Humorist (1918–1921)

The legendary English jockey Steve Donoghue loved and adored his mount Humorist. He said, "I loved that little stallion as I would love a child. In every race, I rode him with all the tenderness I could. It was his love for me that made him fight so bravely and win the biggest race, in spite having only one intact lobe in his lung. He was the most courageous horse who ever lived."

Only three weeks after winning the Derby in 1921, Humorist died. No one had realized that the colt was suffering from an advanced tubercular lung condition.

Phar Lap (1926–1932)

Phar Lap was the first racehorse from Down Under to become internationally known. Bred in New Zealand and with an unremarkable pedigree, the big-framed chestnut set off on an amazing career. The color of his coat got Phar Lap nicknamed "the red terror" by his competitors, but his trainer and groom affectionately called him "Bobby."

The day before the Melbourne Cup (Australia's most important race meeting) horse, trainer, and groom suffered the shock of their lives: an assassination attempt intended to prevent the horse from starting. Fortunately, Phar Lap suffered no injuries–indeed, he won the race.

The story of his success traveled as far as America and his owner was invited to a high-stakes meeting in Mexico. So Phar Lap traveled by boat to San Francisco and then another 397 miles in a trailer until he finally reached Tijuana. Coming from Australian winter to Mexican summer, he could never have achieved top form. Worse still, he was also suffering from an injured hoof. Accordingly, he was last in the field after the start and yet, by the end, he had managed to pass all his competitors, beating them by two lengths and even setting a new record for the track.

The Australian Wonderhorse (as the newspapers called him) was due to run his next race in America, but before he arrived for it, Phar Lap died under suspicious circumstances, barely five years old.

Seabiscuit (1933–1947) and War Admiral (1934–1959)

Seabiscuit was a famous grandson of Man O'War, although his racing career began so unsuccessfully that car vendor Charles Howard, who planned to establish a racing stable, bought him for just $8,000.

Nobody doubted Seabiscuit's talent, but he was too lazy and lethargic for a racehorse. Fortunately, Howard found the right partners for his Thoroughbred in trainer Tom

On November 1, 1938, the "match of the century" took place at Pimlico, in Baltimore, MD. The two best racehorses at the time, Seabiscuit (right) and War Admiral, competed against each other. It was only neck-and-neck for a few meters.

Smith and jockey Red Pollard. Shortly after changing hands, Seabiscuit attained his first major successes, usually by fighting himself spectacularly through the entire field, from the very rear to the front.

Seabiscuit's biggest rival was War Admiral, the best sprinter ever sired by legendary stallion Man O'War. The two mounts competed only once, on November 1, 1938, in Maryland, but this date is known in the annals of horse racing as the "Match of the Century". To the bookmakers, War Admiral was the uncontested favorite, especially since Seabiscuit's regular jockey was injured. But immediately after the start it was evident that things were not taking their expected course. The two horses were the only entries, and contrary to his usual habit, Seabiscuit immediately sprang ahead, quickly leading by an entire length. War Admiral managed to catch up, but Seabiscuit proved to be an indefatigable fighter and accelerated yet more. He defeated his challenger by four lengths and broke the racetrack record. It was a sensation.

In the following year, War Admiral retired to stud and Seabiscuit's career very nearly drew to a close, too, when the six-year-old stallion suffered a severe tendon injury. No one believed he would ever race again. He returned to his owner's yard where his former jockey, Red Pollard, was himself recovering

from a severe fracture and took the opportunity to look after the horse himself. For an entire year, they trained movement, power, and stamina, until the racehorse was back in top form. The jockey, who was still unable to walk properly, convinced Howard, the yard owner, to let him mount Seabiscuit himself. After a few initial setbacks they were soon back to their successful performances and decided to try the important Santa-Anita meeting once more. After a highly dramatic race and several risky maneuvers they finally achieved their coveted victory. They had delivered a truly heroic feat—perfect material for a major Hollywood feature film.

Shergar (*1978)

Shergar was a Thoroughbred of the Aga Khan's stable, and in professional circles was considered one of the greatest racehorses of all time. During his career, the stallion won numerous important graded stakes, including the Epsom Derby, where he led by an amazing ten lengths.

In 1983, while already serving as a breeding sire, Shergar was abducted from the stud in Ireland. A demand for a £2 million ransom (about $5 million) was transmitted to a local broadcasting station, but as it was assumed that the IRA was somehow involved, the owner rejected the idea of paying the ran-

Shergar, one of the greatest racehorses of all times, was abducted from the stable of his owner, Aga Khan, and was never found.

som. Sadly, the fate of this valuable horse has never been discovered, even though officials were able to follow a trail as far as Japan and Saudi Arabia.

Dubai Millennium (1996–2001)

If his career had lasted just a little longer, Dubai Millennium might have become the most outstanding racehorse of the new century. When it came to conformation and character, his breeder and owner, Sheikh

Mohammed bin Rashid al Maktoum, crown prince of Dubai, had never seen a more perfect horse. Of ten races, Dubai Millennium won nine, including the most lucrative flat-race meeting in the world, the Dubai World Cup. But when he fractured his leg, his sporting career came to an abrupt end. He got back on his feet and was successfully employed as a sire, but very shortly afterward succumbed to the mysterious grass sickness.

Anti-Stars

A true anti-star on the German turf was King of Boxmeer (*1999). During his career, the gelding managed to gain five victories. However, he did not go down in history for his success but due to his stubborn character. There were flat-race meetings when he would simply remain in the starting box. Once he ran 100 feet, then suddenly halted and threw off his jockey, bucking wildly. King of Boxmeer had an enormous fan club on the internet, but his trainer was almost certainly not one of them. The female counterpart to King of Box-

meer was the Japanese mare Haruurara (*1996). She failed to win a single race out of 100, and if there was a "Least Successful Racehorse Ever" title she would certainly deserve it. Surprisingly, the races in which she is entered are very popular with Japanese spectators and often sold out. The Japanese love this mare because she always gives her best, in spite of the demoralizing results. Winning is not everything, after all. Meanwhile, Haruurara has become a major media star, gracing high profile advertisements, and is slated to perform in a feature film—about her own life.

In spite of his short career he will remain unforgotten: Dubai Millennium, with his jockey, Frankie Dettori.

The precursor of the "one-armed bandit" is this automatic betting machine dating from 1936, installed in England. Those seeking to bet inserted a coin, turned the winder, and received a betting slip.

I Bet...

Wagering is a highly lucrative, multi-billion dollar business, here and abroad. Around 25 percent of the turnover is needed to cover the costs of the organizers and to finance the prize money.

Betting is especially popular in Asia. Japanese racing alone has an annual turnover of $1,600 billion. The racecourses of Sha Tin or Happy Valley (both in Hong Kong, where races are held three times a week) give the impression that betting is a kind of national passion. On the home stretch, one can hardly see the horses through the blizzard of betting slips flying through the air.

Flat racing was introduced in the USA in the seventeenth century. The race meeting at Saratoga is the oldest continuous meeting in the United States. The regulations set up by the English Jockey Club are generally accepted by racing commissions throughout the world. The US Thoroughbred Racing Association (TRA) helps maintain the integrity of the sport, while the Horsemen's Benevolent and Protective Association helps fund breeders and yards.

Frenchman Pierre Oller introduced pari-mutuel odds in 1865. Pari-mutuel means something like "betting among ourselves." In other words, a bettor is not wagering against the organizers of a race meeting but against all the other bettors. Bets are pooled and the odds on each horse are determined by the amount invested by bettors, and the sum won depends on the odds. A win-wager of $2 with odds of 1:1 will garner $4 dollars. For win odds of 5:1, $12 are paid; win odds of 50:1 bring in $102 dollars, and so on.

> "Horse-sense is something a horse has that prevents him from betting on people."
>
> Father Matthew, Roman Catholic priest

Different Ways of Betting

Win: You win if you correctly identify the winner of the race (the horse that comes in first). On the betting slip, each horse is always identified by its number.

Place: You win if the horse you wagered on comes in either first or second.

Show: You win if your chosen horse finishes in first, second or third place. This is the easiest bet to win, so the payoff is accordingly not as high as with more difficult bets such as the exacta, for example.

Quinella: You win if you identify the first two horses to finish. Order does not matter.

Exacta: You win if you identify the first two horses to finish and in the correct order.

Superfecta: You win if you identify the first four horses to finish and set them in the correct order.

BETTING

Wagering in the United States is based on the pari-mutuel system. This was introduced in the USA in 1939 and ensures uniform betting on all major American racetracks. Totalizators (electronic betting machines) show the total wagering in the win, the amount bet on each horse, and the results on big boards called tote boards.

Generally, jockeys are not permitted to wager on races they enter, but horse owners can certainly wager on their own horse and jockey. For Thoroughbred races, there are three ways to bet on a horse: win, place, and show. In the US, the minimum wager for each bet is $1. There is no upper limit, and you can enter as many bets as you please. Stakes are graded according to the prize sum. Money won on a racecourse is tax-free unless the win exceeds odds of 300:1. The track managers pay taxes on the total money bet, the handle, and the racetrack collects roughly 20 percent of the handle to pay for upkeep, prize money, and other costs. Bets can now be made on

The Japanese are unquestionably the most enthusiastic bettors in the world. After every race, the ground is covered in betting slips.

touch-screen terminals called SAMs (Screen Activated Machines) instead of by filling out an old-fashioned slip.

THE TOTALIZATOR AND ODDS

The totalizator calculates all the bets entered (this includes bets made on the racecourse and in the bookmakers' offices, where bets may be placed in advance). The odds are posted on monitors and on the tote board. They are updated every 30 seconds and show how much money, relative to the total win pool, is bet on each horse in the race. A totalizator may only be run by the organizer of a race meeting registered with the racing association.

Monitors show every race as it takes place so that bettors can watch the progress of their horse(s).

The Quintessential Racehorse

Race Profile: English Thoroughbred

Height: 59–67 inches

Colors: predominantly bay or sorrel, rarely gray or black

Description: elegant and fast, the best bred racehorses

Origin: England

A fast-paced age needs fast-paced horses. For over thirty generations, the English Thoroughbred has been developed exclusively for performing at flat-race meetings. All horses are registered in the internationally recognized Thoroughbred Stud Book published by Weatherbys. Over the years, requirements for the performance of the horses have changed: the first flat races of the seventeenth century were held over 30 furlongs (3¾ miles) to 6 miles, and jockeys weighed between 110 and 168 lb. But those days are long over. Today's flat races run a distance of 5 furlongs (just over half a mile) to 2 miles. Classic races, such as St. Leger, with a distance of 14 furlongs (1¾ miles) have lost some of their former attraction. Today a horse's staying power is less important than its ability to accelerate dramatically within a fairly short distance.

Above: Secretariat was an exceptional racehorse in the 1970s. He won almost every meeting with a track record and even achieved the Triple Crown–a series of races including the Kentucky Derby, Preakness Stakes, and Belmont Stakes.

Below: For sheer power and elegance, no horse can match an English Thoroughbred at full gallop. These horses love speed and movement by nature, and it shows.

Every living English Thoroughbred descends through the male line from one of three foundation sires: the bay stallions Byerley Turk, Darley Arabian, and Godolphin Arabian. These were brought to Britain by English officers and aristocrats and were then crossed with native breeds.

Byerley Turk was the first to be employed in breeding, in 1689. Legend has it that British Captain Byerley bought this Akhal-Teke stallion from a Dutchman for 100 gold guineas. The Dutchman, in turn, had acquired the horse during the Turkish siege of Vienna. Captain Byerley used the horse as a war mount in the 1690 war in Ireland and later entered him for race meetings under the name Byerley Turk.

Darley Arabian also owes his name to the gentleman who purchased him. The British Consul to Syria, Thomas Darley, found the Arab colt in Aleppo and had him taken to Britain in 1704. Legend has it that he gave the most influential foundation sire of the English Thoroughbred breed to his brother Richard in exchange for a new gun. Darley Arabian was kept at the family stud, where he covered mares for nearly thirteen years. About 90 percent of all English Thoroughbreds trace their lineage back to him.

Godolphin Arabian, the third influential sire, went through an astonishing odyssey. He was sent to the court of French King Louis XV as a gift from the Sultan of Morocco, but the French king appreciated the more voluptuous lines of baroque horses rather than this small Barb stallion with tiny ears, slightly plump neck, and impetuous temperament and passed him on to be used as a cart horse. He was eventually discovered, abused and in poor shape, on the streets of Paris by the Englishman Edward Cokes who purchased him and took him to Britain, where he finally arrived in the stud stable of Lord Godolphin. Lord Godolphin originally intended the stallion to serve as a secondary sire, but when his fickle broodmare Roxana refused the main sire, Hobgoblin, the under-appreciated stallion was finally given his chance. The progeny proved so excellent that he was ultimately promoted to main sire of the stud.

Although his pedigree is mysterious, Eclipse was fundamental for the English Thoroughbred studbook. This engraving from 1820 shows the exceptional stallion on the right with Shakespear, possibly his sire.

Only horses that have proved themselves in the races (a sort of efficiency test) are entered into the breeding program. Three hundred years ago, horses had much longer to develop peak performance. Where today's colts and fillies enter their maiden race as two-year-olds, they would once have been six years old or more.

ECLIPSE

Eclipse is said to be one of the most influential stallions in the Thoroughbred studbook. He was a great-great-grandson of Darley Arabian and was born on April 1, 1764, during an eclipse, which is how he got his name.

His sire is not known precisely because the broodmare, Spiletta, was accidentally mated with not one stud, but two, Shakespear and Marske. In the General Stud Book Marske was registered as Eclipse's official sire.

After the death of his breeder, the Duke of Cumberland, Eclipse was sold at auction and was very nearly gelded. His new owner, William Wildman, had considerable problems with the hot-tempered new arrival and apparently seriously considered having him castrated. The consequences for the English Thoroughbred as a breed if he had gone ahead with this are unthinkable!

Eclipse first saw a race track at the age of five. Never having run a single flat race, he instantly proved his potential to racing connoisseurs. The outspoken favorite won his first race on May 3, 1769. Eclipse was second to none, or, as Colonel O'Kelly who had watched the race put it, "Eclipse first—the rest nowhere!" O'Kelly bought the wonder horse for the price of 1,750 gold guineas—1,675 guineas more than Wildman had originally paid.

It paid dividends, though: during the eighteen months of his racing career, Eclipse competed at eighteen important race meetings and delivered outstanding victories every time. Eclipse became a living legend and was extremely valuable and sought after as a sire. O'Kelly earned the record-breaking sum of 30,000 pounds in stud fees alone. Of Eclipse' offspring, 344 were winners of a total of 860 flat races. Although Eclipse died on February 27, 1789, his name lives on. Even now, most English racehorses are descendants of his.

When a racehorse gets going, it reaches an average speed of 25 mph, and on the home stretch can even sprint almost 40 mph.

Fairness above all: this is the trotting racers' code of honor. Dangerous maneuvers with the sulky are strictly forbidden and will lead to disqualification if they hinder other competitors.

Move those Hooves!

Harness racing became popular rather later than flat racing, although there were early efforts to establish the sport. Archaeologists have found evidence suggesting that some form of harness racing was known in Asia Minor in as early as ca. 1300 BCE, but it was anything but an internationally popular sport back then. The Romans did not list harness racing in their program of public entertainment, but in the fifth century BCE they did coin the term *tormentor* (trotter). This referred to a British horse breed that would later become influential in the breeding program of today's trotter.

Harness racing only picked up in the eighteenth century. The first harness race was held in Europe (in Scandinavia, to be precise), where coldbloods were harnessed to sleighs. However, these first representatives of the sport bore no comparison to the elegance and speed of Thoroughbred racehorses. Lighter horses were needed—horses that would have a flat and ground-covering motion in trot,

Mini Trotters

The idea of miniature trotters originated in Sweden, where children and teenagers have been driving sulkies for many years. In Australia, junior harness racing began in 1975. Today there are many courses and stables, in America and abroad, that offer junior races. Children's harness races are as strictly regulated as those of the adults. Ponies with a height of up to 38½ inches run 3 furlongs, while those standing 39–42 inches run a distance of 3½ furlongs.

Miniature trotters are harnessed according to the same system as their full-size cousins and the sulky is built as a correspondingly small version of the standard sulky.

that were fast, had staying power, and a fighting spirit. Clever breeders began experimentally combining a range of promising lineages and upgrading them with English and Arab Thoroughbreds. Trotters have a special motor activity, their strength lying in second gear, so to speak, i.e., the trot. On hard ground, they can reach astounding speeds of 31 mph and more.

England discovered the charm of trotters in 1750 and developed its own breed, the Norfolk Trotter. Many countries then sought to breed their own harness racehorse. The most successful breeding programs were in Russia, France, and the USA. The American Standardbred was highly influential on all modern lineages. In France you can still see trotting races to saddle and other countries are testing this curious version of the sport, too. In America, harness races are held

Horses competing at the White Turf harness race at St. Moritz, Switzerland, must be sure-footed and fast. For this race on snowy ground, sulkies are mounted on runners.

in two gaits, the trot and the pace (a faster variant in which horses are less likely to break the gait). Usually, a trotter is harnessed to a two-wheeled cart called a sulky. The tack is extremely fine and designed to support the horse as much as possible, as is the individually fitted horseshoe. Blinders ensure that nothing distracts the horse's attention. Some horses are so susceptible to noise that their ears are padded with foam before the start. The foam is affixed to a string and the driver can pull it out during the race. Following the demands of animal rights activists, this foam material may not be removed any later than 330 yards before the finish line, because the sudden noise level can have the effect of an acoustic whip.

Special tack and equipment can help ward off many irritations. This hood protects the horse's ears and eyes from insects.

Wearing Blinders

Since horses are nervous animals that startle easily and then take flight, blinders were introduced at the onset of the industrial age, when ever more motorcars were filling the streets of the larger cities. The drivers of the Viennese Fiaker coaches in Austria, and the German businessman Bolle from Berlin, both realized (independently) that some protective device was needed. Bolle, who began his career in the late nineteenth century with three horse-drawn milk wagons and quickly extended his holdings to 297 wagons, depended heavily on calm horses that would not shy and spill the milk. He therefore had blinders made for the horses (which, incidentally, cost more than the drivers' caps).

Wearing blinders originally restricted the horses' line of site. Wearing blinders is now a common expression in social and political contexts. Someone who fails to acknowledge dangers or negative aspects, or who shrinks from making courageous and controversial decisions, is reproached as wearing blinders. Similarly, taking the blinders off can indicate clear sight, courage, and planning ahead.

But Do Not Gallop!

Getting in line behind the starting gate is a tricky moment. The drivers must find their position quickly and their horses must hit their stride. The specific position on the track is decided by draws.

The trot is, of course, only the second-fastest horse gait. So why does a trotter not try to win its races by breaking into a gallop? That is a good question. Presumably, it's not that the horse is unaware that it could go much faster at a gallop. We can safely assume that it knows nothing of the "You gallop, and you lose" rule. There is the driver, of course, back in the sulky pleading, "Please don't gallop!" Whatever their secret, breeders have successfully developed a horse breed that feels most comfortable in the trot gait and thus picks up the most speed in this gait.

Apart from talent (something a horse must be born with), it also takes endless training, professional care, and some mechanical tricks regarding the tack to bring a winning trotter to the track. Headstrong colts and fillies, and greenhorns, do try out a few galloping steps every now and then. This is neither fun nor successful, though, since a trotter that passes his competitors at a gallop will be disqualified by the race organizers, who monitor the race from a car driven alongside the course. Three or four galloping steps are tolerated if the horse does not cover more ground than usual by doing so and if it does not gallop through the finish line. Otherwise, galloping causes ill will all around. Untalented progeny from a trotting breed will probably also fail at other sports, as trotters are usually poor at dressage and at flat racing. That said, however, some trotters have been trained as satisfactory show jumping horses.

Above: The world's most successful sulky driver is Heinz Wewering from Castrop-Rauxel, Germany. He holds the world record for professional harness racing and is instantly recognizable with his characteristic golden helmet.

Below: Many people have a passion for harness racing. German horsewoman Rita Drees has held the amateur world record (which she has since bettered every season) since 2005.

THE ORLOV TROTTER

The Orlov Trotter is one of the most unusual horse breeds. With their swinging gaits and incredible knee action, they were once the pick of the bunch. Their powerful hindquarters guaranteed the required thrust and their legs were strong and robust.

These fabulous animals were created by Count Aleksey Grigoryevich Orlov, a Russian admiral and indefatigable horse breeder. Orlov, who served as commander-in-chief of the Russian fleet that defeated the Turks in 1770, apparently had sufficient leisure time to devote to horse breeding. From one of his many journeys, he brought back with him the gray Arab stallion Smetanka and paired him with a Danish Fredriksborg mare. The result was a colt called Polkan, which was just the beginning of Orlov's program.

He was determined to create the perfect harness horse: powerful, robust, and with great endurance—especially in the trot, as this gait costs horses the least energy to maintain. Furthermore, the horse should have an elegant appearance, since it was destined to draw members of the nobility, such as himself, across the Russian countryside.

He then paired Polkan with a Dutch Harddraver mare and presented the resulting colt, Bars, to the ravished specialists. The progenitor of the Orlov Trotter breed, Bars (Snow Lion) personified the best qualities of all the breeds that were used to create him: the beauty and movement of a Thoroughbred, the robust conformation of the Frederiksborg, and the enormously ground-covering trot of the Harddraver.

Orlov Trotters dominated harness racing for decades until they were surpassed and ultimately pushed aside by a new American breed, the Standardbred. Even today, however, the Orlov Trotter remains a well-known and respected breed that is increasingly employed in driving.

Win 'til You Drop

Both of the world records in sulky racing are held by Germans. In June 2003, professional harness racer Heinz Wewering won his 14,899th victory, which made him the new record holder. To achieve this astounding tally, the horseman who can always be recognized by his distinctive gold helmet had to participate in no fewer than 43,000 starts.

In January 2005, Rita Drees claimed the world record for amateurs with her 2,071st victory. Since both Rita Drees and Heinz Wewering usually run several races a week, every new victory raises their record higher still.

The harness racehorse owner Marion Jauß decided to send her trotter, Bodyguard of Spain, into retirement the instant he had achieved a world record. When he won his 37th consecutive race, she sent him home so that he could retire from the racing world an undefeated champion.

High Level Gymnastics

Dressage is known as the *haute école* (high school) of riding. To amateurs, dressage can seem like a closed book although the basic rule is actually quite simple: "Controlled, comfortable motion on horseback," as Eric Lette, former chairman of the FEI (*Fédération équestre internationale*) dressage committee and judge of the Olympic Games in Sydney once said.

To the horse, dressage is something like high level gymnastics. Dressage demands the mount's obedience and cooperation, as without the horse's ready participation none of the exercises could be performed. The basic features of dressage are mastered by every rider: without them it would be impossible to communicate with the horse from the saddle, whether for show jumping, racing or simply leisure riding.

The early stages of European dressage were discussed with the Lusitanos and Lippizaners (pages 52–55). In later centuries, the most important rules were published by Frenchman Robichon de la Guérinière in 1733, and they still apply in modern dressage. According to Guérinière, the key lies in the correct, balanced seat. The well-balanced rider gives his or her four-legged partner all the necessary commands simply through slight changes in balance and gentle leg movements. Conversely, an unbalanced rider will even hinder the horse from finding its own balance.

The accusation that dressage does not correspond to a horse's nature can be refuted simply by watching horses move in the paddock. Even the very young already show the movements that are later developed as exercises.

The exercises performed in dressage are based on the natural movements of the horse. This also applies to side steps and passage. The fast trot, which every colt and stallion performs naturally, was developed into the parade gait.

In the eighteenth century, the art of riding was taught at special university colleges and the equerries (trainers) held the title of professor. In the nineteenth century, cavalry schools emerged as the most decisive institutions. The French founded their famous elite school at Saumur, which is still highly renowned, and the Germans established the Army Institute in Hanover.

In light of this tradition, it is hardly surprising that the first competitors wore military uniforms when dressage was first accepted as an Olympic discipline in Stockholm in 1912. Long famous

Isabell Werth, the most successful dressage horsewoman in the world, and her Hanoverian Anthony showing an expressive trot. The rider is only exerting a minimal influence, as she conducts the lesson with only one hand.

for their backward seat, the English adopted the Spanish upright seat during the twentieth century. It was a blend of Spanish, English, and Italian (forward seat) ideas that impacted American military dressage, and has continued in sporting circles after the disbanding of the US cavalry in 1948.

The Promise of a Gigolo

A gigolo need not be handsome, but he must please, and the sorrel Hanovarian Gigolo certainly did please, many times over. Isabell Werth first mounted Gigolo when he was six years old, and immediately felt at home. His owner, Dr. Uwe Schulten-Baumer, decided to train the horse and thus began an astonishing career.

Gigolo retired from the world of professional sports in November 2000 at the age of 17, having earned millions. No other dressage horse in the world has ever won so much prize money or captured as many titles. He won sixteen gold medals in interna-tional competitions, including four Olympic medals. He never let Werth down and the pair set new standards in dressage.

Gigolo did put on some airs and graces, but only outside the arena. He expected special treatment from everyone: it upset him deeply, for example, if he was not the center of attention. He also insisted on the privilege of opening his stable door by himself, whenever he pleased. In return, he always gave his best in competition. Just seconds before entering the arena, he could be in such a tantrum that his supporters' hearts would sink. Yet the instant he began the first exercise, he would be fully focused and seem to simply hover over the arena. Gigolo and Werth were the first pair in dressage to succeed in the most advanced school on the ground: switching from fast gallop into the pirouette, an extraordinary movement. The music chosen for his freestyle exercise was *Just a Gigolo* and he moved with such expressiveness that he won individual gold at the Olympic Games in Atlanta and at the World Championships in Rome. Before each event, his owner-trainer Dr. Uwe Schulten-Baumer would personally groom Gigolo's mane, and then wait at the arena gate to welcome him back with a special treat.

When Gigolo celebrated his retirement in Stuttgart, Germany, over 7,000 people came to give him standing ovations, and many tears were shed as he took his last laps of honor. Gigolo certainly seemed to enjoy all the attention.

The tension and collection required when performing in the dressage arena is followed by relaxation, which the horse achieves by stretching.

Natural Rhythm

Children riding ponies and great riders in the arena all start with the same lesson: their horse must be responsive and move rhythmically.

Each gait has its own beat. The walk is the slowest basic gait and requires little energy of the horse. The walk is a four-beat gait, meaning the hooves touch the ground one after the other. The trot is a two-beat gait: the legs move forward in a diagonally opposite footfall, followed by a suspension phase when all four legs are off the ground. Trotting lets horses move fairly quickly for a long distance without tiring too much. The fastest (and most exhausting) gait is the gallop, which ancestors of our riding horses used in flight. A slow gallop is called a canter. This is a three-beat gait: the outside hind leg touches the ground, followed simultaneously by the inside back and outside front, and finally the inside front—after which there is a suspension phase.

In dressage, exercises are performed in each of the gaits. The goal is to show the natural movement of the horse in harmonious perfection. Horses are poetic movers, but differ in their natural talent. A rider must only ask of a horse what it is able to achieve. By giving the best possible aid and training these gymnastic exercises, a horse will develop a refined motion and stay fit and healthy. In order to keep it from getting bored and to enhance its beautiful conformation, a mount needs some demanding exercise, but it should never be overtaxed.

A pirouette should always be performed with brio. Here, legendary stallion Donnerhall pirouettes in canter, turning on his own axis, with his full weight on the hindquarters.

Freestyle in Dressage

Traditionally, the last day of a major dressage competition is horse dancing. For two days, the audience has attentively watched the competitions of Grand Prix and Grand Prix Special, with background music that sounds rather like the soundscape at the shopping mall–although most people probably would not notice if there was an announcement of special offers at the deli counter.

But the final day compensates for all this. On this day, dressage is more than a feast for the eye; it is a delight to the ears as well. Riders have spent months training in the arena, but they have spent equal amounts of time in the sound studio, seeking out the right music to match their freestyle exercises. The choreography is put together first. The exercises are required, but the dressage competitors decide on the order, level of difficulty, and use of space.

After the choreographed tour is videotaped, rider and music specialist get together to identify a score that will perfectly match the freestyle, accentuating the highlights and perhaps playing down the weaker parts.

The choice of classical or popular music is entirely a matter of personal taste. Since the riders will listen to this music repeatedly while training and during the competition, they ought to like it. The arrangement as a whole must also fit the character of the horse, of course–possibly even alluding to its name. For Isabell Werth, there was one song that went without question when she performed with her star athlete Gigolo. *Just a Gigolo* was always incorporated in the music for their freestyle tours. When Nadine Capellmann won her greatest victory with her Westphalian Farbenfroh, the 2002 World Championships, the music was a medley of German pop music. The queen of freestyle tours, Anky van Grunsven of the Netherlands, had several songs by Edith Piaf arranged for her performance with Olympic champion Salinero. In the background chorus, the horsewoman herself could be heard singing along.

World-class professional riders do not use ready-made music spliced together from various CDs, but have music arranged and sometimes even specially recorded by an orchestra. This musical extravaganza can cost as much as $13,000. An amateur or leisure equestrian can find far less costly alternatives among the recordings of the major philharmonic orchestras.

Anky van Grunsven holds the record for the best ever freestyle scores. She won her first World Record at the Olympic Games in Sydney, with Bonfire. The pair was awarded a score of 86.05% by the judges (which meant the gold medal), and Isabell Werth placed second. Bonfire's successor was Salinero, who won the Olympic Championship in Athens. With him, van Grunsven even raised her personal best during the World Cup Finals 2005 in Las Vegas, with a score of 87.725%.

Perhaps the most memorable freestyle tour of all time was performed by Ulla Salzgeber during the Olympic Games in Sydney. Three minutes into her performance, there was suddenly absolute silence. Since she and her gelding Rusty knew the music by heart, they simply kept up their rhythm and went on with the performance until they were called off. There was no obvious reason for the technical problems: during the previous day's sound check the CD had run perfectly. The judges conferred about what to do, and finally chief judge Eric Lette decided that Ulla Salzgeber should be given a second chance at the end of the run-through, but should only perform the part that the judges had not yet seen. Ulla Salzgeber is known to have strong nerves. She made the best of her unplanned break and ultimately won the bronze medal.

The Piaffe is a diagonal movement of the legs, like a trot on the spot. Above, Anky van Grunsven with Salinero, the pair who won the Olympic Dressage at Athens.

Absolute perfection is displayed in the Passage, with the horse showing utmost collection in the frontal and upward movement.

The Flying Change is an exercise performed in the Grand Prix, the most demanding of competitions. The horse makes a transition in canter from left lead to right lead.

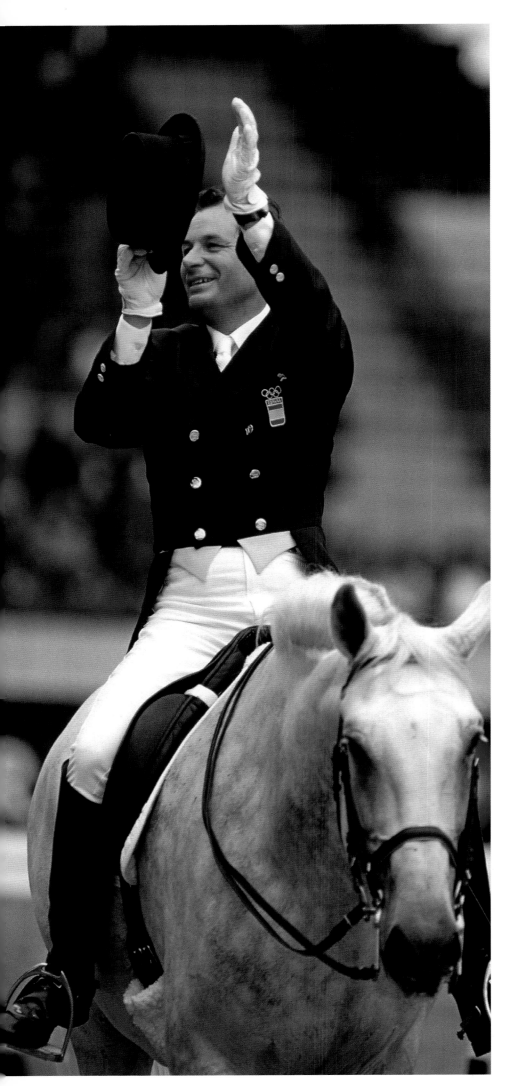

In Top Hat and Tails

A bright yellow polo shirt, brown jodhpurs and riding boots, topped with a baseball cap—a dressage specialist will only be seen in such leisure wear when training or off duty.

In formal competition, participants may only enter the show ring if they abide by the dress code. Today, a tennis player is only required to wear white when playing at Wimbledon, but the Dressage Association still insists that everyone entering competition must wear the traditional black-and-white attire. Competitions at the Prix St. George level and above expect a rider to wear a black tailcoat teamed with white jodhpurs, black top hat, and black boots. In the classes beneath this level, a dark jacket and top hat are required. A bowler hat may also be worn as alternative headgear.

These regulations have often been an issue but the only result of all the wrangling is that a dark blue tailcoat is now also permissible. Evidently, classic English riding and classic clothing regulations do belong together, and perhaps this is not such a bad idea, after all. Just think of the colorful outfits tennis players wear nowadays outside of Wimbledon...

THE HATTER

Every item of headgear was originally designed as a protection, not decoration. Even the ancient Greeks had professional hat makers because no one wanted to wear those heavy helmets all day long. In the Middle Ages, the hat and every kind of headgear was used to define one's social and professional status, such as membership in a guild. From then on, hat makers and milliners became increasingly inventive, creating various designs and using numerous kinds of feathers to decorate the hats according to purpose. Hats became official emblems. Dukes and princes had their specific headgear just as academics have their mortarboard. The pope would even consecrate the hats of religious warriors, tall objects embellished with golden tassels and silk lining.

The top hat was invented in the USA in 1797, and by the 1820s it had become extremely popular. At first exclusively manufactured in America, the top hat soon arrived in England and France, as well. Legend has it that the first gentleman to wear a top hat in public in Britain had to pay a fine for causing public offense.

Nonetheless, the new headgear was increasingly successful. In Germany, for example, members of the upper middle class were very pleased with the top hat. In the nineteenth century, anyone wanting to make a good impression in society wore a topper. It was less well received by the students and laborers, however, who derisively called it an *Angströhre* (pipe of fear).

In every country, the top hat was worn on special occasions and accepted as the essence of good taste. At weddings and christenings, receptions and funerals, wearing a top hat was an unwritten law. In many cases, it was requested explicitly.

For dressage, men and women alike wear a relatively low-crowned top hat—just another sign that dressage is in a class of its own.

A meaningful outfit: those who master dressage at the St. George level have the privilege–and requirement–of wearing the traditional tailcoat in competition.

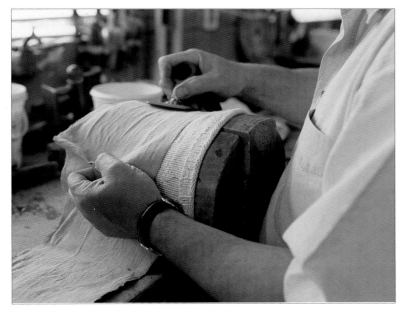

The de Winters from the Netherlands are the last hatters to manufacture top hats according to the traditional technique. Their clients are dressage riders from all over the world. First, impregnated flannel is ironed onto a wooden form.

Since a top hat must withstand all kinds of weather, it must be assembled with great attention to detail. Every part of the hat is treated with pure shellac, a resinous solution made of rubber. Above, the brim.

Once the brim is mounted to the substructure, another wooden form is pounded into the substructure. This ensures the stability necessary for further steps.

Next, the substructure of the top hat is prepared. The hatter irons on pure natural silk fabric.

Then the silk fabric is ironed onto the brim. The hatter must take special care when molding the brim onto the form.

Finally, the master hatter inspects the new top hat. All it needs now is to dry for four weeks. This hat is custom made and is a perfect fit for its new owner, who has a lifetime guarantee and repair service free of charge.

Steep, High, and Wide

All sorts of sports were developed in Great Britain, including soccer, flat racing, and show jumping. The first organized competition for jumping fences and other obstacles was held in Dublin, Ireland, in 1864. In comparison to dressage, show jumping is a relatively young equestrian discipline. At this first competition in Dublin, the winner, who jumped a brick wall—the qualification height was 4 ft 6 inches—received a cup and a whip worth 15 pounds Sterling. Today, the world's best show jumpers compete for prizes of approximately $300,000 (or even a sports car). The spark flew from England to other countries and show jumping became the most popular of all international equestrian disciplines. The prize sums speak for themselves, as do the vast numbers of spectators at show jumping events.

Initially, jumping horses were merely required to take a few obstacles that were either high or deep (oxers, or spreads). The aim was to test a mount's ability for hunting or as a cavalry mount.

The riders were, at first, more hindrance than help for their horses. For a long time, a seat was favored that was completely incompatible with the motor activity of the jumping horse. With backs straight, the horsemen leaned backward, stretching their legs out forward. This obstructed the horse both during take-off and landing. Italian cavalry captain Federico Caprilli was the first to try to relieve the horse's back of a rider's weight. During the jump, he smoothly rose up from the saddle and adjusted his center of gravity toward the front. He also loosened the reins to allow the horse enough freedom of movement to realign its balance. It was Caprilli who set the first world record in high jumps in 1902, taking a fence 6 ft 7 inches high. Soon other riders who adopted his style were also winning competitions, while those who favored the traditional backward dressage seat found they had lost the edge in show jumping.

The oxer poses a double challenge, because this obstacle is both high and wide. The distance between the front and the rear poles can be as long as 6 ft 6 inches.

Olympic Champion by Armchair Decision

When chronicles are written too quickly, they may be out of date by the time they are published. The Olympic Equestrian Events in 2004, in Athens, offer an unfortunate example of this. One year later, the definitive winners of the show jumping class were re-established. After Waterford Crystal tested positive for illegal medications, his rider, Ireland's gold medalist Cian O'Connor, eventually accepted the disqualification that the *Fédération équestre internationale* (FEI) had handed down. This meant Brazilian rider Rodrigo Pessoa now took gold, Chris Kappler took silver for the USA, and Germany's Mario Kutscher was awarded bronze.

The final placing of the teams was also much delayed and only settled before the CAS (Court of Arbitration for Sports). After be-ing awarded gold during the Olympic Games in Athens, the German team slid to bronze when Ludger Beerbaum's stallion Goldfever showed traces of illegal medication. Beerbaum was disqualified, costing Germany the gold–to the benefit of the USA.

An armchair decision also took the individual gold medal from Germany's Bettina Hoy, as well as gold medals from the German team event riders. During the final jumping class, Bettina Hoy accidentally crossed the starting line too early. Initially this fault was not penalized, but following a series of international protests the CAS decided to invoke the penalty. As a result, Germany slid to third place and the gold medals all had to be returned to the International Olympic Committee. The gold medals were then awarded to the American team, and the silver to Sweden.

Rodrigo Pessoa took silver at the Olympic Games in Athens but was subsequently adjudicated the gold medal, after the gold medalist was disqualified.

Mighty Jumpers

Olympic medals were awarded for horses jumping heights and spreads during the Paris Olympic Games in 1900, for the first and only time. The gold medal was awarded for a cleared height of 6 feet and an oxer (or spread) of 20 feet.

During the next fifty years, numerous riders pushed that height and spread to the very limit. In 1906, the Frenchman Capitaine Crousse and his horse Conspirateur cleared 7 ft 8 inches in Paris. In 1938, in Rome, Opposo and his Italian captain Antonio Gutierrez flew over an obsta-cle 8 feet high. Nine years later, Capitano Alberto Larraguibel Morales from Chile set a new record by clearing a height of 8 ft 1 inch in Viña del Mar, with his 15-year-old Thoroughbred Huaso. This record remains uncontested and will probably remain so, because high-jump obstacles constructed like ramps are no longer used for show jumping.

Today's challenge is the wall. It is built vertically and is therefore much more demanding. The exact jump-off has to be appraised in detail. The world record holder, with a height of 7 ft 7 inches, is Willibert Mehlkopf. He cleared this spectacularly high jump with his horse Wabbs during the 1985 CHIO, the biggest international show jumping tournament, held in Aachen, Germany.

High-jump competitions are very popular spectator sports. These competitions have become rare treats, but when they do take place, they are both exciting and entertaining. Large-frame horses that have difficulties with the tight turns required in normal show jumping get their opportunity to shine in these events.

The Right Take-Off

Like dressage, show jumping was first part of the 1912 Olympic Games in Stockholm, Sweden. The first Olympic course had twenty-nine fences with a height of up to 4 ft 6 inches and a maximum spread of 13 feet. To negotiate all the obstacles in the allotted time, horses had to move at least 330 yards/minute.

The speed required for championships has not increased since, but the height of the obstacles has: by as much as 1⅓ ft. Originally, horses had to negotiate immovable obstacles that loomed before them like houses. The poles were fixed, making the risk of injury and accidents quite high. Today poles are attached loosely and come off easily to ensure that a horse that hits a pole will not become tangled in the fence. In the Athens 2004 individual finals course, there were thirteen fences to be negotiated in the second circuit and they were perilously lightly attached. There was such a heavy wind blowing that Sweden's Rolf-Goeran Bengtsson on Mac Kinley could only negotiate obstacle Nr. 11 on the third attempt, because the top pole flew off twice before their eyes.

Over the years, the style of the obstacles has remained the same. Now as before, verticals (fences with poles above each other) require

An acrobatic high jump: to jump this 5 ft 2 inch vertical, Coester catapults himself almost vertically into the air. Rider Christian Ahlmann is adjusting optimally to his horse's movements.

Below: no horse wants to land in the open water. To keep the hooves dry, this pair has to clear a length of at least 13 feet.

The show jumping course at Athens 2004 included 13 demanding obstacles. They were designed specifically for the Olympic Games and feature typically Greek motifs.

Below: Ludger Beerbaum and Champion de Lys successfully mastered the challenge. Not many competitors manage to negotiate the German Hamburg Derby's 10-ft rampart. This pair has already won this deeply traditional examination twice.

a very high jump; spreads, or oxers, require a jump that is both high and wide; and an open water, or ditch, requires a wide jump. Modern show jumping courses test horses' responsiveness as well as their jumping ability. Every so often, designers set the obstacles such that the horse's normal stride won't fit the distance. In these cases, for example when the distance is six and a half strides, the rider must help the horse adjust its stride by shortening or lengthening—only then will they find the perfect take-off point. Another novelty today is the virtual absence of straight approaches to the obstacles; tight turns and changes of direction lead from one jump to the next.

Thorough dressage training is indispensable to a successful show jumper. Communication between rider and mount should be subtle and precise. The horseman must always think a few steps ahead. Since he knows the entire circuit, he can plan the next jump while tackling the one before. Mastering a course takes more than a fast horse with excellent jumping qualities: the horse must also be sure-footed, agile, and attentive.

Before taking this oxer, Ludger Beerbaum made Goldfever accelerate to produce sufficient drive to jump cleanly over this two-fence spread.

The High Flyers

There is a saying that goes *"A horse without a rider is still a horse, but a rider without a horse is no longer a rider."* None of today's or yesterday's show jumping heroes would have made much mark without their compatible quadruped partners. At least half the success is due to the horse, and it can take a long time to find a truly ideal combination—some riders never find their perfect jumping partner. There are a few high flyers, for whom everything clicks perfectly.

Barely stoppable: the Holstein Classic Touch is a jumping miracle, here ridden by Ludger Beerbaum.

Hans Günter Winkler and Halla

Even today, fan mail still arrives for Halla, the famous mare that won Hans Günter Winkler two Olympic gold medals and two World Championships. It is largely due to this pair that show jumping became popular again in Germany after World War II.

Halla was the daughter of a trotter, and no one would have called her a beauty. Her rider sometimes called her "the goat," though he was referring to her stubborn character rather than her appearance. But she was a great fighter and very intelligent when it came to tackling demanding challenges. She started performing on the circuit at a rather mature age, having

begun her career as a racehorse. She had so little success that it was decided to try her as a jumper. After several detours she arrived in Winkler's stable, where the pair initially had trouble. "After a year and a half of intense training, Halla finally understood that jumping was not only about wide obstacles, but high ones, too."

During the 1956 Olympic equestrian events in Stockholm, Halla's performance was so extraordinary that she took every horse lover's heart by storm. Hans Günter Winkler had injured his groin during the first circuit and had to take heavy painkillers before the decisive second circuit to be able to ride at all. An individual and a team gold were both at stake. Winkler led his mare with the tremendous jumping ability to the obstacles as precisely as he always did and Halla took over from there, securing the victory more or less by herself.

Of course we will never know if the mare realized how important this round was, but that does not diminish her exceptional performance and popularity. This show immortalized her to such an extent that the German equestrian federation banned the name Halla from ever being used for another horse.

Rodrigo Pessoa and Baloubet du Rouet

The chestnut stallion was first ridden competitively by Nelson Pessoa, but it was with Nelson's son Rodrigo that Baloubet's career took flight. Medallists in every Olympics since 1996, the pair also achieved the unprecedented feat of winning

the World Cup final three times: in 1998, 1999, and 2000. Pessoa was ranked #1 in the world by the FEI/BCM in 2000, while Baloubet was elected best horse in the world in 2004. Both continue to compete.

Alwin Schockemöhle and Warwick Rex

This pair's joint career was comparatively short, but it was intense and they were extremely successful. The truly great bay horse, with a height of 73 inches, arrived in Alwin Schockemöhle's stable in 1974. The two got along wonderfully from the start and by the following year were already European champions. No obstacle was too high for Warwick Rex, who also had a very calm character.

These qualities helped horse and rider become Olympic champions in 1976. Alwin Schockemöhle and Warwick Rex were the only pair out of forty-nine entries to negotiate the entire circuit cleanly in both rounds. This was especially impressive because the course was exceedingly demanding. Among other obstacles, there was a ditch 16 ft 5 inches long and five oxers spread to 6 ft 7 inches. On top of this, the weather became a challenge. When the pair entered the Bromont stadium as the last competitors, a thunderstorm broke out. But thunder and lightning were a mere sideshow during the determined and genial round they performed.

Only a year later Alwin Schockemöhle and his quadruped star bid the sporting arena farewell—Schockemöhle's backaches had become unbearable and he retired.

Conrad Homfeld and Abdullah

Conrad Homfeld is a canny American rider who made his career with a Trakehner stallion. Homfeld's major successes cannot be separated from the large-framed, spotless gray Trakehner stallion Abdullah.

The gray beauty was already 14 years old when he came to Homfeld and in the early stages, the horseman had to cope with a range of disasters. When in 1984 the pair

German post-war heroes: Hans Günter Winkler with his renowned wonder mare Halla.

surprised everyone by winning second in individual competition and gold for the team at the Olympic Games in Los Angeles, Homfeld's dry comment was "We've finally become friends." More titles followed: individual World Equestrian Games first in 1985, team World Champion in 1986, and second for individual. After this victory, Abdullah quit the competitive world and served in a stud.

Homfeld never managed to gain similar victories with other horses. In the end, he quit professional riding and became an innovative show jumping course designer.

A star despite having never won the Olympic gold: Milton under English horseman John Whitaker.

John Whitaker and Milton

Few pairs have been as beautiful to watch as John Whitaker and the snowflake-white Milton, although their circumstances–which ultimately cost them their chance at the Olympics–were tragic. John Whitaker took over the Bradley's gray mount in 1984. Caroline Bradley had trained and ridden this incredible jumper until her untimely death. In the arena, everything seemed to run smoothly for Whitaker and Milton. They won wherever they appeared.

Thus, Milton was the only favorite for the 1988 Olympic Games in Seoul. But the Bradleys could not bring themselves to enter Milton for those Olympic Games because their daughter had been barred from the Olympic team after the British Horse Association had declared Caroline a professional. Only in 1992 did they consent to Whitaker and Milton entering Olympic competition in Barcelona–but by that time the gelding's athletic zenith already lay behind him.

Franke Sloothaak and Weihaiwej

At the 1994 World Equestrian Games held in the Netherlands, no one could fail to notice these two. Franke Sloothaak and Weihaiwej started by securing first for the team and then, as if it came quite naturally, won individual gold. And this in spite of the fact that the dappled sorrel mare with her unusual blue eyes was a taxing ride, because she was often distracted by her surroundings. Sometimes people in the audience felt personally challenged by her as she cantered by the lower rows of seats in an indoor arena, looking them right in the eye.

Her lack of concentration was more than compensated by her tremendous jumping talent, and she went down in history as a superlative high flyer.

Ludger Beerbaum and Classic Touch

If anything ever stood in the way of Classic Touch, it was not an obstacle but her own ambition. The high-

A blue-eyed world champion that will never be forgotten: Weihaiwej and her rider, Franke Sloothaak.

strung mare needed no urging forward; she needed a skilled rider to hold her back with the lightest possible touch. Those who got along with her could count on her in every way, but those she didn't like she would literally toss aside.

This jumping wonder of Holstein lineage got along best with Ludger Beerbaum. The pair caused the German team's relatively poor placement in the 1992 Olympic Games in Barcelona, but they were not really to blame. A bridle strap broke in the middle of the course; Beerbaum had to dismount in full swing, which disqualified them and put their team in 11th place. The finals, however, would be their biggest success: starting in last place, they secured the gold, and both seemed to relish their triumph during the lap of honor. This was their last joint victory, because even before the Olympics began, Classic Touch's owner had announced that his own son would ride the mare in the future.

Hugo Simon and E.T.

All who witnessed Hugo Simon and E.T. fighting for victory in a tied entry with a shortened course knew that they were witnessing something stellar indeed. Risk-taking tight turns at full speed without a second's loss followed by cleanly taken verticals–these are the feats that made the pair famous. In 1998 they placed first at the Aachen tournament, winning the record prize sum of $1.5 million.

E.T.'s show jumping winnings are unmatched. He adored jelly beans and bananas, a treat he preferred to receive from his groom Margit, whose loving care had been crucial to the horse's spectacular performances. So when Simon decided it was time to retire E.T. from the world of sports, he gave the mount to Margit as a parting gift.

Meredith Michaels-Beerbaum and Shutterfly

Meredith Michaels-Beerbaum is famous for her daredevil riding style. The tiny horsewoman–a mere 5 ft 3 inches tall–tears around the course at high speed despite having taken some severe falls. This California native prefers unusual mounts. She has lived and worked in Germany since 1991 and is married to another show jumper, Markus Beerbaum.

Always a favorite with audiences, her career got a major boost at the beginning of the new century. Together with the spirited Hanovarian bay Shutterfly, she was ranked German Mistress in the Championate Equipe, won the World Equestrian Games, twice won the Rider's Tour (the show jumping series with the highest prize money), was voted Rider of

the Year, and in 2005 won the prize at Aachen, Germany.

The horse was discovered by Paul Schockemöhle, who recognized his talent and recommended the connection to Michaels-Beerbaum. Though his mane was always neatly combed to one side, the gelding's name at the time was Struwwelpeter (tousle-head). Meredith Michaels-Beerbaum renamed him to allow his American owners to call him by name more easily.

Below: New name, new beginning. Meredith Michaels-Beerbaum riding Shutterfly, formerly known as Struwwelpeter.

A horse with out-of-this-world ability, he won millions in prizes and was crazy for jelly beans: E.T., ridden by Hugo Simon.

The annual CHIO (World Equestrian Festival) is held at Aachen, in the world's most modern outdoor riding arena. Over 300,000 spectators attend these games, which are regularly voted 'Best Tournament in the World' by both the riders and the drivers.

The World Equestrian Festival

To any horseman or horsewoman, the CHIO is the Wimbledon of the equestrian sports world, not only because the event is held on turf, but because winning the medal, the Großer Preis of Aachen, is the equivalent of winning the Tennis Grand Slam Tournament. CHIO is short for *Concours Hippique International Officiel* (World Equestrian Festival), and it is the only international equestrian event in the world where Nations' Cups are held in the four disciplines of jumping, dressage, four-in-hand driving, and eventing. It ranks on the same level as the World Equestrian Games, and the competitors at Aachen are among the equestrian elite. Approximately 400 horses and 150 riders and drivers from twenty-four nations compete for prize money amounting to $1.8 million. This makes CHIO the most highly remunerated riding tournament in the world.

Charlemagne

Aachen owes its fame and long tradition to this mighty medieval monarch, who not only made Aachen an imperial spa town, but apparently bequeathed its inhabitants his special love of horses.

It is a fact that Charles I was crowned emperor by Pope Leo III in Rome on December 24, 800, but there is no truth in the legend that his horse found the buried hot springs (by stamping on the spot with his hooves) that eventually led to the foundation of the spa town of Aachen (whose Latin name is *Aquis*, water). In fact, Roman legionaries were already enjoying Aachen's hot springs a century earlier.

The six-day event, with a budget of over $12 million, is organized by the Aachen-Laurensberger Rennverein e. V. with the aid of some 900 volunteers. This friendly society is proud of its century-long tradition, as their founders organized the very first riding and driving tournament in 1924. On August 1 of the following year, the event was established on the grounds where it still takes place today, a generously designed space whose show jumping arena alone is twice the size of a soccer field. The first grandstand had space for 1,000 spectators and phone connections for journalists. Even though the rain was coming down in sheets, 20,000 eager spectators attended the first event in celebration of the best riders.

Today's most modern equestrian sports facilities can hold over 50,000 visitors. Like Wimbledon, this area is used just once a year, underlining the exclusiveness of the tournament. Every year, celebrities and aristocrats, politicians, business people, and artists come to watch. Some arrive incognito, such as director Steven Spielberg, who watched the dressage freestyle from the grandstand in 2005.

The audience at Aachen has always been enthusiastic, no matter what the weather, and people will make all kinds of sacrifices to make this great festival possible. The show jumping judges have formed an association called Pferdeschwänze (pony tails) and it goes without saying that they use their vacation days to take part in the CHIO. The final day with the popular Farewell to Nations is always sold out a year in advance, and much-coveted grandstand tickets are handed down from generation to generation.

The only event that can compete with the CHIO is the World Equestrian Games (or World Championships). In 2006, the World Championships even took place in Aachen. Four show jumping World Championships and one dressage World Championship had previously been held here. The 2006 tournament was innovative because for the first time competitions were held in seven disciplines: jumping, dressage, eventing, driving, endurance, vaulting, and reining. It lasted two weeks and drew approximately 500,000 visitors.

Above: In many tournaments, the dressage class is treated as an orphan. This is not so in Aachen, however, where the dressage arena is as impressive as the show jumping course. The grandstands are sheltered by a roof and offer seats for 51,000 spectators.

Below: Every available hand waves a white handkerchief during the Farewell to Nations parade, the traditional conclusion of a highly eventful tournament week in Aachen.

Farewell to Nations

The first impression of this blizzard of white handkerchiefs can be confusing. It is, in fact, a highly festive ceremony that requires a strong sense of rhythm and much stamina–plus, of course, the white kerchiefs that spectators need to wave farewell to the athletes, and the hundreds of horsemen and women need to wave to the crowd in response.

Farewell to Nations is the traditional finale of the Aachen World Equestrian Festival, and neither audience nor participants would want to miss it.

This beautiful and moving custom was introduced by Dr. Kurt Sonani in 1953 and has since become a popular interplay between onlookers and those active in the tournament. The audience takes the opportunity to convey their thanks for a week of inspiring sporting performances by horses and equestrians from countless nations, while the participants thank the spectators for their great support during the event.

On entering the arena, a short version of every national anthem is played. After the German host team has entered (last of all), the traditional tune *Muss I Denn* is played and the stadium turns into a sea of white handkerchiefs, from the arena right up to the highest row of seats. The song is repeated without interruption until all the participants have completed their lap of honor and left the holy lawn, which means that in the end every waving arm is numb. There is just enough time to dab away the odd tear furtively and then make sure the tickets are secured for next year.

All-Rounders

Eventing, or horse trials, is called the "Crown of Equitation" for good reason, as it unites the major disciplines in a single class, yet it remains controversial in the world of horsemanship. Animal rights activists protest that the class is far too demanding, though many aspects have been changed over time to make it easier on the horses.

Formerly, the versatility class was referred to as the *militaire*, and this name betrays its origins. Even more than show jumping and dressage, this sport was influenced by European cavalry schools. Originally it was intended as a combined training to test the performance of army mounts. Tragically, many horses died in the process, and it took several decades to establish viable regulations for registered competitions. In 1892, one of the first reported military trials was held, a long-distance ride covering an astounding 360 miles: the winning and second-place horses died of exhaustion shortly afterward.

Women engaged in this officers' sport surprisingly soon. As early as 1932, Irmgard von Opel won an international military trial held in Vienna, Austria. In Europe, English and German women continue to be very active in this class. Bettina Hoy and Ingrid Klimke were European champions, as was Princess Anne, who made it to the top of the world's versatility class alongside her equally well-known husband Mark Phillips and became European champion in 1971. Her daughter Zara won the same title in 2005.

Most eventing riders prefer the Thoroughbred for their speed, courage, tenacity, and the staying power required for the three-day event. Trakehners are also popular, as they share the same qualities.

THREE-DAY EVENT

The first day of this event begins with a 4th-level (M) dressage class. Horse and rider must perform lessons in the basic gaits with many changes in tempo and features such as traversal in trot.

The second day is the most demanding, and those who are not 100 percent fit may not reach the finish line. After many terrible years

Precision work? This horse is so intent that it fails to realize that the horsewoman, who can see what is ahead, will not make it around the flag.

with awful dismounts, injuries, and horse deaths, the International Olympic Committee has used its influence to adjust the trials so that more mounts and equestrians stand a chance of reaching the finish in one piece. At the 2004 Olympic Games in Athens, the two-road tracks and steeplechase were omitted for the first time (the new short format). These were formerly part of the trial and had to be tackled before the actual cross-country race (classic format), which was shortened from 4¼ to 3½ miles. In 2004, all participants could start the cross-country race fresh and strong. Still, though the course is far less demanding, one horse was so severely injured that it couldn't be saved.

The big thrill—and the major challenge—of the cross-country race is that its obstacles are fixed. That is, there are no fences that give way at a touch, as there are in the show jumping arena. If horse and rider do not negotiate the obstacle properly or make a mistake, they risk injury to the horse or even a fatal fall. Water obstacles, or ditches, look especially spectacular, though they are not the most dangerous. Under the new rules, when there are highly demanding fences on

Horses often take off with no knowledge of what awaits them on the other end of the fence—they trust their riders completely.

the circuit, an escape route is offered. This takes longer but is less risky. If a horse comes to a standstill, this is counted as a refusal; a fall leads to disqualification. Riders are protected by a helmet and safety vest. The horse is protected with boots that cover the hocks; the chest and legs are smeared with Vaseline to help it slide over logs.

Successfully completing the course is a major achievement—it is an enormously demanding exercise—but the tournament is not over. After completing the cross-country race, the horses are checked by veterinarians, their legs are cooled, they are given a massage, and then slowly walked about to stave off muscle aches the following day. This is essential because the final tests are still to come: on the last day is the hunter class. Veterinarians check each mount one more time before it enters the jumping arena, consisting of twelve obstacles with a maximum height of 4 feet.

The crown of equitation can only be won by riders who know how to pace their horses' strength and energy for the entire three days of the versatility trial.

Acrobatic jumps like this make it clear why these horses are called all-rounders–versatility or eventing horses can tackle just about anything.

The front legs of eventing horses are thickly smeared with Vaseline to help them slide over the immovable obstacles.

Spectacular and masterly: Mark Todd (above) is one of the best eventing horsemen of the 20th century. Below, Bettina Hoy with Ringwood Cockatoo.

A Helmet with GPS

Nowadays, not even the world of equitation is spared from technological devices. With the help of miniature computers, current information can be obtained about the horse, the ride, and geographical position. With the help of a GPS (Global Positioning System) device on their helmet, riders can access information about their whereabouts, the distance they have already covered, average speed, and the time elapsed. Additional information concerns the physiological performance of the horse, its body temperature and heart rate. This device is designed for use by versatility or long-distance

riders to help make their training sessions as efficient as possible; but it also helps leisure riders trekking in the open country who need to locate themselves. The GPS device is the size of a cellular phone and saves all the data so that riders can later assess and analyze the training on their personal computers.

This artificial horse pilot is in contact with satellites that emit time signals at regular intervals. The GPS helmet receives these time signals. In light of the satellite's own course, the GPS measures the mileage between signals and then sends the precise positioning–which is accurate to within 6 ft.

This aircraft has a huge cargo compartment especially designed for carrying horses. Every horse is well padded to protect it as well as possible from potential injuries during the flight.

Bon Voyage!

When horses travel nowadays, they are far more comfortable than even fifty years ago. There is a whole industry devoted to making four-legged voyagers as comfortable as their biped partners. Luxury horse trailers are more than an unusual affectation. Although a considerable expense, these rolling homes are a worthwhile investment for anyone wanting to travel comfortably with their horse. However, an ordinary horse trailer for everyday use will not break the bank.

Generally speaking, horses don't mind going on an outing. Although some horses do not like to climb into the trailer, this is often because they are afraid of traveling alone. Others enjoy being in the trailer so much they can hardly be coaxed into coming out again.

There should be an air miles program for horses, as the sporting horses that perform at international competitions fly a lot and would surely earn thousands of bonus miles. In spite of the well-established routine, however, there are two very real concerns during every horse's journey: claustrophobia and colic. Horses that suffer from travel sickness can be helped with a prior meal of hot wet bran, which will lead to an empty stomach before take-off. It is also important that horses get plenty to drink during the flight. Finally, if there is someone they trust close at hand during take-off and landing, that person can signal that all is well, even though the ground is shuddering under hoof. Under these conditions, flying can be far less tiresome than spending days aboard a ship or in a truck.

All Aboard!

Avid travelers? Not always. Hours of crossing the sea aboard a rocking ship is anything but fun, in spite of the good breeze. And horses can get seasick, just as people do. Unlike people, however, who (in extremis) can ease their trouble by "feeding the fishes," a horse cannot find relief in this way because it is impossible for horses to vomit.

The explanation lies in muscles in the cardiac sphincter valve leading into the stomach, which only releases when stimulated by food or drink entering through the esophagus on the way to the horse's stomach. If the contents of the stomach press onto that muscle in the other direction, the opening reflex is not stimulated. A horse that is seasick will react instead with increasing body temperature, fever, or worst of all, painful colic.

Operation Olympia

The voyage to the 2000 Sydney Olympic Games was an unprecedented organizational tour de force. Eleven months before the event started, the journey of the 250 horses had been calculated and planned to the last detail. Never before had so many horses been moved halfway around the globe in so short a time.

Owing to Australian quarantine regulations, all the horses had to arrive within five days of each other. Before the journey, all had spent two weeks quarantined in one of thirty-one designated European stables and, on arrival in Australia, another fortnight's quarantine was required. In this case, quarantine meant the horses could have no contact with other animals, and only a select few riders and grooms were allowed to see the precious mounts (who were held inside a double-fenced, regularly disinfected stall). Before they were permitted to go near the horse athletes, every visitor was required to disinfect the soles of their shoes and change their clothes in a locked room. These extraordinary measures were necessary because many animal diseases, dangerous viruses, and germs do not exist in Australia.

The arrangements in Germany were typical and were described for a radio station by journalist Susanne Sgrazzutti, who watched the horses' departure on August 2, 2000. Here are some excerpts:

(Voice of Thomas Hartwig, press spokesman for the German Equestrian Association) "For example, even horse influenza, which a European horse will normally catch at least once in its lifetime, is unknown in Australia. To us Europeans, horse influenza is nothing serious, any more than if you or I had the flu. But there would certainly be disastrous consequences if it was introduced to Australia."

"Australian personnel have made surprise visits to the various quarantine stables to verify that the strict regulations where properly observed. One important aspect of their tracing list is the common woodworm, which does not exist in Australia. Every saddle is suspect, because it partly consists of wood. It is not easy to trace this parasite because few people know what the woodworm looks like–not even an experienced horseman like Olympic champion Ludger Beerbaum." (Voice of Ludger Beerbaum) "Not a clue, I'm at a loss as to what this is all about, really. If the woodworm can be introduced via the saddle tree or in the soles of our boots, it's quite adventurous in a way, and quite a farce."

"This morning, fifty-two horses were loaded into the aircraft belly of a Boeing 747-C, strictly adhering to the quarantine regulations. The horses are facing a journey that will take 26 hours and lead them half-way around the globe. The aircraft, weighing 370 tons, will take-off at an especially low, gentle angle. Although the mounts do not fly first class but have to stand in their containers throughout the long trip, a single ticket costs $66,000. On the other hand, these passengers are entitled to a little more hand luggage than usual, that is, 770 lb each. The most important on-board service is a steady supply of water. The 520 gallons of water now onboard are insufficient for the whole trip. The aircraft will make stops in Dubai and Singapore to take on fuel and additional water."

Transport expert Martin Atoc saw the happy end of 'Operation Olympia' on October 7, 2000. That same day, all the horses, both the champions and the also-rans, arrived safe and sound at Frankfurt Airport, finally touching home ground.

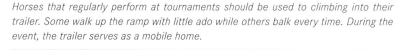

Top-class sporting horses are frequent flyers. They survive long flights unharmed in specially designed transport containers. No stall takes no more than two horses. It is more comfortable (and more expensive) if a horse travels in a stall of its own.

Horses that regularly perform at tournaments should be used to climbing into their trailer. Some walk up the ramp with little ado while others balk every time. During the event, the trailer serves as a mobile home.

A Long Way to Go

In endurance riding, horses have to cover long distances quickly, and the horse's speed and stamina are both tested to the limits. Riding distances upwards of 15 miles also require a clever rider who knows how to manage their horse so that it can pass the thorough veterinary tests that are carried out before, during, and after the ride. The winner of an endurance competition is generally only announced after veterinarians have inspected the competing horses.

Of course, covering a long distance in as short a time as possible is not a new idea. The riding peoples of antiquity and the famous Pony Express riders of the American West were already stimulated by the race against time. From their beginnings as army competitions, endurance rides soon became one of the major sporting challenges and became very popular with the cavalry regiments of the late nineteenth and early twentieth centuries.

One notorious event will always be remembered. This was the ride held by European cavalry officers in 1892. The German officers were to ride from Berlin, Germany to Vienna, Austria. Meanwhile, Austro-Hungarian officers were charging from Vienna to Berlin. Whoever arrived first would win. Austrian Count Starhemberg made

Breeds that go the Extra Mile

A steady character and willing worker who loves to run, a horse with endurance and speed who stands 57–61 inches and weighs 1,000–1,100 lb: these criteria are often met by Arabians. Arabian Thoroughbreds and the breeds crossed with them are the most successful endurance horses, but warmbloods such as Norwegians or Icelandic ponies are also good bets for endurance rides. The mule can be surprisingly successful in very long endurance meets.

As a general rule, if you expect exceptional stamina from your horse to compete in endurance events, it will need several years of individual training. The same is true of people: no one should run a marathon without months of training. Short tours of up to 25 miles should not pose any problem for a healthy horse, as long as the speed is moderate.

A horse can take its first endurance rides of 25 miles when it is 5 years old, and moderate distances of up to 50 miles at age 6. Only after they have turned seven are horses permitted to compete in the major endurance rides of over 50 miles.

One of the most powerful men in the United Arab Emirates and in the international equestrian world is Sheik Mohammed bin Rashid al Maktoum. He takes part in every major endurance competition.

Keep cool: this applies especially to horses that perform to the limits of their endurance. Regular rest periods are mandatory, in which everything possible is done to help the horse recuperate quickly.

100-Mile Rides

An endurance ride covering 100 miles is the crown of the long-distance class, and is particularly popular in the USA. The most demanding of endurance rides is the Tevis Cup (or Western States Trail Ride). Anyone who has covered the 100-mile ride in a single day will agree that it is a tough event. This amateur trail ride is held in Placer County, California, which is both beautiful and grim, leading across the crest of the Sierra Nevada with its steep canyons and cliffs in scorching heat. All who complete the course within 20 hours and pass ten veterinary inspections are rewarded with the coveted silver Completion Award Buckle. The fastest Tevis Cup ride to date–10 hours 46 minutes–was by Boyd Zontelli on Rushcreek Hans in 1981.

Above: Although it is important to avoid overtaxing the horse during an endurance ride, a minimum speed of 8 mph is required. It is also obligatory for the rider to weigh at least 112 lb.

Left: During the mandatory stops, a veterinarian checks the horse's heart rate. It should not exceed 64 beats per minute.

the distance in 71 hours and 26 minutes, but his horse, Athos, died of exhaustion two days later.

Today, responsible endurance riders will have nothing to do with foolhardy challenges that punish their horses. In fact, today's endurance riders spend a long time preparing their horses in training sessions, seeing their horses as four-legged partners that need to train for the competition just as they do themselves.

The inspections performed by veterinarians during the ride, during mandatory rest stops, include the horse's gait and general state as well as an analysis of circulation and metabolism.

The modern sport of endurance began in America and Australia, then quickly spread to European countries like France and Spain, and to the Middle East, where it is very popular. Horse-loving sheiks from the oil-producing states pump millions of dollars into this sport to further its international renown. They regularly organize international championships with multifaceted fringe events in order to realize their goal: turning endurance riding into an Olympic sport.

Heading in the Right Direction–Trail Riding

Experiencing peace of mind, feeling at one with the natural surroundings, the horse, and oneself–this is how trail riders would describe what they love about their hobby. Enthusiasts for this sport are, therefore–by definition–non-competitive. Nothing can shatter the peace as quickly as the unbridled urge to win.

Trail riders cover great distances and steadfastly stay the course, but they are under no pressure to perform. They abide by a single rule, which is the biological clock of horse and rider.

Ideally, a trail rider rises in the early morning and beds down equally early. At noon, a natural energy trough, an extensive layoff is made. At an average speed of 3¼ mph, some 18½ miles can be covered in a day. On horseback one can even venture out on trails that would be far too arduous for a person on foot. Yet trail riding needs training and experience just as much as other classes. A novice who rides for too long will suffer chafed legs and sore muscles at the very least. Riding associations publish lists of approved trail organizers for a vacation on horseback.

Redcoats

Hunting live quarry with hounds was already popular in ancient Greece, and horsemen accompanied by packs of hounds still hunt live animals today. As a result of fierce protests from animal rights activists, however, ever more countries are banning this form of hunting, or limiting it to the chase. Only recently and to great controversy, it was declared illegal in Britain, where the sport has a long and honored tradition. The hunt remains popular, and in the USA it is still permissible to hunt foxes and coyotes (but not to the kill).

DRAG HUNTING

Today, many hunters go drag hunting, where the field follows a scented bag dragged over a course. The trail setter hangs a canister from his saddle that scatters drops scented with fennel, aniseed, herring, or fox over the ground to mark a trail for the hounds. Only a well-set trail that mimics the course a live quarry would run makes the hunt interesting.

The success of the chase depends heavily on the horse. A hunt horse should be calm and unfazed by the baying of hounds, the press of people, and the sounding horn. It should have an easy canter, be able to take sharp turns, be sure-footed and obedient. In America, hunts have a non-jumping category as well as one that jumps fences.

To find a horse with these qualities, breed or place of origin does not count. The field hunters used in England and Ireland are specially trained horses stemming from heavy mares crossed with Thoroughbreds, but they do not belong to any specific breed.

HUNTING RULES

"Prepare for the hunt"—once the huntsman has blown the signal with his horn, the horsemen, field hunters, and hounds start to gather.

Fox Hunting in America
In the USA, fox hunting usually does not end in a kill, but is more of a thrilling chase, which is why some people prefer to call it fox chasing. An animal that does get killed is usually old or sick. Many American farmers allow coyote hunting on their property because this keeps the predators from getting too close to their livestock.

The actual hunt begins when hounds are set loose in thickets called coverts (pronounced "covers"), where foxes lay up during the day. If the pack picks up the scent, it will pursue the fox and the mounted hunters will follow by the most direct route possible. In America, the hunt is abandoned as soon as the fox goes to ground (seeks refuge in a set, or burrow).

Even uninitiated onlookers who happen to pass by will notice that this sport is steeped in tradition. The attire of the horsemen is chosen with great care and follows strict rules of etiquette. Scarlet coats (sometimes called pinks or pinques) are worn by the Hunt Master, Huntsman, and Whippers-In. In England, fully subscribed members also wear them. In the USA they are restricted to fully subscribed gentlemen with colors, while the women wear black or navy. Participants under 18 years of age wear tweed jackets called ratcatchers. The highest honor is to be awarded the hunt button (bearing the hunt crest) by the Hunt Master. The recipient may then wear the hunt collar with the button. The stock (cravat) is indispensable. It is fairly long and tied around the neck in several loops and secured with a stock pin. The outfit is completed with a white shirt, white gloves, white or beige jodhpurs, black boots, and a safety helmet.

To return to the action: before the signal is given for everyone to mount up, the riders confer to settle on the field they will join. The field is divided by the level of horsemanship. Members of the first

Looking forward to the hunt: Here, the leading field gathers with the pack of hounds and the field master. The gentlemen wear red coats, the ladies navy or black coats.

field assume the obligation of jumping every fence or other obstacle on the way. Members of the second field may choose to clear an obstacle or pass it by, while the third field, consisting of novices and young horses, will refrain from tackling any jump.

The next signal calls all riders to doff their hats for the official greeting, accompanied by the horn players. The Master of the Fox Hounds welcomes the entourage and informs participants about special features of the course and grounds. Next, the drag trail is set out for the pack of hounds, which are in the care of the Master of the Hounds (or Kennelman). Once the Huntsman gives the final call by blowing the horn, thus signaling the hunt to start, the hounds run ahead of the first field. As soon as the hounds have picked up the scent, the Master gives the final signal for the chase to begin.

It is an absolute faux-pas to overtake the leaders of the first field or the pack. All participants should remain in their position and keep a safe distance, especially when taking obstacles. Stops for recuperation are ordered by the master; these may even include a picnic. Horses and hounds are given a drink and have time to rest before the session is continued. All these activities are communicated by means of the horns. At the culmination of an eventful chase, the rider who first sees the fox holds up his or her right-hand glove (even in canter) and calls out "tally-ho!" The horns then take up the signal.

The hunting season begins with an open meeting in November. In 2004, there were 318 registered packs of hounds in England and 175 in North America. Each country has a Masters of Foxhounds Association that takes the registrations. The British association was founded in 1881, and the American in 1907. Notable American presidents who have enjoyed fox hunting include George Washington, Thomas Jefferson, and Ronald Reagan.

At the end of the event, the horn players sound their final signal. Both musicians and huntsmen are now winded.

Tally-ho!

The British expression "tally-ho" is cried by the first hunter to spy the fox. It was originally used in deer hunting and was likely introduced to Britain by William the Conqueror, an avid hunter who conquered Britain in 1066.

Mounted hunting emerged in the 16th century, and foxes were killed as vermin control. The golden age of British fox hunting was the mid-19th century, when there were ca. 190 packs of foxhounds.

The sport demands skill of both horse and rider and has given rise to several sports such as steeplechasing. Today, the objective of a fox hunt is to provide a thrilling and enjoyable cross-country ride.

The King of Games, The Game of Kings

Dynamic and spectacular, always bearing in mind the safety of both mount and rider—this is polo, the game of kings. Polo is one of the oldest team sports and is still played in more than fifty countries.

In the third century BCE, the Persians were the first to play a mounted ball game astride their famously agile horses, but it was the Indians who finally gave the game its name. *Pulu* is the Tibetan expression for the bamboo wood which was used in the playing ball for many decades. Polo was already known throughout Asia when British Hussar officers finally introduced the bamboo ball to Europe in 1860. The new sport enjoyed great social acclaim and polo clubs were opened by the score. In 1876, James Gordon Bennett, Jr. organized the first polo match in America, which was held in New York City. When the first German polo club was opened in Hamburg in 1898, the organizers used cardboard dummy horses and strode about the field on foot to explain the rules of the game to the audience.

Polo does cost more than other sports. Apart from the club fee, every player needs at least one relay pony because according to the regulations, after every period of play (called a *chukka*), the riders change mounts. A good Argentinean polo pony—Argentina being the leading country in polo class—costs at least $4,600, to which must be added the running costs for the stable, feed, insurance, farrier, and veterinarian.

Unfortunately, polo only enjoyed Olympic prestige for a few years. The game was only admitted between 1908 and 1936, when it was last registered in the Berlin Olympic Games. In the old glory days, polo was regarded as something exclusive, held in a high-brow social surrounding. Today, however, class differences are only made on the turf and then only in regard to the handicap. As in golf, every player has a handicap which starts at −2 for novices and can be improved to +10, the goal for top-rated players. The sum of the individual handi-

A Well-Known Polo Player: Prince Charles

In Britain, polo is still a highly popular game, in part due to the royal family. Prince Philip used to be a passionate polo player, and Prince Charles has followed in his father's footsteps. In fact, playing polo has quite a long royal tradition. In ancient Persia, learning to master polo was part of any prince's education, and only polo adepts could hope for a career at the court.

The British Crown Prince has frequently come face to face with the tough side of the sport. He has suffered many severe dismounts, and has even had to be hospitalized. He did try to quit the active sport for a while, but found that he missed it badly and took up the mallet once again. He has now firmly decided to retire to the stands and leave the exhausting activity to his two sons, Prince William and Prince Harry.

caps of the players makes up the team handicap. There are four playing levels for the teams: low goal, inter-medium goal, medium goal, and high goal. Depending on the tournament, the team with the weaker handicap is given advance points.

For a left-handed person, there is another handicap in this game, because the polo mallet must be gripped with the right hand. This regulation was introduced for safety reasons, because polo's fast pace makes it rather dangerous. An adroit polo player, however, will manage to get to the ball from any side.

Right: When playing polo, a good sense of distance and plenty of dexterity are indispensable. Galloping up and down the field at a fast pace, it's not so easy to keep track of the ball.

The focus of the game, for which two teams of four players each battle, is the polo ball, which weighs about 4 ounces.

1 HP on Snowy Ground

The latest variation of this very fast-paced team game is polo in the snow. Equipped with spiked shoes, the polo ponies are ready to entertain the enthusiastic jet set that gathers every January and February at St. Moritz, Switzerland. Snow polo is seen as an alternative to the trotting and flat-race meetings on "white turf" and the extremely hazardous skijoring, in which horses are harnessed to a person on skis. The polo circuit is set in a spectacular mountain landscape provided by nature herself: a frozen lake, where the ice cover is 13-16 inches deep and can bear 2,300 tons. The White Turf Racing Association erects grandstands and tents to cater to the every need of the discriminating and distinguished guests.

Naturally, the tent reserved for celebrities is heated—none of the coveted VIPs would attend if there was the slightest prospect of getting cold feet.

Acrobatic exercises on the saddle: during the match, horse and rider lose control from time to time. Many riders come off while trying to hit the ball, but they usually come to no harm.

A Short Guide to Polo

THE RULES

A first-time visitor to a polo match is bound to be impressed by the action on the turf, but it may be hard to figure out what is actually happening.

At its simplest, each of the two mounted teams has four players, each of whom has a mallet that is used to hit the ball. The match is divided into four to eight periods called *chukkas*. Outdoor polo is played on pitches or fields 300 yards long by 150 yards wide. Arena polo fields are one-third this size, and on these fields teams have only three players. To score, players must hit the ball between the opposition's goal posts. In practice it isn't quite that simple—the fact that the regulations consist of a hundred-page manual speaks for itself.

The basic game is governed by right of way. The rider who follows the hit ball in a straight line or who first intercepts the ball's line of travel without blocking other players has right of way. The other players may not disturb him from the front or behind. However, any player may try and push another off to the side, and may use his mallet to prevent another player hitting the ball.

Two mounted umpires direct the game through each chukka (which lasts seven minutes). During the four-minute break after each chukka, the mounts are changed. There is a ten-minute break at half time. Stallions are strictly barred from the game, for safety reasons. If a horse falls, the game is immediately called off. If a rider falls but is not badly injured, the game goes on.

ATTIRE

Safety comes first in polo, which is why a helmet and knee protection are obligatory. The horses' legs are protected with soft wraps, the tail is braided, and the mane is clipped to prevent the 5-ft-long mallet becoming entangled in the horse's mane or tail. The ball weighs approximately 4 ounces. It was originally made of bamboo, but these days it is generally made of compressed plastic.

Apart from jodhpurs and boots, polo players wear a special shirt, which has become everyday leisure wear. This highly practical outfit became widely popular due to the cotton fabric, which was originally cultivated in India and then introduced to America, China, and Russia. Today, any horseman or woman, tennis player, teenager or senior citizen knows the feel of the cool cotton polo shirt. The original high-quality polo shirt suffered when artificial fibers were introduced around the world. Equestrians, however, still prefer pure cotton because its sweat-wicking property makes it more comfortable to wear.

THE MOUNT

A talented, well-trained polo pony is quick and agile, it follows the game as if playing itself, and is responsive enough for the rider to direct it with a single hand. It also needs to be courageous and calm to endure the flurry of balls, mallets, and other players without either refusing to move or bolting. In the USA, where long passes are aimed at the rider who brakes away from the others at full gallop, polo is a much faster sport than in Britain, where the passes tend to be short. America has both women's and men's professional polo leagues.

The best polo ponies come from Argentina, which has in fact been World Champion of polo for over fifty years. The USA is second in the league, followed by Mexico, Britain, Australia, and New Zealand. The Argentine polo pony stems from the horses brought to the New World by Spanish conquerors Cortés and Pizzaro, which were then crossed with English Thoroughbreds. Today, these horses are high-profile export goods.

Spectacular hits underneath the neck of the horse are part of a good polo player's standard performance.

The right of way is given to the pair following the ball in a straight line. The player may not be blocked, but can be forced to the side.

A high-grade polo match is a popular event. Numerous spectators enthusiastically watch the players edge the ball toward the goal posts with very risky maneuvers.

Mid-air parry! It takes spectacular action to change the ball's direction.

Polo ponies are powerful sprinters that can reach top speed in short distances.

Cowboys are often viewed in a romantic light. But this glorification of the old Wild West has little to do with reality. In reality, working as a cowboy is a tough and very demanding job.

On the Cowboys' Trail

The art of reining, or Western riding, lies in the communication between horse and rider, which should be as simple and efficient as possible. Reining was developed through working with cattle herds. Even today, cowboys spend up to twelve hours in the saddle, driving the herds together or separating individual animals.

The interaction between horse and rider happens at lightning speed and is only possible through mutual trust. When driving cattle, a cowboy must be able rely completely on his quadruped partner's "cow sense." Horses are more intelligent than cattle and will instinctively make the right decisions. Advanced reining riders hold the reins in one hand only, as the other is needed for opening gates or wielding the lasso. Further differences between reining and classical dressage concern aids and the horse's collection. A dressage rider works to achieve ground-covering action through continually applied aids given with the legs and weight shifts. In Western riding, by contrast, the horseman or horsewoman only gives

a signal when they want some kind of change in the action. For example, if the horse is going at a trot, it will remain in that speed and direction until it is given a new signal. The reins are not held taut but left fairly loose, and the horse's head and neck are held much lower and further forward than in classical dressage. A Western horse and its rider make a very relaxed and calm team, attending to their work at a smooth pace. But the instant anything

Reining Competitions

Reining is the first Western discipline to be fully recognized by the FEI, and since 2002 has been incorporated in the World Equestrian Games and the European Equestrian Games. Formerly restricted to the United States and Latin America, reining has become equally popular in Europe, where many associations have been founded to organize competitions at various levels (beginners are called rookies). In fact, at the 2006 World Equestrian

Games, Germans took both individual and team first places.

Competition attire for reining is as rigorously prescribed as for classical dressage, but it is very different. The competitors should bear in mind that judges will take into consideration the hat worn, the highly decorated Western shirt and boots, and the tack–a matching set comprising the distinctive bridle, split or romal reins, and deep-seated saddle with wooden stirrups, leather guards, and pommel horn.

The Origins of Western Riding

As every child knows, Western riding was developed by American cowboys. In fact, though, the cattle herders only brought to perfection a style of riding that was already established. The basics were imported by the Spanish conquerors who arrived in the Americas in the sixteenth century, bringing their horses and stock with them. The *vaqueros* of the old world had long since specialized in driving cattle from horseback. In Mexico and in the southwest of what is today the USA, haciendas and ranches with enormous herds of cattle

developed. The Native Americans were the first to adapt the riding style of the vaqueros. Over time, the gauchos and cowboys developed the style further and refined it to answer the needs of cattle working.

The aids are mainly applied through shifts in weight, but voice commands are also important. In practice, an American curb or long-shanked bit is hardly necessary because the weight of the reins alone should suffice to make contact with the muzzle. A well-trained Western horse will react and change direction as soon as it feels the reins brushing against one side of its neck.

Opening and closing a gate is one of the exercises in the Trail class. The task should be performed without dismounting.

happens within the cattle herd, the horse must immediately power up to peak form. The most important lessons of reining, both in daily life and during horse shows, are based on these requirements.

THE LESSONS OF REINING

In Pleasure competition, the judges assess the three gaits walk, jog, and lope (the latter two being the equivalent of trot and canter). They also consider the horse's movement and relaxed responsiveness, and the correct Western horse posture.

In Reining class, flying change in canter is required as well as speedy turns on the haunches in one spot (called spins), and a full halt from a gallop. Since the horse arrives with plenty of speed and cannot help but sliding with the hindquarters, this lesson is called a sliding stop. Other requirements in Reining class are rollbacks (180° turn and gallop) and flawless backward steps.

To test the versatility and nimbleness of a horse, competitors take part in an event called Trail. It consists of a course designed with obstacles that might well be encountered in the open, such as negotiating a closed gate, crossing a bridge or sure-footedly passing over a rocking board such as a see-saw.

In Roping class, the riders must swing a lasso and catch cattle. Time counts in this competition. There are also team roping competi-

tions, where the front man (the header) slings a loop over the cow's head while the heeler gets the cow by the hindquarters. The class in which cattle are isolated from the herd is called Cutting.

Learning to ride Western style is easiest when you have no previous experience of horseback riding. Someone who has been trained in the classical (or English) style of riding will have many habits to unlearn.

Traversal steps, called sidepass, involve moving sideways across the cavaletti without touching them either with front or hindquarters.

Any well-trained Western horse will walk over a rocking see-saw without fuss. This is an exercise that would unnerve classically trained horses–and their riders.

The sliding stop, a halt from full gallop, is unquestionably one of the most spectacular lessons of the Western Reining class.

Many children use vaulting as an initiation to horseback riding. The exercises train one's sense of balance and basic lessons like the Flag are quickly mastered.

A Special Form of Gymnastics

Acrobatics at full canter sounds terrifying, and these athletic exercises on horseback are very demanding. Even performing them in the gymnasium takes a great deal of training and courage. Summersaults and flips, handstands with splits, flying mounts and vaulting over the horse: equestrian vaulting is not for the faint of heart!

The vaulting alone looks like a miracle of airborne grace. But it is a skill that can be learned, and as a competition class it can be entered by individuals, pairs, or teams of eight. The compulsory exercises have evocative names including Basic Seat, Stand, Flag, Flank, Mill, and Scissors. These can be complemented with other exercises for the choreographed freestyle exercise. Judges assess the performance of both vaulter(s) and horse.

Modern vaulting has little to do with its original form. The name derives from the French *la voltige* (jumping across the horse). During the Renaissance, French nobility took a fancy to artful posing on horseback. A little later, vaulting was added to the cavalry schools' educational program, where it was seen as a way to enhance the soldiers' fitness and agility. During the 1920 Antwerp Olympic Games,

Friend and Helper

It has long been known that being with a horse and riding can have a calming effect on people or even further healing. Today there are various forms of equine-assisted treatments such as hippotherapy, therapeutic vaulting and riding, and para-equestrianism.

In hippotherapy, a disabled rider sits on the warm back of a horse, without a saddle. The disabled person must actively respond to the horse's movements, which has a beneficial effect on their muscle tone. It also has a positive effect on the psyche, because it enables the person to move about freely in an upright position, with the help of foreign legs, so to speak.

Horses are excellent therapists and riding has proven beneficial for people with sensory, physical, and mental handicaps. Not only do these people pick up the lessons easily, they also derive great pleasure from them. The North American Riding for the Handicapped Association (NARHA) was founded in 1969 and advises many organizations throughout the USA.

Disabled riders can demonstrate their accomplishments in national competitions as well as international ones, such as the Paralympics.

The Pommel Horse

Originally, the horse was real. Gymnastics and athletic exercises were performed on horseback until somebody came up with the idea of using a wooden substitute. From this evolved an individual discipline that is still part of the Olympic program. The pommel horse has handles that enable male athletes to perform all kinds of exercises, including single and double leg work. Women generally only use the apparatus for mounting and dismounting.

Equestrian Vaulting was one of the disciplines (it was called Artistic Riding), but that was the only time Olympic medals could be won. Nowadays, many youngsters see vaulting as an introductory level before moving on to traditional horseback riding. The American Vaulting Association was founded in 1966.

THE VAULTING HORSE

The vaulting horse is a true athlete. Ideally 63–71 inches high and calm tempered, it steps out in an even, spirited canter and has to bear up to 350 lb of weight on its long, broad back. Without losing its balance, it artfully places every step of the canter for 15 minutes or more. A vaulting horse starts its career on the lunge line at a minimum age of five years. Prior to that, it has to pass a classical training where it learns to obey the aids of the lunger, who is hardly noticeable to viewers.

The tack used for vaulting consists of a padded surcingle with two handles and two foot loops called cossack stirrups, plus a matching felt or foam rubber pad. The horse wears a bridle, caveson, and side reins. The lunge line, which is ca. 26 feet long, is attached to the inside bit ring.

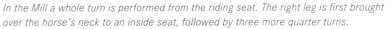

In the Mill a whole turn is performed from the riding seat. The right leg is first brought over the horse's neck to an inside seat, followed by three more quarter turns.

The Handstand requires a strong sense of balance as well as strong arms. The calm, regular canter of the horse is crucial.

There is no room for fear in the Stand. The movement of the horse is cushioned by keeping the knees and ankles loose.

Equestrian Vaulting is an official competition sport. The high point of a championship is the freestyle choreography performed by teams.

Top-class international championships demand fearless performance of heart-stopping exercises that far exceed the demands of the compulsory lessons.

On the Long Lead

Whether warmblood, coldblood, Thoroughbred, or pony—any horse harnessed to a carriage is instantly transformed into a parade horse. For centuries, horses were an essential means of transport, until suddenly an invention changed the world. The instant the first motorcars appeared on the streets, nobody wanted a horse-drawn carriage any more. It was the end of an era, and it almost deprived the horse of its raison d'être, too. Fortunately, the horse was recognized as part of human culture and transport, and found a new life in the worlds of equestrian sports and big social events.

Because there had been several ways of using horses to draw carriages, coaches, and wagons, show driving was introduced as the fourth discipline in equestrian sports. Each mode has its own demands that lend themselves to competition and assessment. Show driving is officially recognized by the FEI. Although it is not an Olympic category, show driving—including individuals, pairs, and teams of four horses—is embedded in a wide array of national and international championships. Meanwhile, the spectacular four-in-hand races have become veritable crowd pullers.

Well-trained carriage horses are extremely sensitive to voice commands. In some difficult situations, the voice commands are much more important than aids applied through the reins.

Teamwork

The driver of a carriage is never alone. When driving four-in-hand, he can select two grooms to accompany him. These know the horses as well as the driver, and when the team takes a sharp turn they help keep the coach stable by leaning out to the opposite side. This action can be compared to sailing in high winds. And if the carriage should ever get stuck, the grooms quickly help push the vehicle back on the track. They will also help calm the horses and unhitch them if necessary. There is no question that it takes excellent teamwork to negotiate a challenging cross-country course four-in-hand.

For a number of years, a neutral fourth person would sit on the box seat beside the driver in major international competitions. This was an extra judge who was responsible for monitoring the negotiation of the cross-country course, as the other judges could not assess the performance adequately from the starting line. This position has been abolished, however, in part because a considerable number of judges got "lost" along the way.

THE TURNOUT

There are various ways of harnessing horses, depending on the type of carriage, the tack, and the number of horses. Gigs or broughams, pulled by just one horse, are very easy to maneuver. A pair means that two horses move side by side, but there is also a variation known as tandem, in which the two horses are harnessed one behind the other. Three horses are either harnessed side by side or with one

leading and the other two behind. The most famous form of carriage drawn by three horses is the Russian Troika draft. Here, the horses are harnessed side by side, but they move in different gaits. While the inside horse trots, the two horses on the outside move in canter. The four-in-hand, with a pair in front and another behind, is often used in competition driving. When the Romans held their chariot races, four horses were harnessed to the quadriga side by side. Five horses were used in Hungary, with three in front and two following. Carriages drawn by eight or six horses were usually drawn by pairs, while the rare team of eleven has one leader and five pairs following.

Competition driving was initially influenced by the British, but in the early twentieth century Benno von Achenbach of Germany developed the style of harness driving significantly. He claimed that harness horses should be trained on the same general principles as riding mounts. For him, the most important aspects of a good horse were subtlety, collection, athletic movement, and responsiveness. The coachman's goal and duty is to make things as easy as possible for the horses, and from the coachman's seat he can only achieve this through voice commands, the reins, and the whip. Von Achenbach, who might be considered the master of modern harness driving, also invented a reining system that enabled contact with each individual horse. The complex arrangement makes perfect sense to a skilled driver, but to a layman that tangle of straps might as well be so much spaghetti. In fact, harness driving is a high art, and a fascinating one. Many enthusiasts find it addictive.

Harness driving involves even more time and effort than show jumping or dressage. There is much to do: the leather tack, reins, and bridles must be oiled; the metal fittings must be polished; and the upkeep of the coach is both time-consuming and expensive. The coach itself is costly, too: a marathon carriage suitable for cross-country driving costs around $13,000.

Splashing through knee-deep ditches with a marathon carriage is highly adventurous and has little to do with what one might imagine as a comfortable coach ride.

In competition, horse driving trials consist of three phases. The first day is dedicated to dressage, and the teams are immaculately turned out in full regalia. The drivers look as if they were heading for Ascot in their morning suits and gray top hats, while the grooms wear livery. The second day of the championship is reserved for the marathon, in which the carriages must complete a cross-country course. Since this includes water ditches and muddy forest tracks, formal attire is exchanged for more practical, waterproof outfits. And just in case of accidents, the drivers and grooms are required to wear helmets. The final competition is back in the arena. This time, the drivers must negotiate an obstacle course marked out with cones. Both dexterity and speed are decisive here, and, of course, the teams again present themselves in their formal best.

All in one hand: there are several kinds of harness driving, from a simple gig drawn by one horse to a carriage drawn by eleven—in which case the driver has his hands full.

When a horse's active career is over, it is time to relax and enjoy. Ludger Beerbaum's band of retirees, here show jumping mare Ratina Z (left) with champion Rush on, enjoy easy living on the paddock and are always pleased to see their former boss.

Career's End

A horse that is ready to retire from active sporting is not necessarily very old, and even an old horse is not necessarily weak. In some cases, the age of a horse can only be verified on inspection of its teeth. After years of grinding, the chewing surface wears down and there may even be a tooth missing. An old horse may also acquire gray hairs in its mane, tail, or face; wrinkles may start to appear around the muzzle, and the eye cavities deepen—none of which matters in pragmatic terms. Experts still cannot agree on whether or not horses care about their appearance. Women riders are more likely to believe it than men, for all the difference it makes. Appearance aside, it remains true that horses aged 20 or more do show signs of slackening. Old age is simply a fact of horses' lives, as it is for humans.

None of that, however, addresses the mount's physical or emotional fitness. Plenty of time in the pasture, the congenial company of other horses, and tender loving care will ensure that any horse carries its age well. In the past, when horses spent almost all their time outdoors and led a more robust life, they could easily reach the age of 40. Today, a 30-year-old horse is already considered something of a Methuselah.

A good horseman or horsewoman can tell when it is time to stop riding a horse. Generally speaking, even an old horse can still be saddled up and put through its paces, although naturally one should avoid over-demanding lessons. Easy dressage lessons maintain a horse's flexibility and should be carried out on a daily basis.

Once the horse's back has sunk it is time to leave the saddle in the tack room for good—but even this does not prevent the old fellow from enjoying mild exercise. Now it is time to repay the horse for years of safe and willing performance by taking it for walks, possibly along an easy forest trail. A senior horse will also usually be the one to maintain peace and order when a group of horses is turned out on the pasture.

FAMOUS RETIREES

Unfortunately, not every horse is lucky enough to be well provided for in old age. Too often, a horse with bones that are too tired to perform a jump or piaffe is treated very unkindly, either cruelly rejected or even sent to the butcher. But top-class competition horsemen and women usually treat their old friends in an exemplary way, and would never allow their former stars to end their days in isolation. No matter how busy a professional stable may be with its competition horses, there is always time to care for the veterans.

Paul Schockemöhle, for example, always came to have a chat with his former wonder horse, the Hanoverian Deister. The two won the European Championships three times. When Deister, who was

The successful mare Ratina Z showed such a perfect jumping technique that her breeder, Leon Melchior, decided to immortalize her in action. He used this photo as a blueprint.

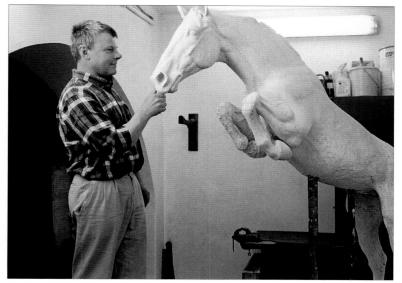

A sculptor made a plaster model based on the photo, which he then used as the prototype for a bronze statue.

famous for his idiosyncratic way of jumping, left the professional circuit in 1989, he had earned his master prizes worth almost a million dollars. At the time, this was an exceptional amount of money. Deister lived to the grand old age of 29.

Ludger Beerbaum, too, takes special care of his senior citizens. He even bought back the mare with which he had begun his sporting career as a teenager. The mare, who was by then 24 years old, was treated like a royalty. The prima donna in the veterans' club, without question, is Ratina Z. She has amassed more medals in Olympic, World Equestrian, and European show jumping championships than any other horse. When she became a retiree, she quickly began a second career as broodmare. Soon after her emotional farewell at the end of the 1999 World Equestrian Games in Aachen, she went on a journey to Mexico. By means of embryo transfers, several surrogate broodmares later gave birth to her foals. At the end of 2000, she returned to her riding partner Ludger Beerbaum, who runs a stable

There are two copies of the statue. Fans of Ratina Z can admire the bronze mare at Ludger Beerbaum's stable in Riesenbeck, Germany, or at the breeder's stud of Zangersheide in Belgium.

in Riesenbeck, Germany, where she is now enjoying the company of the highly attractive equine millionaire Rush on. Rush on was two-time German champion and amassed prize money totaling well over a million dollars. He could also be embarrassingly stubborn at times, however. Once he refused to jump down the big mound at the German Derby in Hamburg. Beerbaum, who would not consider forcing a horse, waved his white kerchief and left the arena with a gracious smile.

The dressage genius Rembrandt was equally stubborn. Even before winning the first of his four Olympic gold medals, he knew he was one in a million, and acted accordingly. Nicole Uphoff tells us that even at the age of 23, a year before he died, he fell for a lady pony and indulged himself by spending whole days in the paddock with her.

Desert Orchid was a highly successful English racehorse whose popularity derived at least in part from his love of performing to the crowd. When he retired in 1991, his public appearances continued and his presence at charity events attracted huge crowds and raised thousands of pounds. When even these had to be curtailed, his love of the crowd continued, and he greeted visitors from his stall until he died peacefully in 2006, at the grand old age of 27.

Comanche

Comanche was long famous as the sole survivor of General George Custer's command at the Battle of the Little Bighorn, Montana, on June 25, 1876.

The bay Mustang Morgan with a little white star on his forehead was born wild. In 1868 he was rounded up, gelded, and sold to the US Army Cavalry. Over the next nine years, he saw much action and sustained many wounds that he bore with courage (he was named after his first battle, when his fighting stamina caused a serious wound to go undetected until after the battle). But none was as bad as those that nearly killed him at Little Bighorn. It was two days before he was discovered and shipped to Fort Lincoln, North Dakota, where he slowly recuperated.

Comanche was formally retired, but he remained at Fort Lincoln, where he developed a taste for beer and roamed freely. He regularly toured the country and was a great crowd-pleaser, leading processions as the caparison (riderless, draped in black, and with reversed boots in the stirrups). When the cavalry was ordered to Fort Riley, Kansas, in 1888 Comanche went with them and continued to receive full honors as a symbol of the tragedy at Little Bighorn until November 1891, when he died at about 29 years of age.

Comanche's preserved body is on display at the University of Kansas Museum of Natural History. He was not, in fact, the *sole* survivor of General Custer's last stand, and the plaque that used to say so has now been removed.

Growing Up with Horses

Even tiny tots are smitten with horses. Happiness is having a pony at your side.

Crazy About Horses

Wherever you go in the world, you will see the same phenomenon on entering a riding stable: girls and more girls! For many young girls, nothing can match their love of horses. They are drawn to them like moths to a candle. No computer game could lure them away from the chores of feeding, grooming, cleaning the stall—and riding. Granted, there will always be some boys who ride, but the girls are generally in the majority, which may (or may not!) please the boys.

What causes the girls' passion for horses and ponies? This phenomenon has been the focus of scientific research and scholars have suggested an explanation. Apparently, females are either born with or encouraged through socialization to develop the desire to nurse and care for other beings. Even toddler girls can be seen cuddling and hugging their teddies and other toys, and any pet that doesn't make itself scarce quickly enough will be caressed and hugged at length.

But there is absolutely no cause for concern if a girl is smitten with horses. Experts are emphatic it is an absolutely natural phase in girls' development when they swap their dolls for ponies and start

Ride a cock-horse
to Banbury cross
To see a fine lady
ride on a white horse
With rings on her fingers
and bells on her toes
She shall have music
wherever she goes!

working on those manes. Often, the quadrupeds are the last cuddly friends the girls have before they become adult women. Between the ages of six and fourteen, growing girls can meet various emotional needs by spending time with horses. On the one hand, a horse is a powerful and strong partner that gives the girl a sense of being protected. On the other hand, she is the driving force in command of the huge horse, and this gives her a sense of confidence in her ability to hold her own among headstrong creatures stronger than herself. More often than not, her interest in horses comes to an abrupt end when a teenage girl meets her first boyfriend—when suddenly she prefers to spend her evenings in a disco rather than a horse stall. Having said that, of course, there will always be life-long horse fanciers who may even make a career on horseback.

Incidentally, the love affair between horses and girls really only began in the mid-twentieth century. Before that—before the ubiquity of the automobile and the motorcycle—riding had been a predominantly male preserve, and only a few women took part in equestrian sports competitions.

Perhaps this accounts for the fact that even today there are more top-grade horsemen than horsewomen, although the number of ladies in competition sports such as show jumping and versatility is rising steadily.

The horse bug usually attacks young girls. On reaching their teens, however, they often shake off the infatuation and move on.

The Theories of Sigmund Freud

In the eighteenth and nineteenth centuries, medical research and discoveries were mostly concerned with healing the physical sickness of people. The scholars throughout the world were astounded when suddenly a previously unknown neurologist from Vienna came up with a set of new theories. Austrian doctor Sigmund Freud was the self-confident scholar who claimed to have analyzed spiritual and psychological phenomena and was now offering to heal "sick souls."

Among other things, Freud studied a five-year-old boy who was afraid of horses. Why would a horse become a threat for the boy? Freud came up with the idea that the boy must have recognized something in the horse that reminded him of his father, of whom he was more or less afraid. The father was less loving to him than his mother was, and the horse

seemed to the boy like some dangerous alien creature that would usurp his place at his mother's side. Freud called this psychological phenomenon the Oedipus complex, and thus made history. Of course, Freud also examined the relation between girls and horses. He made a connection between horseback riding and female sexuality, seeing the size and power of a horse as sexual factors. Freud's daughter, Anna, even interpreted girls' love of horses as a form of penis envy.

Neither theory need be given undue attention, as both have been disproved. At the time, though, Freud's theories were highly acclaimed and were used to explain many complex mechanisms of the human psyche. His revolutionary ideas also influenced art and literature. Writers and philosophers consulted Freud. When poet Rainer Maria Rilke, for example, was feeling desperate, he asked Freud for advice. The

novelist Thomas Mann held a eulogy entitled "Freud and the Future," and even Albert Einstein was eager to discuss various matters with the astute scholar.

But Freud's most ardent admirer and follower was his own daughter, Anna. She published her father's oeuvre in eighteen volumes, and in doing so, succeeded in overturning professional circles in Europe and Northern America all over again. Anna herself established a research-based childcare center in the UK, because she was convinced that the traumatic experience of the boy who was afraid of horses was the key to a competent interpretation of childhood traumas. Thus was Oedipus returned to the fore. Incidentally, the original hero of Greek mythology did not fear horses, but he did kill his own father (whom he did not know) and marry his mother without realizing who she was.

Toy Horses

In the art of the Renaissance, and even in relatively modern photos from the early twentieth century, children's gender can often only be identified by the toys they hold. Girls inevitably held dolls, while little boys bestrode a rocking horse or hobby-horse (a wooden horse head fastened to a stick). Before the advent of motorcars in the twentieth century, boys needed a horse to play at knights, cowboys, Indians, or heroic figures from adventure novels. In the past hundred years these interests have changed, and it is now girls who are more likely to be deeply fascinated by horses.

The toy industry has long since realized the potential of young female customers and there are now a dazzling variety of horse-related items available, from simple plastic horses to elaborate wooden stables, and from fabrics to horse-decorated accessories like jewelry and window shades.

Practice makes perfect! This little cowboy looks ready for the prairie.

Toy horses can be found in every size, shape, and color—there is something for every taste.

Hobby-Horses

The Middle English word *hoby* means a small to medium-sized horse. Among traditional English Morris Dancers, one or two will wear a costume called a hobby-horse and interfere in the dances to amuse the crowd.

For children, however, a hobby-horse is something to ride. It consists of an imitation horse head at the top of a long stick, and children swing one leg over it and gallop around in circles (or not) pretending to be riding a real horse. Adults who continually repeat themselves on one subject are also said to be riding their hobby-horse.

Soft cuddly horses are prized by children. If having a real horse is just not possible, one as appealing as this will help soothe the pain.

Horses in Children's Classics, Past and Future

Black Beauty

Anna Sewell's *Black Beauty* is a much-loved children's classic. Originally published in 1877 as *Black Beauty: The Autobiography of a Horse*, it features a stunningly beautiful black horse as a first-person narrator that relates the ups and downs in the life of a horse. It is an exciting and moving story that encourages people to be less cruel towards animals.

Fury

The story by playwright and children's author Albert G. Miller about the young orphan Joey Clark and the black stallion named Fury grew to cult status after the TV series of the same name in the 1960s. Joey reads in the paper that a mustang named Fury has been caught and is being kept at Jim Newton's Broken Wheel Ranch. The curious boy sets off to see the horse and finds happiness in various ways. The wild stallion and the boy immediately become friends, and the rancher is so taken with the boy that he adopts him. When it is rumored that Fury is responsible for a man's death, it is up to Joey to prove his best friend's innocence.

The Black Stallion

Walter Farley wrote fifteen volumes about a black Arab stallion who saves the life of a young boy named Alec and later turns into a famous American flat-race horse. The first book of the series was published in 1941, titled *The Black Stallion*. In countless interviews, Walter Farley emphasized that he had been an avid horse lover even as a young boy and had started his first book about the Black Stallion at the age of 11. His son, Steven, continued the father's legacy and in 1996 began to publish additional stories about the Black Stallion, his friends and offspring.

Flicka

My Friend Flicka is the title of a book by Mary O'Hara, written in 1941. It was filmed shortly afterward and a remake was filmed in 2006. It is the story of the friendship between a dreamy young boy named Kenneth McLaughlin and a wild Mustang filly called Flicka. In the second volume, *Thunderhead*, which was published in 1943, Flicka gives birth to a colt named Thunderhead. A third book, *Green Grass of Wyoming*, was published in 1946. In this book, the young Kenneth has grown into a mature adolescent.

Heartland

Lauren Brooke's Heartland series features highly emotional plots designed specifically for horse-crazy girls. The stories relate the heartrending story of Amy Flemming, a 15-year-old American girl who has to learn to cope alone after the loss of her mother. Fortunately, she has inherited her mother's talents of being able to help traumatized and frightened horses through alternative methods. Being with horses helps Amy overcome her own grief. The story offers an interesting view of the psyche of horses.

Misty of Chincoteague

Marguerite Henry has written many enduring horse stories for children, but the *Misty* series is her classic. Set on an island off the coast of Virginia and Maryland, the story tells of a boy and a girl and a band of wild ponies led by an extraordinary mare, Phantom. Through her foal Misty, born wild and adopted by two children, the conflicting needs of people and the wild are powerfully shown.

The Saddle Club

The Saddle Club is a horse-book series published between 1988 and 2001. American author Bonnie Bryant and several ghostwriters wrote more than 100 volumes about three girls—Lisa, Stephanie (Stevie), and Carole—who are united in their love of horses. The trio has adventurous challenges and must prove their horsemanship before overcoming all kinds of difficulties. Themes include responsible treatment of horses, fairness in competition, and friendship and standing by one another.

Those who are not yet ready to ride could always play at coachman.

Welcome to the Circus!

When the curtains are raised and beautifully trimmed horses trot into the arena, children's eyes widen and sparkle, growing nearly as wide as the circus arena itself. The word *circus* can be traced back to ancient Rome, where round arenas were given the name circus. Even in ancient Greece and Rome, the crowd couldn't remain seated when horses performed artistic movements. Trick horse riding—when horses gallop around inside a narrow tent, the centrifugal force of the tight circle aiding the riders in their athletic performances—is spectacular in effect. One person to realize this was English riding instructor Philip Astley, who in 1769 opened the first circus, in London. He designed the circus ring with a diameter of 42 feet, which remains the norm today. This was the start of a new era for the circus, featuring innovative acts such as trick horse riding, acrobats, tightrope walkers, clowns, and jugglers.

Venetian-born Antonio Franconi, whose circus performed in Paris, raised horseback riding in the circus to the *haute école* level known only in the Spanish Riding School in Vienna. He also introduced various dressage performances with other animals.

In fact, freestyle dressage performances including elements with fire and water became so popular that venues were constructed

This pony is pretending to be a puppet on a string. The trick only works because Pignon has successfully coaxed his horses to work with him rather than forcing them.

especially for these spectacular horse shows, such as the London Hippodrome. The circus experienced a great wave of popularity. Traveling circuses toured all over North America and built circus theaters in many cities they visited. Modern circus entrepreneurs introduced a combination of menagerie and vaudeville with horses, as well as wild animals such as elephants, lions, tigers, and camels. In 1825, Joshuah Purdy Brown was the first to use a gigantic canvas tent for his circus performance. The American circus was revolutionized by P. T. Barnum's Museum, Menagerie & Circus, the first to travel by circus train.

Horse shows at the circus delight both young and old, which is why circuses large and small usually feature a horse act.

As a result of his exceptional horse dressage acts—which are achieved entirely without force—and also because of his exceptional and rather idiosyncratic horses, Pignon's horse shows are world famous.

Animals used to perform for fear of being punished, but those days are long gone. Today's circus audiences can be sure the animals are treated well. Contemporary animal trainers use the insights of modern dressage, analyzing the natural behavior of the animals and respecting their individuality. Voice and body language are all a horse trainer needs to ask spirited stallions to put on astonishing performances. The audience is thrilled as horses rear onto two legs and walk on their hind legs, then immediately return to their place in the circle before performing the next exercise, such as kneeling down or curtseying. With no halter, the horses could bolt at any time, but they will not. They obey their trainer because they accept him as highest in rank.

The art of equestrian display is quite rare, because the trainer needs special talent in building a relationship with his horses. Jean-François Pignon is renowned for breathtaking equestrian displays; Pignon and his magical white horses put on perhaps the best show in the world.

Pignon's horseback comedy, Le Padron, includes a band of 15 horses as well as 23 artists and a dozen musicians. It is a romantic story about two quarreling clans and their reconciliation.

Horse Musicals

These days, horses have even conquered show business. Their well-trod stage is not made of wooden boards but of sand, where horses feel most comfortable. After intense training, these horses do not mind the limelight, colorful spotlights, loud music or sound effects. And like human performers, they seem to feed on applause.

The plot of a horse show might be the fight of good against evil, or the story might be set in a dream world. In 1995, Swiss-born Dieter Speidel produced one of the first horse musicals in Zurich. Circus pioneer Franz Althoff picked up the idea and organized a horse musical in cooperation with Günther Fröhlich. Setting a custom-designed tent and extravagant stagecraft around Goa, Prince of Darkness, they toured numerous cities. This was followed by Equi Magic, the story of a little girl's dream journey.

Various breeds belong to the ensemble, but most are baroque horses like Friesians and Andalusians. Apart from classical dressage exercises there are also acts with cowboys, horse stunts, and other equestrian displays. Sometimes the riders have brief speaking parts, and there may be live music and singing. Musicals and gala events featuring horses (such as Appassionata) have seen such a boom in Europe that even the biggest venues are sold out. Increasing numbers of children who go horseback riding yearn to perform in similar shows, and even small riding stables are organizing horse musicals. This lets young enthusiasts enjoy watching their horses perform to music without having to pay extravagant ticket prices.

There is a saying that goes, "Happiness is found on the back of a horse." Passionate riders would instantly agree, with one caveat: happiness is found not only on horseback, but anywhere in close proximity to a horse.

Friends for Life

If the only important issue were whether to ride English style, Western, or Iberian, the would-be rider might just as well buy a motorbike.

All those who take it upon themselves to spend time with a horse are fully responsible for the creatures entrusted to them. This statement is part of the rules and regulations issued by the German Riding Association. It means that before deciding to take up horseback riding or even buy a horse, it is essential to understand that time in the saddle is only part of the time spent with the horse, and a relatively small part at that. Learning to ride can only lead to satisfactory results if the rider is sensitive to the other creature, getting to know its character and its needs and taking care of it appropriately.

What makes people want to spend so much time with a horse? Do men enjoy the action and the camaraderie, and women the whispers and closeness before and after the ride? Although some riders do behave in this clichéd manner, the relationship between horse and rider is anything but this simple. Olympic dressage champion Isabell Werth has described the relationship in this way: *The communication is a constant learning process. The goal and the challenge lies in developing a mutual language, in finding a thread that will lead you through to every individual horse.*

All riders must accept the fact that they cannot simply force their will on a horse. If it should come to a showdown of physical strength, the horse would win in any case. Even a pony or a foal can easily put

a grown man out of action if it gets panicky. So the hierarchy has to be settled in some other way, because it is essential that the rider is boss. Otherwise, life can get very complicated and even dangerous for horse and rider. It is no joke working with a horse that knows its powers and uses them to act against a person's will, so riders must win the horse's trust by treating it with gentleness and understanding and by presenting appropriate challenges—because a bored horse will begin to rebel. Only clear, precise directions will produce the desired results. If your own behavior is ambiguous, the horse will become insecure. Horses and ponies are sensitive creatures that need to be treated fairly, and they quickly learn to distinguish praise from blame. A sudden unwarranted outburst of fury from the rider is inexcusable, and will severely damage the relationship with the horse. A good sportsman will always seek the fault in himself before blaming the mount, and this is usually indeed where the problem lies. Even successful riders must face setbacks. "Dealing with horses is as complex, individual, and personal as life itself," says Ludger Beerbaum, who has won several Olympic show-jumping competitions. And if there is an apparent sore point in the training session, it's always a good idea to change plans and relax. It may seem too obvious to consider, but riding out together in the countryside can often work miracles.

Spending time at a riding stable makes it clear to everyone when the chemistry is right between horse and rider. As soon as the person to whom the horse relates most closely enters the stable, the quadruped will recognize their footsteps, and it will whinny and come to the door to greet "its" person and receive the anticipated apple or other treat. When the rider is a stressed townie who has just come

BOOT, SADDLE, TO HORSE, AND AWAY!

Rescue my castle before the hot day
Brightens to blue from its silvery gray,
Boot, saddle, to horse, and away!

Ride past the suburbs, asleep as you'd say;
Many's the friend there, will listen and pray
"God's luck to gallants that strike up the lay—
Boot, saddle, to horse, and away!"

Forty miles off, like a roebuck at bay,
Flouts Castle Brancepeth the Roundheads' array:
Who laughs, "Good fellows ere this, by my fay,
Boot, saddle, to horse, and away!"

Who? My wife Gertrude; that, honest and gay,
Laughs when you talk of surrendering, "Nay!
I've better counsellors; what counsel they?
'Boot, saddle, to horse, and away!'"

Robert Browning, 1812-1889,
from *Cavalier Tunes*

Many riders enjoy riding out much more than training in the arena. This is especially true for people tied to an office with little leisure time, who savor extended rides in the country or along the beach, great relaxation for humans and quadrupeds alike.

from an exhausting day in the office, this enthusiastic welcome is particularly therapeutic. Horses do many things well, but they never feign. They are free of envy, are usually of a cheerful disposition, and they are anything but cold and calculating. Their only vice may be an insatiable appetite. Horses being the way they are, spending time with them is an enormously positive experience for the human soul.

Straight from the Horse's Mouth

There are many sayings that originated in the world of horses. Getting information *straight from the horse's mouth* means it comes from the highest source and is not to be questioned. It stems from the fact that a horse's true age can be determined with certainty by examining its incisors.

To *tell something to the horse marines* means to tell an absurd story others do not believe, while one who *belongs to the horse marines* is an awkward new recruit who lacks necessary skills.

The proverb *you can lead a horse to water, but you can't make him drink* means that you can provide an opportunity, but there comes a point when a person will not be influenced or forced by any means to take advantage of it.

A *dark horse* is a person whose capabilities are not generally known and who will wait for the right moment to reveal them to the best advantage. *Get down off your high horse* is a warning to stop acting superior to others; people can also *climb onto their high horse* or *get knocked off of their high horse*.

Your horse will become a genuine partner if you refuse to look on it as a mere sports apparatus and instead acknowledge it as a creature with its own mind. A good riding instructor will point this out during the very first lesson.

Well Equipped

Before mounting a horse, it is important to have all the necessary equipment. Only then will you be able to really enjoy your ride. Certain body parts must be properly protected to prevent abrasions, blisters, and bruising through riding.

Riding pants, called jodhpurs or breeches, are indispensable for regular riding. They can only have been devised by someone who knew what suffering is. Unlike ordinary pants, their seams do not run along the inside of the leg; instead, they are on the outside to prevent the legs from getting sore. Leather panels on the insides of the knees or running from the seat to the ankle help maintain the legs' grip on the saddle, because leather on leather is not as slippery as fabric on leather. Also, while riding pants must be comfortable, they should not pucker. Jodhpurs can be found in various colors—and even patterns—to suit every taste. For competition entry, however, the rules specify white or light beige-colored pants.

The lower third of the jodhpurs is covered by riding boots, which can be made of leather or rubber. Leather is more expensive, but a novice rider will be fine with ordinary rubber boots or Wellies, as long as they are not too wide in the shaft. Ankle boots can be worn with jodhpurs whose leather panel extends to the ankles. Another popular alternative is leather half-chaps. These are leather panels fastened around the lower leg with velcro. One vital aspect of shoes for horseback riding is that they must have a small heel to prevent the foot from sliding forward through the stirrups. They should not have a tongue, though, because this can be quite dangerous if the feet get entangled in the stirrups during a fall.

Hands are also vulnerable to soreness, especially for novices who do not yet know how to hold the reins properly. Gloves of leather, or with padded fingers, will meet this need, especially for those with sweaty hands.

Protecting the head is the most important factor of all and should not be taken lightly. Children should never mount a horse without an appropriate and well-fit helmet fastened under their chin. Many adults ride without a helmet, which is really quite negligent. Even the best rider can fall off a horse, and safety always comes before looking good.

The most important items of riding attire are a safety helmet and good shoes. Special riding pants are practical because the seams are on the outside of the leg and thus prevent sores. Whether you need gloves and a whip depends on the horse.

Bootjack

A bootjack is a wooden appliance with a U-shaped heel grip to help pull off riding boots; one can be found in every riding yard. When the wealthy still had armies of personal servants, the original bootjack was a man who waited for the horseman to return and dismount. The bootjack would then turn his back on the master, swing one leg over the boot, grab it by the heel, and wait to be kicked in the buttocks—a simple means for pulling off the tight boot which is still used today if the wooden bootjack is missing.

A bootjack of either kind is needed because a rider's body warms up while riding, which tends to make the legs and feet swell; the boot shaft becomes too tight to just slip off after the ride. We have to believe the human jacks were relieved when the wooden kind appeared on the market!

Depending on the weather, temperature, and event, there is a choice of jacket, vest, and coat (called a tailcoat in the UK and a shadbelly in the USA). In competition, every participant is expected to wear a coat. There are various colors for the various disciplines. In dressage, for example, the classic outfit is a black coat, whereas in show jumping the coat is red. But the range of coat colors to be seen in jumper classes is expanding all the time, and some participants in dressage now wear navy. Leisure riders may wear any kind of jacket, as long as it has side vents to allow it to stretch over the hips. For riding cross-country, choose one that is waterproof and windproof and has a hood. If the climate is too warm for a jacket, a vest is the best alternative. Bear in mind that a mere polo shirt may not be warm enough at full gallop.

The riding attire market is served by specialist manufacturers that cater to every need and taste. The possibilities range from the practical and relatively inexpensive to costly elegance and luxury.

Western riding spurs may look fearsome, but when attached to the boots of an experienced rider, they are far more innocuous than they seem. The little wheels at their end tend to make them roll off a horse's flank rather than sticking into its body.

Winning and Dishing Up Spurs

In the Middle Ages, winning one's spurs was the highest goal of any horseman, because it meant he had gained the rank of knighthood. These spurs were usually made of gold and would have to be won by competing in various tournaments and skirmishes. The macabre other end of the story is that some knights would later degenerate into robber barons— and lose both their head and their spurs when they were eventually captured.

Even today it is said that someone has "won their spurs" when their efforts are recognized.

In Scotland, when food was becoming scarce, the lady of the house would serve a plate of spurs, or dish up spurs, for dessert as a signal that it was time to raid England and fetch more cattle.

Riding Aids: Whip and Spurs

Like medieval knights, today's riders must also win their spurs. That is, they must become good horsemen and women before being permitted to wear spurs. Only someone with a controlled seat can be certain they are not constantly pricking the horse's sides. Generally, the riding instructor will tell students when they are advanced enough to wear spurs. To avoid injuries, one should always start with dull spurs (see photo).

Even a novice can handle a short whip or riding crop of approximately 3 feet (and some school mounts make its use indispensable). Advanced riders use a longer whip for dressage in an indoor arena and a short crop for jumper class and when riding cross-country.

In the end, however, whip and spurs are nothing but additional aids. They are meant to complement the aids given by the rider, not replace them, and they must never be used to hurt the horse.

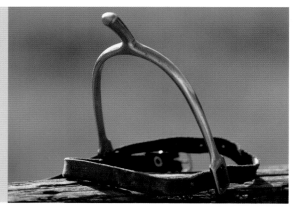

Bridles and Hackamores

There are few differences between the riding tack used by ancient Romans and the bits and bridles of today, though we do have more choice. All are based on the same principle, which is to communicate a change of tempo or direction to the horse. These messages are sent via physical pressure against the horse. The horse senses the pressure either on the bridge of the nose or inside the mouth. The hackamore (training halter) puts pressure on the nose, while a bridle puts pressure on the mouth via the attached bit. Even this brief description shows what a highly sensitive affair this is, because the pain barrier can be reached quickly and (unfortunately) breached easily.

Snaffle bits are the most commonly used. As a rule of thumb, thick, jointed bits are more gentle than thin, straight mouthpieces.

The range of bridles on display in a tack shop or store can be daunting at first, but they can be reduced to four basic categories: snaffle, curb, double bridle, and bitless bridle (halter or hackamore). A bridle has nothing to do with fashion or appearance—it must be carefully chosen to suit the needs of the individual horse. Above all, it should fit the horse's anatomy, and it should never be intimidating. If the mount becomes afraid of the bridle, this can lead to irreparable harm.

Most working horses are ridden with a bridle that has a mouthpiece, called a bit. There are a range of bits made of metal or rubber, and they can be attached to a snaffle, curb, or double bridle. The bit is placed in the horse's mouth. As long as the bit is the right size, it will not disturb the horse in the least, as there is plenty of room between its jaws. As it happens, horses have a space just behind their front incisors, like a missing tooth, and this is where the bit is placed. When the rider pulls the reins, the horse feels the pressure on the gums, or bars. The most widespread bit—used by novices and

There are numerous possibilities for choosing a bridle. The one pictured here is a standard bridle with snaffle bit and leather reins. The bridle should be appropriate for the horse and fit well. Always check the condition of the bridle, because a broken strap can lead to serious injuries.

Proverbs!

Changing horses in midstream means to alter plans or views in the middle of a project.

Beating a dead horse means trying to bring up a subject that no one is interested in.

To eat like a horse is an expression for people who eat a great deal, even if it doesn't show.

Hold your horses is said to someone who is moving ahead too fast (carriage driving).

To be on a high horse is to be overbearing and arrogant.

To *lock the stable door after the horse has bolted* (or been stolen) is to take precautionary measures too late.

To set the cart before the horse is to do things in the wrong order.

A horse of a different color is a person that is completely different from others.

Someone with *horse sense* has a plain, good sense.

Horses for courses means choosing people with appropriate talents for the task in hand.

A willing horse never wants work means that a willing worker will never lack for things to do, as lazier people will be happy to offload their own work onto him or her.

The 15 points of a good horse: Wynkyn de Worde made a list published in 1496 stating that a good horse should have three properties each of a woman, a man, a fox, a hare, and of an ass. These are: fair breast, hair, and easy to move (woman); boldness, pride, and hardiness (man); fair tail, short ears, good trot (fox); great eye, dry head, running well (hare); as well as a big chin, flat leg, and good hoof (ass).

The bosal works without a bit. A skilled rider like show jumper Jürgen Krackow can ride astonishingly successful courses even with such a gentle bridle.

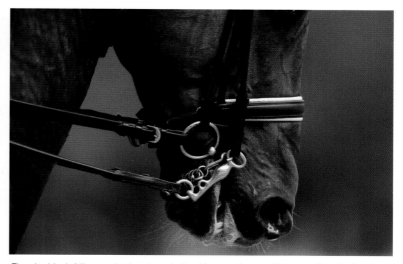

The double bridle can be harsh and should never be used by a novice. Professional dressage riders apply it gently, and for high-grade competitions this bridle is a must.

professionals alike in English riding style—is the snaffle. There are different forms of snaffle bit, the most common having a single joint to ensure the pressure is applied relatively gently. The double-jointed snaffle bit is even more gentle on the horse. Where the snaffle functions by putting direct pressure on the mouth, the curb works through a system of levers. Curbs have shanks on the mouthpiece that create leverage and apply pressure to the poll, chin groove, and mouth of the horse. The curb bit is usually made in a single piece, and is not jointed.

The bit is attached to the bridle, of which there are also myriad variations. It always consists of a crown piece behind the ears, which is directly attached to the bit ring. The browband, caveson across the nose, and throat latch make sure the bridle stays in place.

The double bridle (and the Pelham bit) should really only be used by skilled horsemen. It requires the aids to be given very subtly and if applied by a novice can seriously hurt and damage the horse. The double bridle gives the rider four reins in hand. Two reins are thicker and are attached to the bradoon (a modified snaffle bit), while the two finer reins lead to the curb and are called curb reins. The horse has two mouthpieces with shanks at the side and a curb chain running underneath the chin. The double bridle allows the rider to put pressure on the jaw, the head, and the chin of the horse. Depending on the form of the curb bit and how much space the horse's tongue has inside the mouth, the curb can also apply pressure on the gum. This might all sound like an apparatus for torture, but in fact double bridles are required for advanced-level dressage tests and allow a very subtle communication between rider and mount, which is essential for top-class competitions.

The Pelham bit is a variant of the curb and consists of a single mouthpiece attached to shanks. It can be made of metal or rubber, and works on the same principle as the double bridle.

Laymen tend to think that a bitless bridle is more gentle, but this is not the case. The mechanical hackamore, which is predominantly used in Western riding styles and for show jumping, puts pressure on the horse's nose, which is very sensitive, by means of long metal shanks that work as leverage.

The liberty neck ring was developed by Canadian horsewoman Linda Tellington-Jones. It should only be used by a pair that knows and trusts each other well. Neck rings are available in various sizes.

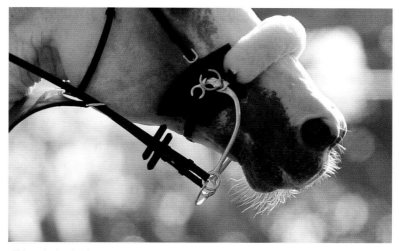

Although the hackamore works without a bit, it can nevertheless be extremely harsh and painful because the horse's nose, where the hackamore exerts pressure, is highly sensitive.

"To bite on the bridle"
"To take the bit between the teeth"

The true hackamore, on the other hand, is certainly the gentlest way of haltering. It consists of a braided noseband (called the bosal), which is connected to a rope. The rope takes the place of more customary reins and ends in the rider's hands. The noseband is fairly loose and held in place by a leather strap that runs along the crown. This bridle can only be used when horse and rider are a well-trained team, because the opportunity for acting on the horse is much reduced.

Saddled Up

A rider's seat depends heavily on the kind of saddle used. There are many possible ways of cushioning horse and rider. While it is important that the rider should feel comfortable, the crucial factor when buying a saddle is that it is suited for the body of the horse. If the saddle rubs against part of the horse's back and the problem goes undetected for too long, the horse will get bad sores. In that case, the rider can choose between staying off the horse's back for a while, or using the oldest method in the world—going bare back. Bareback riding is certainly an experience not be missed, but is far less comfortable than riding with a saddle.

Comfort is probably the reason riding peoples invented saddles in the first place. The Scythians strapped rugs onto their horses, while the Sarmatians developed the first wooden saddle tree. Saddles were created in response to the needs of the time. The knights of the Middle Ages, for example, needed very different saddles from the cavalry officers of the seventeenth and eighteenth centuries.

Today's standard English saddle was largely influenced by Italian riding instructor Federico Caprilli, who always worked to ensure perfect balance between horse and rider, regardless of the movement. To achieve this when jumping, for example, the horseman rises up in the stirrups and shifts his center of gravity forward to relieve the

Stirrups

Without question, the most practical item ever invented by saddle makers is the stirrup. It allows for greater comfort and better balance for riders, which means that they can remain in the saddle much longer without becoming exhausted. The improved balance also helps prevent falling off the horse too easily. The seat-stabilizing property of stirrups was particularly appreciated in battle by the cavalry, who were continually fending off foot soldiers trying to unseat them.

It is believed that stirrups were invented many centuries ago in Mongolia. Attila, the famous king of the Huns, is said to have ridden with stirrups that would hold either the entire foot or simply the ball of the foot. Prior to that, however, Indians had invented a kind of precursor to the stirrup consisting of a small leather latch to hold just the big toe. That toe stirrup is still used in Asian countries such as India, Malaysia, and Singapore—even for flat racing.

jumping horse. To make this movement easier for the rider, a special jumping saddle was developed in the mid-twentieth century.

Now there are different saddles for every equestrian discipline. Whether it is for eventing, reining or dressage, the aim is always to help the rider achieve a perfectly balanced riding seat. There are special, extremely light weight saddles for racehorses, and of course saddles for ponies. For those with a soft spot for the old days, it is also possible to purchase a side saddle as originally used by women riders.

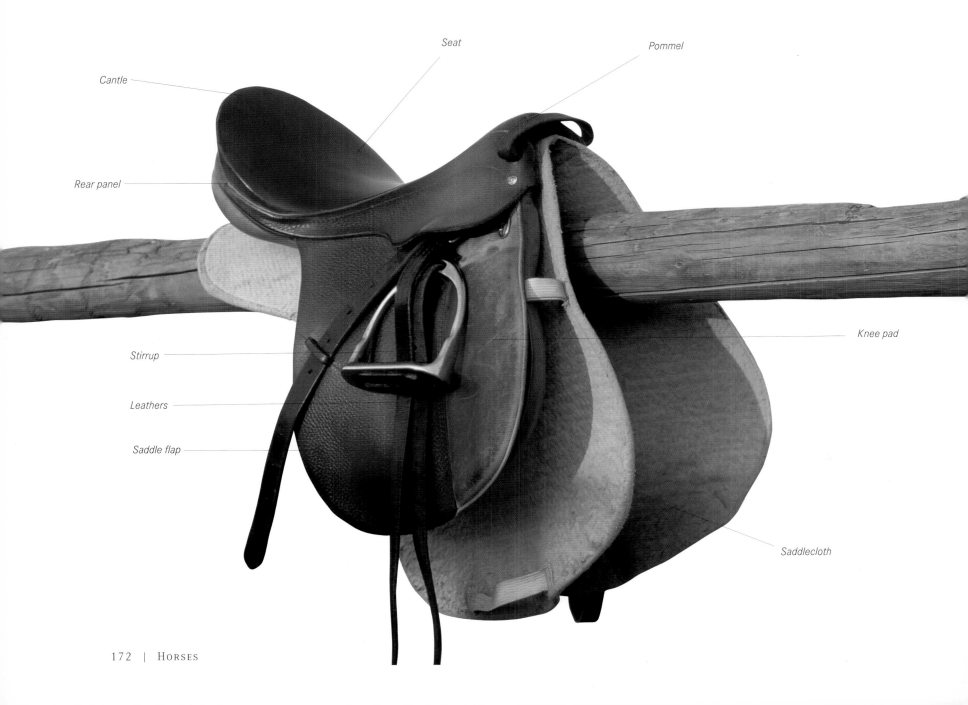

Seat

Pommel

Cantle

Rear panel

Stirrup

Leathers

Saddle flap

Knee pad

Saddlecloth

The first stage in making a new saddle is cutting the leather. An appropriate stencil for the desired saddle is laid on the leather and its shape traced with a pencil. Specialized sharp tools are used for cutting the leather.

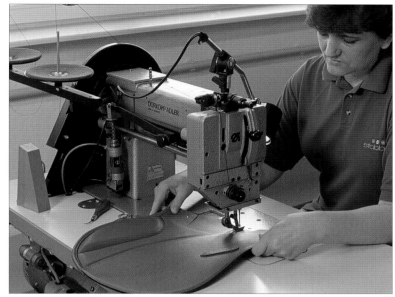

The separate leather pieces are carefully sewn together with a heavy-duty sewing machine. A special, extra durable yarn is used.

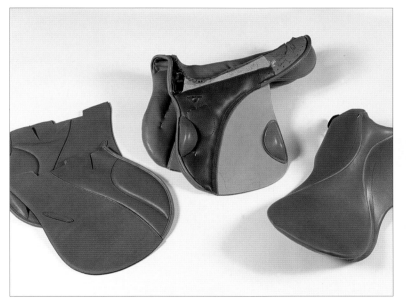

The main parts of the saddle are ready to be put together: saddle flaps (left), saddle tree (center), and seat (right).

The pre-sewn leather pieces are now mounted onto the saddle tree. To prevent abrasions on the body of the horse, the saddle is then upholstered.

The saddle is almost complete. With a very strong needle, the final seams are sewn closed by hand.

The completed saddle is then placed on a horse-shaped barrel and inspected. If it passes muster, the saddle is ready for the store–and for horseback.

Food and Drink

When we say somebody eats like a horse, we mean someone who eats indiscriminately and in great quantity. In fact, though, a horse's stomach is acutely sensitive, and in relation to the volume of the whole body, it is also relatively small. A horse's stomach only holds about 3–3½ gallons. For this reason, a horse (which would never stop eating if left to itself) should not be allowed to eat too much at a time. To avoid overworking the stomach, horses should be fed three times a day.

That small stomach is anything but a design flaw. On the contrary, the first horses that lived in the vast steppes would spend their days peacefully grazing, moving about at a leisurely pace and nibbling at the sparse grass. This continual feeding is not available to most horses today, but it is the origin of the ideal of several small meals rather than two large ones. Best of all would be to serve up five meals a day—but this is beyond the personnel capacities of most riding stables, and three meals do very well.

There is no uniform dietary plan for horses. Each horse must have its own regime, because what suits one could well be wrong for another. Much depends on the individual digestion of the horse and, of

The Problem with Oats

A horse that eats too many oats will soon feel a slight tickle in its stomach, which could turn into a full-blown irritation. The horse will become fidgety and excitable. This power grain is not listed as a doping substance, but it does contain a lot of dopamine, which has the effect of increasing activity levels. This, at least, is what doctors say about horses that have eaten too many oats.

course, on the amount of work it is required to do. A sporting horse will need a greater quantity and different type of food than one who is owned by a leisure rider, and a broodmare will need more feed than a gelding.

A leisure horse that is exercised no more than two hours a day will need about 2½ lb of concentrated feed, plus approximately 2½ lb of roughage per 2½ cwt (280 lb) body weight. A horse weighs approximately 10 cwt (½ ton, or 1120 lb), which means it needs 11 lb of oats and 11 lbs of hay per day. If the stall footing is made of straw, the horse will most likely nibble some of that, too. Some horses absolutely adore eating straw, but none should eat more than 6 lb extra straw per day.

It is very important that the horse has easy access to water and can drink whenever it feels like it. A horse will easily drink an average of 8–10 gallons a day or more. An automatic drinking trough makes things much easier for horse and groom.

In the end, it is the same for people and for horses: food and drink can soothe the soul.

Hay is for Horses

Horses pay keen attention to hay, perhaps because they have to eat relatively slowly. Because horses only have one small stomach, they need to eat often, and also to chew much longer than other ruminants, such as cows. With such prolonged repetition it is important to prevent boredom. Research has shown that horses perk up noticeably when they are fed more than three times a day, or when the hay is placed in more than one location, or—best of all—when several varieties of hay are offered!

Picnic at the pasture. Many horses like their roughage straight from the bale. Just be careful that they don't eat too much out of sheer appetite.

Horses cavorting about the paddock have not necessarily had an overdose of oats—but it is certainly possible, as oats boost their energy.

"You can keep your litter and your hay
and your oats. Long live the thistles of the field,
for there you can play the stallion to
your heart's content."

François Rabelais, French author

A Horse's Appendix

The equine appendix, which has a capacity of about 8 gallons, is so enormous that it is difficult to conceive of the excruciating pain a horse with appendicitis must suffer. The comparison to our own situation must stop there, however, since we humans can easily live a normal life without our appendix, while for horses it is an indispensable part of their digestive system.

A range of microbes are required to properly break down food in the intestines. These are found in the appendix. and while busily processing the food, they also break down the cellulose (which makes up the larger part of the food) as a by-product. These microscopic creatures are highly welcome, because if the horse could not digest its food properly, it would starve despite having a full stomach.

Be careful not to overdo it with handing out these treats: too many juicy apples can lead to colic.

Horses love carrots, and the vegetables are also an important source of beta carotene.

Many horses adore bananas (which should be peeled before the horse eats them).

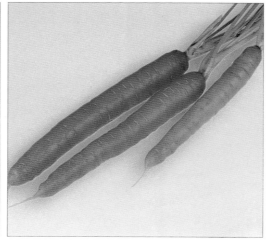

A stall that opens to the outside ensures plenty of fresh air, a nice view, and ideally, fun with the neighbors.

Stall Beautiful

Would you move into a dark hole without daylight or fresh air? Probably not. Or what if your home was so small that you would prefer to spend every possible daylight minute outdoors? You probably wouldn't like that, either. Think of it from a horse's perspective, and treat your horse as you would yourself: don't make it live in conditions that you would not accept for yourself. It is not that your horse will want a sunny balcony, roof terrace, or seaside view—but the climate within the stable must be good.

The most important factor for ensuring a healthy climate in the stable is making sure that plenty of fresh air is circulating. To prevent infections and respiratory diseases, there should be a humidity of between 60 and 80 percent and a constant, light breeze. Cleaning out the stall regularly—removing the horse manure and adding fresh bedding material—is the best means of ensuring your horse's well-being.

Upright Housing

Before the end of World War II, horses were generally kept in large communal stalls and were tied up to stand next to one another with only a pole in between them. At that time, the concept of animal rights was almost unknown. A horse employed in military service simply had to be at the ready, and this was the most practical solution. The horses were tied to a long rope and had a maximum space of 10 x 6 ft. There was little room for them to move about. It should also be pointed out, though, that military and agricultural horses were out working all day and were only in the stall at night. So their living conditions worked better in practice than might be expected—although they would not do for today's horses, who sometimes spend 23 hours in the stall, waiting for their rider to appear.

Horses feel most comfortable in a light and airy surrounding, but unfortunately it is a minority of horses that live in sunlit stalls. The minimum appropriate amount of daylight can be gauged as about 1 square yard of window per horse. As for the size of the stall, it can be measured by the rule of thumb of multiplying the square of the horse's or pony's height at the withers by two. In other words, the one-room-apartment of a horse standing 16.1 hands (65 inches) should be close to 60 sq ft: $(2 \times 65^2) \div 144 \ (1 \ \text{ft}^2) = 58.68$. If the horse's stall is much smaller than this, the horse could become jammed when it lies down to sleep at night, and need help to get back to its feet.

Horses enjoy watching what goes on around them and having eye contact with their neighbors. Of course, these neighbors are not always the best of friends, and they easily quarrel around feeding time, but the social contact is very important for herd animals and will make for some entertainment on a long winter's day.

These days, providing running water should be a matter of course. Horses are thirsty creatures and they must have easy access to plenty of fresh, clean water. An automatic drinking trough should be attached to the wall at a height of about 3 feet. This will allow the horses to drink whenever they wish, day or night. The manger should be set at approximately the same height and filled with foodstuff three times a day. Additional straw makes a welcome between-meals nibble.

The stone floor of a box should be covered with a thick layer of footing, as it serves as a mattress for the night. The footing usually consists of straw, but for horses that tend to consume the carpeting, wood shavings may be used instead. A thorough visual inspection is mandatory before moving any horse into a new stall: every corner must be checked for sharp edges and all power lines and light switches must be out of reach. Remember, the last to leave puts out the light, and this really should be a person.

These stalls are very elegant and comfortable. Although the new resident will be "behind bars," every stall with a footing of wood shavings offers plenty of room for moving about.

Equine Feng Shui

Feng Shui for the office, the living room, the bedroom, the garden, and the balcony—undoubtedly, there will also be Feng Shui for the fridge at some point! By that time, though, the invisible energy sources and the people who specialize in locating them will have long conquered the riding yards. The idea has great potential, as horses are said to be highly sensitive to the free flow of energy.

The first principle of Feng Shui is to allow a free flow and consequently an improvement of the Qi (or Chi), which stands for life energy. The idea is to keep your immediate surrounding free of straight, pointed, or even sharp outlines, because these are thought to foster the Sha, which is negative energy.

But applying Feng Shui at a riding yard involves something other than these formal issues (which would be difficult to resolve, anyway). No matter how strongly a person believes in the power of Qi and Sha, they are hardly going to make major structural alterations merely because the entrance is in the wrong place.

Feng Shui for horses seeks instead to improve the well-being of every horse—which can be negatively affected by a variety of things. There are always cases when a horse behaves inexplicably and the veterinarian is stumped. For example, it is quite common for a horse to balk at entering its stall, and to seem very tense and nervous once inside. This is exactly the kind of situation that lends itself to Feng Shui. The specialist will probably arrive with a dowsing rod and make some specific inquiries, possibly suspecting a very strong energy field underneath the stall. A water vein, for example, would explain the horse's restlessness. The issue is quickly clarified with the help of two metal batons. These are held loosely as the dowser walks through the stall. If there is indeed a water vein, the batons

Feng Shui

Literally translated, Feng Shui means "wind and water." The ancient Chinese art of bringing one's habitat into harmonious unity with nature is over 5,000 years old.

The origin of Feng Shui lies in Taoism, one of the three major Chinese philosophies. For centuries, the Chinese have been taking aspects of Feng Shui into consideration when constructing new buildings and even cities.

In the modern capitals of Asia, it is routine procedure to call in a Feng Shui consultant when designing new offices. Businesses in America and Europe are also increasingly interested in Feng Shui advice. The goal is to allow Qi, the positive life energy, to flow freely, while hindering the negative energy, Sha.

will draw together and cross, as if by magic. In the face of such evidence, it is hard to cling to disbelief—although many do.

Today, dowsing is called radiaesthetic evaluation, and Feng Shui consultants will advise that energy fields detectable in this way create disturbances to which horses (and some people) are highly sensitive. They explain that these energy fields cover the entire earth like a network, and that while some creatures enjoy powerful energy radiance, others feel very uncomfortable in such an environment. Cats, for instance, who are known to enjoy snuggling up on top of the television, cope well with high energy, as do bees and ants, who prefer to build their hives and anthills on top of highly energetic fields. Horses, dogs, and humans, on the other hand, cope less well with powerful energy fields and prefer resting in fields with lower radiation. That is why they can feel uneasy if the energetic field in their immediate environment is too powerful.

Like any human home, Feng Shui requires that a horse's or pony's stall be free of negative energy fields. When the life force flows freely, horses are fitter and healthier.

The Feng Shui consultant who finds such an energy field in a home will advise the owner to move the furniture. In the riding yard, most practical response for the troubled horse is to move it to another stall, where it will almost certainly calm down.

Critics claim that the dowsing rods' movement is caused by the ideomotor effect, a term coined by W.B. Carpenter. The ideomotor effect is used to explain musculature movement which is involuntarily suggested by the mind of the dowser. This unconscious

When horses behave in unaccountable ways, a Feng Shui consultant may use dowsing rods to seek out any energy fields that might have upset them.

Not only does the biotensor deflect excess energy, it also identifies the best foods for a particular horse. Whether the horse agrees with the findings, of course, is another matter entirely.

motor behavior is said to explain the movement of the rods. Passionate dowsers will counter this by pointing out that they are simply concentrating on a static point. In Asian culture, this static point has a very evocative name: the *Gateway of the Gods.*

The biotensor is a special kind of dowsing rod that can help deflect excess energy from the horse.

Geopathology

In a broad sense, geopathology analyzes rays emanating from the earth that can lead to diseases. Energies with a negative impact on the well-being and health of people and animals alike can have their origins in water veins, metal deposits or cracks and clefts in the rock substrate. These harmful energies can seriously influence the nervous system, sleep habits, and immune system, especially when situated near resting or sleeping areas.

For centuries people have been using dowsing rods and pendulums to trace these invisible ley lines and energies. The effects and results of dowsing cannot be scientifically proven, and remain controversial among scientists.

Most horses and ponies are not bothered by mud or cold weather. In fact, quite a few horses turned out with a blanket soon try to get rid of it. Who needs a blanket when they are moving around, after all?

Rustic Life

"Open day every day"—could a slogan like this persuade someone to rent a place for their precious horse? Anyone with any imagination would probably take an immediate interest, because keeping a horse outdoors on the pasture can be wonderful if the conditions are right. Life in a single stall is not very entertaining, as the amount of fresh air, light, and social contacts a horse can enjoy is rather restricted and greatly depends on the timetable of the owner. Lack of fresh air and exercise will result in a horse becoming increasingly bored and also more sensitive. The idea of outdoor residence is to provide shelter when necessary, while allowing the horse more self-determination and freedom of movement during the day.

The shelter is a large one, closed on three sides to protect the horses from wind and rain. Depending on the particular group of horses and which one is dominant, it may be advisable to make a second entryway, as the dominant horse will sometimes seek to prevent a less favored member of the group from taking shelter inside. With a second door, the weaker horse has a back way in and does not have to stand in the rain. Although this kind of behavior is a disadvantage, an equine living community is exactly right for a horse's natural lifestyle, on the whole—before they were domesticated, horses always lived in herds, after all. Of course, the horse

Horses that are turned out regularly are not concerned in the least about muddy ground, whereas those who spend most of their life in an indoor stall may actually shy at a puddle.

owners and yard managers must make sure the constellation within a band of horses that share a pasture is generally peaceful. Usually, horses only stand together in groups when the weather is bad. In good weather, each horse goes its own way as it indulges in its natural pastime: grazing. This means that every horse is following its own route, taking the odd leisurely step, nibbling at the grass, trying some herbs, and walking on when the previous spot has been eaten bare.

The ground surrounding the shelter is usually covered in wood shavings to prevent soggy earth on rainy days. Even the most robust horse would eventually become ill in such conditions. This means the grazing area starts a little further on, away from the shelter. The pasture should offer plenty of space so that there is always an abundance of grass to feed on. Cleaning out has to be done just as regularly as in a stall, and if there is no creek or other running water on the plot, several drinking troughs must be installed, because horses drink anywhere from 6 to 15 gallons every day.

Some horse breeds, like the Icelandic, are traditionally kept in the open throughout the year, but after a short period of settling in, any horse will be content with this rustic lifestyle, simply because the leisure activities are perfect.

The paddock is the open pen in front of or close to the stalls, and usually has little or no grass covering. It is a place where horses are able to get a breath of fresh air, stretch their legs, and move about.

This pasture must be equine paradise. There is plenty of space for romping around or staying out of each other's way, and the horses can be alone or in little groups. The abundance of grass prevents any competition for food.

Admiring this Welsh Cob in action, could anyone suggest that horses and snow are not a fortuitous combination?

Fit and Healthy Throughout the Year

A horse on a snow-covered pasture is anything but an object for sympathy. It will not freeze to death out there. Treating horses too

much like humans does them no good—indeed, such behavior can be harmful to them. Naturally, a sporting horse that is sweating from hard work should never be left standing in a draught or turned out without a blanket. But in most cases, it is the creatures that spend too much time inside that get ill—just as is often the case with people. Horses that have grown used to the sinking temperatures by spending several hours a day outside in all kinds of weather are hardy enough for the winter.

Humans need to wear breathable, insulating clothing in the cold season. Horses do not. They have all the protection they need naturally. The horse is an absolute climate specialist among all

Change of Coat

When the temperatures start to drop in autumn and the days grow shorter, horses gradually start to prepare for the coming winter by growing an especially thick coat of fur. In fact, their short summer coat simply grows twice as long.

To complete the horse's winter outfit, wooly hair pushes into the gaps in their regular coat, and the trapped air creates a layer of natural insulation. The actual

change of coat, when new hair grows, takes place not in winter, but in the springtime. First, the wooly hair so necessary in winter dies off and falls from the coat in thick tufts, and then the winter-length normal hairs slowly but surely come loose, one after the other.

The mane, tail, and guard hairs around a horse's eyes and muzzle are permanent and do not change with the rest of the coat.

Icelandic horses are a classic hardy breed—which is no wonder, considering the climate of their native Iceland.

mammals, and is well able to adapt to extreme weather conditions. Their countless blood vessels regulate the warmth of the skin and ensure a constant body temperature of 98–100°F. Thus horses can even survive temperatures of –40°F, far below what would kill most cattle. Although there are very few bands of wild horses left in the civilized world, they are a proof of equine hardiness.

The blood flow to a horse's skin is controlled by circulation. Usually, the skin is held at a minimum temperature, so that the body can keep as much warmth as possible inside. In cases of emergency, though, the skin is warmed up to prevent freezing. If a horse has been turned out regularly, it will be accustomed to these changes of skin temperature and will feel comfortable. And as long as it has enough roughage available, it can fuel its internal heating system, because the digestion process that takes place in the colon generates additional heat. Through this method, any horse will survive the winter unharmed.

Once a horse has come to know the smell and feel of snow, it will move quite happily through the white carpet, whether it is mounted or alone. The only problem that might arise is caused by its shoes, as the snow sticks more easily to shod hooves, which can cause it to develop an uneven gait and lose its surefootedness.

Even if the cold winter is followed by a very hot summer, the horse is ready. In this case, the blood vessels work so hard that up to 4 gallons of sweat can be produced by the numerous sweat glands when needed, and this helps to cool off the skin. All in all, horses are astonishingly good at adapting to various conditions, as they have proven over centuries of living with and without human help, and as they will continue to do in the future.

Below: Hard as it may be to believe, horses are not made of porcelain. Once they are used to it, they take to cold weather very well and even enjoy being in the snow. Of course, this also goes for indigenous or wild breeds like the Przewalski horse.

Above: After energetic romping in the snow, icicles can form on the whiskers and mane. But that does not bother most horses—this black Fell pony evidently couldn't care less.

A Coat for
Every Situation

Breed Profile: Curly Horse

Height: 63–67 inches

Colors: all colors, even piebald and skewbald

Description: various horse types

   with a curly coat

Origin: USA

Equine Cushing's Syndrome
Apart from Curly horses, there are others with an exceptional coat. Unlike the Curlies, which are usually very fit, these horses suffer a particular disease called Equine Cushing's Syndrome (ECS). Horses with Cushing's have hypercortisolism, meaning they have excessive levels of the hormone cortisole in their blood. The disturbance can present as a wide array of health problems, both physical and psychological. Other symptoms may include an unusually long coat that turns curly and excessive sweating.

This hormone disorder is most often provoked by a slow growing tumor on the pituitary gland (hypophysis). If the disease is recognized early enough, the horse can be treated with a mild hormone therapy and will be able to live with no further symptoms for many years.

As yet quite a rarity, but they do exist: horses with curly coats. They look as if their owner spent the whole night giving them a perm, but in fact Curlies are a natural mutation. The hair follicles are not rounded but oval, which turns the coat to crimps and curls. It is thought that these horses grow their winter coat as a way of adapting to the extremely cold winters of their natural habitat, the mountain regions of North America. Curly hair keeps a horse extra warm, as the curls trap air close to the skin, building a warming and insulating layer. Curly horses can have a range of coat types. Some tend to be crimped, others are tightly curled, but they all have in common a curly mane and tail, curly hairs at the pasterns, and curls inside their ears. Typically, they also feature long eye lashes that look as if someone has treated them with curling tongs. Straight Curlies are another type of curly horse. These have a straight, smooth coat even in winter with just a few kinks in mane and tail.

Although Curly horses are not very well known, they have been around for a very long time. It is known that when the Native Americans lived in North America they engaged in fierce battles over the Curly horses that lived like Mustangs in wild herds, but it was not until 1898 that the first breeding program was established. Rancher Peter Damele adopted the Curly horses and most of today's Curlies can be traced back to Damele's stud book.

Damele made no attempt to keep the breed pure, however, and many breeders of Curlies, especially in the USA, have been less concerned with the pedigree than the coat. Any horse with curly hair could be registered as an American Bashkir Curly Horse, and Curlies have been crossed in haphazard fashion with other breeds, resulting in a wide variety of colors, sizes, and types. Standing 51–67 inches at the withers, there are Curly ponies, elegant Curly Saddlebreds, and Curlies of the Quarterhorse, Mustang, and coldblood type. As can

While some Curly horses have a crimped coat, others actually have tiny curls that could be the envy of many a horsewoman.

Curlies are delighted to be turned out in snow and cold weather. Their wooly coat protects them as they gallop across the pasture.

easily happen when breeders pay too much attention to one particular feature (such as the coat), the breeders of Curlies must accept criticism for not having properly considered features such as a correct conformation or the character of the offspring. Many breeders have now restructured their breeding programs to focus on breeding well set-up Curlies of a specific type.

Curly horses are good looking in the field—but they also look impressive under saddle, both in show jumping and in dressage competitions. And because Curlies are perfect all-rounders, some of them are also highly skilled at the rack (a special pace), while others have good cow sense and are thus welcome in Western disciplines. Being tough, with good stamina, calm nerves, and a steady character, Curly horses are also ideal partners for trail riding.

Attention, Allergy Sufferers!

Curly horses have become extremely popular with people who suffer all kinds of allergic reactions when riding regular horses. No sore patches, red eyes, or runny nose result from contact with a Curly. As if these horses did not already have plenty of special features and talents, they are also the perfect match for allergics.

Contrary to popular assumption, it is not their long, curly hair that makes these horses hypo-allergenic; the secret lies one layer deeper. Although many people tend to think that allergies are caused by animal hairs, they are actually triggered by allergenic proteins such as dander from the animal skin.

These allergenic proteins are smaller in Curly Horses than with other breeds, and there are also fewer of them, so people who are allergic to other horses can ride a Curly without experiencing adverse effects, even if it has a smooth, straight coat.

Curlies have a different smell from other horses–they smell of wool. Their coat has a high percentage of sebum. Even when it is carefully groomed form top to bottom, you will feel the sebum when stroking the coat of a Curly Horse.

In winter, the coat of a Curly is kinked or covered in little curls, while in summer the coat may simply be smooth. The mane and tail remain curly all year.

ACKNOWLEDGMENTS

Author's acknowledgments

Special gratitude to my father, Horst Sgrazzutti, who reinforced my resolve to accomplish the exceptional; and to my mother Liane, who made my first riding lessons on a pony possible. Thanks also to my "Berliners," who accompanied this book with good will, and finally to Sabine Hartelt, who first aroused my interest in the field of equestrian sports and with her power inspired me to actually write this book.

The publisher would like to thank the following for their advice, assistance, support, and photographs:

Daniela Söhnchen
Curly Horses Germany
Die Curly Horses Zucht in NRW
Scheideweg 34
42499 Hückeswagen, Germany
Tel: +49 (0)700 – 76 46 24 36
www.curly-horses-germany.de
E-mail: curly-info@t-online.de

Fritz and Sylvia Krümmel
Trainers of Iberian Horses
Lengelshof 1
40883 Ratingen, Germany
www.fritz-kruemmel.de

Minitraber Team
Karola Döme
Wenningkamp 3
48599 Gronau, Germany
www.minitraber.de

Aachen-Laurensberger Rennverein e.V.
Albert-Servais-Allee 50
52070 Aachen, Germany
www.chioaachen.de
www.aachen2006.de

Top Hat Maker L'Hiver
H. W. de Winter
5405 AR Uden / The Netherlands
www.lhiver.nl

Cologne Zoo
Dr. Waltraut Zimmermann
Riehler Straße 173
50735 Cologne, Germany
www.zoo-koeln.de

Joh's Stübben KG
Ostwall 185
47798 Krefeld, Germany
www.stuebben.de

Reiterhof am Waldrand
Regina and Michael Fuchsberger GbR
Willmarser Str. 30
97640 Stockheim, Germany
www.reiterhof-am-waldrand.de

Rückepferd Max with Ernst Winkelmann
47929 Grefrath, Germany

Baldssuhn Hufbeschlag
Thomas Baldssuhn
Moenicher Heck 4
52396 Heimbach, Germany

Stutenmilch-Gestüt Sickinger Höhe
Dr. Guth
Hintereckstr. 11
66506 Maßweiler, Germany

Burg Satzvey
53894 Mechernich-Satzvey, Germany

Angelika Fengels
Lanter 2
46569 Hünxe, Germany

Nationales Zinnmuseum Ommen
Markt 1
7731 DB Ommen
The Netherlands

Heinz Hoevelmann – Trabfotoagentur
Feldstr. 24
45661 Recklinghausen, Germany
Tel: +49 (0) 2361–689892
www.trabfotos.de
E-mail: heinz.hövelmann@trabfotos.de

Jacques Toffi
Beselerstr. 27 a
22607 Hamburg, Germany
www.toffi-images.de

PICTURE CREDITS

All photos by Jürgen Schulzki / Cologne, except:

Archive of the German Horse Museum / Verden (all): 98

Archive of the Trakehner Association / Neumünster: 99 (c.l.; c.r.)

Braatz, Peter / Aachen (www.360pixel.de): 136

Corbis: Richard T. Nowitz 10/11, Stapleton Collection 12 (t.), Buddy Mays 12 (b.), Bettmann 15 (t.), Tedd Gipstein 15 (b.), Gianni Dagli Orti 16 (t.), Araldo de Luca 16 (b.), Archivo Iconografico, S.A. 18 (t.), Werner Forman 18 (b.), Historical Picture Archive 19 (t.), Ted Spiegel 19 (b.), Bettmann 20/21, Christie's Images 22, Swim Ink 2, LLC 23 (t.), Julian Calder 23 (t.l.), Bob Thomas (b.c.), Bettmann (b.r.), Tom Brakefield 26 (t.), Sean Sexton Collection 27 (t.), Bettmann 31 (t.l.), Bettmann 33 (t.), John Gillmoure 33 (b.), Adam Woolfitt 35 (t.), Wally McNamee 36 (t.), Bureau L.A. Collection 37, Burstein Collection 39, Kit Houghton 42 (b.), Kevin R. Morris 43 (t.), Yann Arthus-Bertrand 43 (b.), Bettmann 46 (b.), Ludovic Maisant 49, Corbis 52, Bob Krist 53 (t.), Kit Houghton 53 (b.), Tim Thompson 54 (t.), Jerry Cooke 54 (b.), 55 (c.l, c.r.), Larry Lee Photography 55 (t.), Yann Arthus-Bertrand 64 (t.), Bettmann 78, Robert Holmes 79 (t.), Archivo Iconografico, S.A. 19 (b.), Bettmann 80 (t.), Geoffrey Clements (b.), Jonathan Hession/Touchstone/Bureau L.A. Collections 81 (t.l.), Bettmann 81 (t.r.; b.), Araldo de Luca 83 (t.), Hulton-Deutsch Collection 84 (t.), Franz-Marc Frei 85 (t.), Bettmann 86 (t.), Cat's 86 (c.), Corbis 86 (b.), Bettmann 87 (t.), Carl and Ann Purcell 87 (b.), Craig Aurness 88 (b.), Carl and Ann Purcell 88 (t.), Corbis 89 (b.), Bettmann 90, Richard Cummins 91 (t.), Dave Bartruff 91 (b.), Bettmann 92, Quadrillon 93 (t.), Régis Bossu/Sygma 93 (b.), Gianni Dagli Orti 94 (b.), Archivo Iconografico, S.A. 95 (b.), Hulton-Deutsch Collection 96, 97, Kit Houghton 100 (t.), Reuters 100 (b.), Kit Houghton 101 (t.), Craig Aurness 101 (b.), Carl and Ann Purcell 102, Nik Wheeler 103 (t.), Lukas Schifres 103 (c.) Najlah Feanny 103 (b.), Reuters 107 (b.), Arnold Cedric/Sygma 109 (t.r.), Bettmann 110 (t.), Hulton-Deutsch Collection 111 (b.), Tim Graham/Sygma 112 (t.l.; t.r.), Kit Houghton 112 (b.), Caren Firouz/Reuters 113 (t.), Franck Prevel 113 (c.), Joe Skipper/Reuters 113 (b.), Bettmann 114, Hulton-Deutsch Collection 114 (t.), Reuters 115 (b.), Hulton-Deutsch Collection 116, Michael S. Yamashita 117 (t.), Layne Kennedy 117 (b.), Kit Hughton 118 (t.), Corbis 118 (b.), Bettmann 119 (c.), Bettmann 134 (c.), Hulton-Deutsch Collection 140 (b.), Tim Graham 146 (t.), Darrell Gulin 150 (t.), John and Lisa Merrill 158/159, Craig Aurness 162 (t.), Scheufler Collection 163, David Stoecklein 169 (t.), Ron Sanford 176 (t.), Paul Almasy 176 (b.), Kit Houghton 177

Ditter, Irina / Cologne: 181

Döme, Karola / Dülmen (www.minitraber.de): 120 (b.)

Hövelmann, Heinz / Recklinghausen (www.trabfotos.de): 122, 123

Lufthansa Foto: 140 (t.), 141 (b.l.)

Martinez, Claudio / Cologne (www.martinez-design.de): 17 (b.)

Melchior, Leon / Lanaken: 157

Schloss Johannisberg / Geisenheim-Johannisberg: 89 (t.)

Schupp, Holger / Aachen (www.holgerschupp.de): 142 (t.), 143 (t., c.l.)

Söhnchen, Daniela (www.curly-horses-germany.de): 184, 185

Stempell, Kyra / Bedburg: 26/27 (illustrations), 40/41 (illustrations)

Strauch, Michael / Eschweiler (www.foto-strauch.de): 137 (b.)

Toffi, Jacques / Hamburg (www.toffi-images.de): 62, 63, 104/105, 106, 107 (t.), 110 (b.), 119 (b.)., 121, 124, 125 (t.), 126, 127, 128, 130, 131, 132, 133, 135 (t., b.), 136, 137 (t.), 138, 139, 142 (b.), 146 (b.l., b.r.), 147, 148, 149, 152 (b.), 154, 155, 156, 164 (t.), 165 (t., c.), 167 (t.), 171 (t.l., t.r., b.),180 (b.)

Zimmermann, Waltraut Dr. / Cologne (www.koelner-zoo.de): 28/29

LITERATURE AND SOURCES

Schnieper, Xaver, ed. *Pferde in Dichtung und Farbaufnahmen.* Lucerne, 1966.

Busch, Wilhelm. *Kritik des Herzes.* Munich, 1940.

Binding, Rudolf G. *Reitvorschrift für eine Geliebte.* Hildesheim, 1995.

Dossenbach, Monique and Hans D. Trans. *The Noble Horse.* London: Bounty Books, 1998.

Duve, Karen and Thies Völker. *Lexikon berühmter Tiere.* Frankfurt, 1997.

Edwards, Hartley. *Saddlery.* 2nd rev. ed. Kent, UK: J. A. Allen, 1991.

Harrison, Lorraine. *Horses: From Noble Steeds to Beasts of Burden.* London: Watson-Guptill, 2000.

Isenbart, H.-H. and E.M. Bührer. *The Kingdom of the Horse.* New York: Time Life, Inc., 1969.

Köhler, Hans Joachim. *Tempelhüter. Symbol der Trakehner Pferdezucht und des Landes Ostpreußen.* Stuttgart and Hamburg, 1995.

Pourtavaf, Ariane and Herbert Meyer. *Die Brücke zwischen Mensch und Pferd.* Warendorf, 1998.

Every effort was made until the time this book went to print to correctly identify all copyright holders and sources. In case of any discrepancies or omissions, please provide the publisher with this information so it can be included in future editions.

INDEX